The Unbalanced Mind

The Unbalanced Mind
Pope and the Rule of Passion

Rebecca Ferguson

Lecturer in English
St David's University College
Lampeter

upp

UNIVERSITY OF PENNSYLVANIA PRESS

First published in the United States in 1986 by the
University of Pennsylvania Press, Philadelphia

First published in Great Britain in 1986 by
THE HARVESTER PRESS LIMITED
Publisher: John Spiers
16 Ship Street, Brighton, Sussex

British Library Cataloguing in Publication Data

Ferguson, Rebecca
 The unbalanced mind : Pope and the rule of passion.
 1. Pope, Alexander —— Criticism and interpretation
 I. Title
 821'.5   PR3634

  ISBN 0-7108-0973-5 (Great Britain)

  ISBN 0-8122-8027-X (United States)

Printed in Great Britain

In memory of Alfred Smith

In lazy Apathy let Stoics boast
Their Virtue fix'd: 'tis fix'd as in a frost,
Contracted all, retiring to the breast;
But strength of mind is Exercise, not Rest:
The rising tempest puts in act the soul,
Parts it may ravage, but preserves the whole.
On life's vast ocean diversely we sail,
Reason the card, but Passion is the gale;
             (*An Essay on Man*, II. 101-8)

Whether we dread, or whether we desire,
In either case, believe me, we admire;
Whether we joy or grieve, the same the curse,
Surpriz'd at better, or surpriz'd at worse.
Thus good, or bad, to one extreme betray
Th' unbalanc'd Mind, and snatch the Man away;
For Vertue's self may too much Zeal be had;
The worst of Madmen is a Saint run mad.
       (*Imitations of Horace; Epistle I vi*, 20-8)

Contents

Acknowledgements x

Introduction xi

A Note on Texts and Abbreviations xv

One 'The best of passions': the *Elegy to the Memory of an Unfortunate Lady* and *Eloisa to Abelard* 1

Two 'What stranger Cause': Pope's *Iliad* and *The Rape of the Lock* 32

Three 'Steering betwixt extremes': *An Essay on Man* 64

Four 'This clue once found': the Ruling Passion and the *Moral Essays* 95

Five 'Th' unbalanc'd Mind': the *Imitations of Horace* 122

Six 'Kind Self-conceit': *The Dunciad* 157

Conclusion 186

Select Bibliography 189

Index 202

Acknowledgements

I should like to express thanks to Professor John Chalker of Westfield College, London, for the patience and judicious care which he showed at all times when I was preparing this work as a PhD thesis, and also to Professor Peter Dixon who likewise gave me much help in the early stages. For spirited conversations and helpful leads on Pope I am grateful to Frank Stack of Southampton University and to Warren Chernaik of Queen Mary College, London; and I owe a particular debt of thanks to Mrs Elsie Davies, who produced the typescript for this book with remarkable speed and efficiency, as well as to my parents for their invaluable help with the proof reading.

Introduction

'The frequency with which Eighteenth-Century writers placed man and his reason at the mercy of his passions, particularly his ruling passion, suggests that the age of reason might with more justice be called the age of passion', Kenneth Maclean observed in his early study of *John Locke and English Literature of the Eighteenth Century*.[1] His remark would scarcely provoke astonishment among present-day scholars of the period, for whom the cliché of the rationalistic 'Peace of the Augustans' has steadily receded into myth. In recent years, some close attention has been given to the theory of the passions expounded in Pope's *Essay on Man*—particularly to the influential 'ruling passion' theory — and through these assessments Pope's position in relation to the philosophy of his time has been usefully clarified.[2] No full-length study has yet been made, however, of Pope's obviously deep interest in the meaning of 'passion' as it is expressed and developed in the body of his works as a whole. It should be seen as significant that his ambitious 'opus magnum', stemming from the *Essay on Man*, was never completed — 'what I gain on the side of philosophy', he once complained of the project to Swift, 'I lose on the side of poetry' — yet as I hope this study will show, the suggestions of the poetry and the philosophy cannot be drawn apart. 'Passion' is a subject which is central to Pope's writings and thought as a whole, embracing not only those works which are most explicitly concerned with moral philosophy (which would include, of course, the *Imitations of Horace*), but also the psychological depths of *The Rape of the Lock*, and the strikingly 'proto-Romantic' cast of his two early poems, *Eloisa to Abelard* and the *Elegy to the Memory of an Unfortunate Lady*, both of which exalt the power and the claims of emotion with conscious extravagance. Pope's interest in the idea of a 'ruling passion', too, cannot be confined to the framework of the poems which were connected most directly with his 'opus magnum' project; the notion was indeed flourished before Spence as a 'New Hypothesis' in 1730, but it had been taking shape in Pope's mind for many years before that date, and had an important place in his conception of the causes of conflict—both conscious and unconscious — within the individual personality.

The aim of this study is to be suggestive rather than comprehensive or schematic, although in the outline of chapters I have chosen to follow approximately the chronology of Pope's writings in order to gain some sense of the progressive development of his interests and ideas. Within the mingled philosophy and satire of the *Essay on Man* itself, Pope's discussion of the passions is as interesting for its imaginative expansiveness and for the nature of its implications as for its intellectual propositions (which are by no means rigorously self-consistent), and I have tried to bring out this dimension of the work in my account of its processes of argumentation.

The meaning of the word 'passion' for Pope and his mentors is discussed in chapter three, but while it is not easy to give a condensed and straightforward definition, it may be helpful here to put forward a broad description of the term, and of the contexts in which it was pursued. In a general sense, 'passion' may be taken to signify impulse, and especially motivational impulse, encompassing also its more modern meaning of 'intense emotion'; it might be defined as denoting the affective or emotional capacity of the soul, although many contemporary treatises on the subject attempt to draw rather variable distinctions between what are called the 'passions' and 'affections'. 'Passion' is a term which is constantly employed in seventeenth- and eighteenth-century psychologies, steadily departing from the Renaissance faculty psychology and the physiological division of 'humours' towards less confidently rationalistic analysis of the 'perturbations of the mind' such as melancholy, hysteria and insanity. In the field of ethics (very closely connected with that of psychology, indeed in this area frequently undistinguished from it) it was equally crucial, representing the central problem of motivation; Pope describes the passions as 'modes of self-love', individualistic desires and aversions, and it was the question of passion defined as self-interest and its relationship to virtue which chiefly exercised the moralists. Lastly, 'passion' was also much invoked in the vocabulary of literary criticism, denoting the capacity of the writer to feel and to convey emotion to his reader or audience (whether the empathy of pathos, tragic 'pity and fear', or the hostilities of satire). It naturally became a central term in affective aesthetics, as it was in discussions of the art of character-writing (another minor branch of psychology) and of the efficacy of satire. Pope's interest in all of these applications of the terms was, as I hope to show, very alert, and he was evidently well-informed on many points of topical debate. From the mid-eighteenth century, the directions taken in moral philosophy and psychology tended to lead away from the well-worn 'passions' analysis; but it would be fair to observe that, looking beyond the condensed arguments of the *Essay on Man* to consider the diversity and complexity of his works as a whole, Pope emerges as one of the most cogent and perceptive writers on the subject, drawing out the more challenging possibilities of the ideas available to him with a comprehensive intelligence and a highly independent imagination.

Notes

1. Kenneth Maclean, 1936, 47-8.
2. I am indebted throughout this study to the work of Miriam Leranbaum, *Alexander Pope's 'Opus Magnum', 1729-1744* (Oxford, 1977), and Douglas H. White, *Pope and the Context of Controversy: The Manipulation of Ideas in 'An Essay on Man'* (Chicago and London, 1970).

A Note on Texts and Abbreviations

Unless otherwise stated, the text of Pope's poems used throughout is that of the Twickenham Edition (general editor John Butt; 11 volumes, 1939-69), abbreviated as 'TE', followed by volume number, as follows:

Volume I (1961) — *Pastoral Poetry, and An Essay on Criticism*. Edited by Émile Audra and Aubrey Williams.

Volume II (third edition, reset, 1962) — *The Rape of the Lock and other Poems*. Edited by Geoffrey Tillotson.

Volume III (i) (reprint, 1964) — *An Essay On Man*. Edited by Maynard Mack.

Volume III (ii) (second edition, 1961) — *Epistles to Several Persons—Moral Essays*. Edited by F. W. Bateson.

Volume IV (second edition, 1953) — *Imitations of Horace, with An Epistle to Dr. Arbuthnot*. Edited by John Butt.

Volume V (third edition, 1963) — *The Dunciad*. Edited by James Sutherland.

Volume VI (reprinted, 1964) — *Minor Poems*. Edited by Norman Ault, completed by John Butt.

Volume VII, VIII (1967) — *The Iliad of Homer*. Edited by Maynard Mack, Norman Callan, and others.

Volume IX, X (1967) — *The Odyssey of Homer*. Edited by Maynard Mack, Norman Callan, and others.

Volume XI — *Index* (1969).

Other abbreviations used are:

Anecdotes: Joseph Spence, *Observations, Anecdotes and Characters of Books and Men*, edited by James M. Osborn (2 vols, Oxford, 1956).

Correspondence: *The Correspondence of Alexander Pope*, edited by George Sherburn (5 vols, Oxford, 1956).

Dryden, *Poems*: *The Poems of John Dryden*, edited by James Kinsley (4 vols, Oxford, 1958).

Dryden, *Essays*: *'Of Dramatic Poesy' and other Critical Essays*, edited by George Watson (2 vols, 1962).

EC: *The Works of Alexander Pope*, edited by W. Elwin and W. J. Courthope (10 vols, 1871-89).

Spectator: *The Spectator*, edited by Donald F. Bond (5 vols, Oxford, 1965).

Swift, *Prose Writings*: *The Prose Writings of Jonathan Swift*, edited by Herbert Davies (12 vols, Oxford, 1939-55).

Periodicals

ECS	*Eighteenth Century Studies.*
ELH	*English Literary History.*
HLQ	*The Huntington Library Quarterly.*
JEGP	*Journal of English and Germanic Philology.*
JHI	*Journal of the History of Ideas.*
MLN	*Modern Language Notes.*
MLQ	*Modern Language Quarterly.*
MLR	*Modern Language Review.*
PMLA	*Publications of the Modern Language Association of America.*
PQ	*Philological Quarterly.*
REL	*Review of English Literature.*
RES	*Review of English Studies* (n.s.: new series).
SEL	*Studies in English Literature, 1500-1900.*
YES	*Yearbook of English Studies.*

CHAPTER ONE

'The best of passions':

The *Elegy to the Memory of an Unfortunate Lady* and *Eloisa to Abelard*

The period around 1717 has been aptly characterised by Reuben Brower[1] as Pope's 'Ovidian' phase, when there emerges a marked susceptibility to tender feelings which is brought out particularly in his letters to the Blount sisters and to Lady Mary Wortley Montagu. Both the *Elegy to the Memory of an Unfortunate Lady* and *Eloisa to Abelard*, published in that year, are unique among Pope's works in presenting a direct and sustained engagement in emotion, forging an empathy between the reader and the 'narrator' of each poem which is not qualified by any dimension of irony; in this respect, they should be seen as complementary works. Byron's extravagant eulogy of *Eloisa* ('if you search for passion, where is it to be found stronger?')[2] is reflected more soberly in Pope's letter of March 1716 to Martha Blount, in which he refers to the composition of the poem pointedly as though it embodied his own emotions:

> I am here studying ten hours a day, but thinking of you in spite of all the learned. The Epistle of Eloise grows warm, and begins to have some Breathings of the Heart in it, which may make posterity think I was in love. I can scarce find it in my heart to leave out the conclusion I once intended for it.[3]

For Pope, the aim of both poems is to engage the reader sympathetically in their fluctuations of emotion,[4] and in this affective and psychological emphasis their Ovidian cast is dominant; the influence is particularly striking in *Eloisa to Abelard*, which is closely modelled upon Ovid's *Heroides*.[5] Alongside their affective emphasis, however, it is equally significant that Pope chose to moralise the Ovidian theme of love betrayed, to introduce what he terms in the 'Argument' to *Eloisa* 'the struggles of grace and

1

nature, virtue and passion'; these key terms express interests which are greatly elaborated in his hands, and the overall movement of both poems is designed to embody a crisis of values as well as an urgent emotional response. This synthesis has raised difficulties for the interpreter; the affective bias of *Eloisa* in particular seems to heighten its moral ambiguity, since through the dramatic vacillations between 'virtue and passion' Pope has been taken to draw the reader's sympathies towards irreconcilable values. There is no clear resolution to Eloisa's struggles, and thus the final significance of her dilemma has been the subject of some contention among recent critics, many of whom feel that the poem must reach a point of conclusion within its own moral terms.[6] My central concern in this discussion is to consider the relationship between the moral framework and the emotive aim of both the *Elegy* and *Eloisa*, and in particular the correspondence of the human and the divine explored in each.

As one would expect from their Ovidian cast, both poems are especially sharply focused upon the experience of loss, which is encountered as a crisis in psychological and ethical terms, and death also provides the final perspective in both. However, Pope's deepening of these themes can perhaps best be characterised by observing that the subject of each of these poems is not so much the extinguishing of passion as its abiding potency and its value; the meaning of passion is explored in each with a dual emphasis on its overwhelming force in human nature and on its apparent tenuousness in the face of eternity. Thus the terms 'virtue and passion' set in relation to one another are crucial to both; Eloisa is directly engaged in the striving between Christian dictates and the dictates of her own nature, both of which call forth seemingly contradictory claims for what might be termed 'virtue', sacrifice and endurance, and although for the 'Unfortunate Lady' that crisis has already been resolved by suicide, the poet engages himself in these issues anew in a passionate defence of her heroism. It is the mind of the speaker which absorbs our attention and directs our responses throughout, and we are immediately made aware that his emotion is pitted against a very different, hostile order of values. Two aspects of the *Elegy* thus assume particular importance; the nature of the poet's close relationship to the Lady, and the view of her action of suicide (the subject of some outrage to Dr Johnson)[7] which he puts forward.

It is the final verse-paragraph of the *Elegy* which overtly draws our attention to the poet, presenting a meditative close in which he resolves his diatribe against the Lady's persecutors to reflect upon his own mortality. D.C. Mell has argued cogently that the poem, following the theme of *Lycidas*, finally turns to the subject of the artist's own power of imagination and the tenuous standing of his creation, and that the wider problem encountered is that of universal impermanence.[8] But he also acknowledges the central point of contrast with Milton's perspective, and that is the focus on the individual death of the Lady and the specific circumstances of her death from which these reflections take their root; it is the intensity and rhetoric of the poem, and the dramatic images of the Lady herself, which make the most forceful impression on the reader. The very extravagance of this intensity has led Howard Weinbrot to the doubtful suggestion that Pope meant to cast the 'poet' as the Lady's lover, fulminating against the hypocrisy of her relatives and of the established Church in a vain attempt to exorcise his own justified guilt at her death, an argument which serves to distance the emotionalism of the writing.[9] The proposition is surely untenable, yet it does point towards what I would see as a carefully subdued intimation of love on the part of the poet for the Lady; for the greater part of the poem the reader is indeed held in doubt as to the speaker's identity and hence as to the grounds of his close concern in the Lady's fate. And it is through this intimation, consistently held in abeyance, that the closing verse-paragraph achieves a subtle and moving shift of tone and perspective; at that point the speaker comes forward in his personal identity as 'poet', whereas the lover is never mentioned within the poem at all. The poet here more firmly represents one who has a particular sensitivity to the Lady's plight and to the fact of her death, and the bond between them is such that he naturally relates the contemplation of her death to thoughts of his own mortality; the bond of mortality is thus in part a witness to the bond of humanity. We are left in no doubt that the Lady is 'belov'd' by the poet, but the meaning of the word as it appears in the final line is in fact more diffuse than before, and curiously more poignant. The poet has identified himself as the last feeling link between the Lady's memory and an indifferent world, and it is for this above all that we are made to feel that his voice is important. He does not emphasise his role as imaginative creator, or meditate upon the transience of his art as such, but upon the absolute finality of physical death and the rupturing of his tender and devoted relationship to the Lady as a consequence. The balanced half-lines which open the verse-paragraph are rhetorically structured to emphasise this fragmenting of a formerly close correspondence by the intervention of death:

> Poets themselves must fall, like those they sung;
> Deaf the prais'd ear, and mute the tuneful tongue.
>
> (75-6)

Although that reflection has been raised to the abstract level, personal intimacy is again brought out in the lines which follow, stressing the painfulness of individual loss:

> Ev'n he, whose soul now melts in mournful lays,
> Shall shortly want the gen'rous tear he pays;
> Then from his closing eyes thy form shall part,
> And the last pang shall tear thee from his heart,
> Life's idle business at one gasp be o'er,
> The Muse forgot, and thou belov'd no more!
>
> (77-82)

The poet's response is a magnanimity of tenderness rather than a recognition of duty; his is the '*gen'rous* tear', in pointed contrast to the 'mockery of woe' already satirised in the world. In the pathos of this valediction, above all, the poem does indeed belong to the speaker.

Within the full range of the poem, the speaker's declamations are in a sense both personal and public, 'sentiment in the heightened rhetorical style',[10] a fusion of voices which is particularly reminiscent of Ovid's manner. By this fusion, the Lady's own passion is as it were set forth on a public stage; she shares the fate of Ovid's heroines, of betrayal through 'loving too well', and as in the *Heroides*, 'honour' is an issue of vital concern. The conceptions of honour and of heroism towards which the poet guides us are unorthodox; Brower emphasises the predominantly 'Roman' ethos of the poem, the recognition of the dignity of suicide as an action demonstrating Stoic fortitude in the face of an intractable choice (here presented in terms of the choice between life-in-death rather than death-in-life). Yet this fortitude is impelled not

by the Stoic's dispassionate rejection of life's fleeting values, but
on the contrary by an ackowledged extremity of emotion; there is
a deliberate complexity embodied in the lines which elevate and
lament the Lady's actions:

> To bear too tender, or too firm a Heart,
> To act a Lover's or a *Roman's* part.
> (7-8)

Passion and resolution are seen as closely analogous, and both are
identified with a power of generous aspiration which is ambiguously referred to as 'ambition'. Eloisa, in her outburst upon
Abelard's enforced emasculation and retreat, makes a connection
between the powers of love and of ambition in a relatively worldly
sense:

> There stern religion quench'd th'unwilling flame,
> There dy'd the best of passions, Love and Fame.
> (39-40)

and this conception seems to be distinguished from the clearly
mundane and reductive 'Fame' ('reputation') of l.80: 'Fame,
wealth, and honour! what are you to Love?' The speaker of the
Elegy takes up the issue of the Lady's 'Ambition', which has been
invested in her capacity for overwhelming love and testifies to her
heroism:

> Why bade ye else, ye Pow'rs! her soul aspire
> Above the vulgar flight of low desire?
> Ambition first sprung from your blest abodes;
> The glorious fault of Angels and of Gods:
> Thence to their Images on earth it flows,
> And in the breasts of Kings and Heroes glows!
> (11-16)

The heterodoxy of this outcry is manifest, but the claim is made
with a conviction and conscious daring which demand the
reader's consent;[11] the whole passage in its implications seizes on
the contention of both the *Elegy* and *Eloisa*, that such greatness of
spirit could not be merely a fortuitous and futile gift, but must in a
mysterious way testify to the communion of the soul with heaven.

The striking fusion of the Christian and pagan at l.14 ('The glorious fault of Angels and of Gods') serves to strengthen the force of that contention. To accentuate the power of the passage, Pope contrives a shift of subject to the common order of the passive, lethargic world in satiric terms:

> Most souls, 'tis true, but peep out once an age,
> Dull sullen pris'ners in the body's cage:
> Dim lights of life that burn a length of years,
> Useless, unseen, as lamps in sepulchres;
> Like Eastern Kings a lazy state they keep,
> And close confin'd to their own palace sleep.
>
> (17-22)

It is in fact the body which is said to blunt and constrict the soul of the unaspiring — the Lady's passions, far from having a fleshly bias (as her relatives and detractors might aver), bring about a sublimation above the 'dregs' of this earth and define the true quality of virtue. It is this concept of virtue, now tending towards the Platonic, which renders heaven the 'congenial place' of the soul rather than the haven forbidden to her in orthodox Christian terms; the reversal of values for which the poet argues extends to a redefining of the idea of salvation.

Passion and compassion are presented as naturally complementary, and the strength of compassion is matched by the strength of bitterness by which the Lady's enemies are as it were banished and exorcised. The poet's own compassion is imaginatively transposed to the 'pitying sky' and to the empathy of nature which adorns the grave: 'There shall the morn her earliest tears bestow' (l.65). This universal tenderness has the power to transmute excommunication to a new sanctity, and death itself to a more serene and pervasive life than the living themselves can attain to. It is in fact the characteristic of the passionless living to be charged with death; the imagery of incarceration and the tomb at ll.17-20 is trenchant, and rises to the retributive frenzy of death envisaged by the poet in his tirade against the persecutors (ll.35-46):

> So perish all, whose breast ne'er learn'd to glow
> For others' good, or melt at others' woe.

By contrast, the second vision of the Lady herself (though at the point of death) is invested with all the attributes of vibrant life, and even of eroticism:

> See on these ruby lips the trembling breath,
> These cheeks, now fading at the blast of death:
> Cold is that breast that warm'd the world before,
> And those love-darting eyes must roll no more.
>
> (31-4)

For the speaker, the pitch of his invective is in a sense cathartic and is gradually resolved into the conciliatory assurances to the Lady of ll.47ff. and the resignation of the final paragraph; the structure of the *Elegy*, like that of *Eloisa*, is dominated by a succession of emotional responses brought out by a train of psychological association (the suggestion of 'Race' at l.28 leads to the outburst of rage against the Lady's relatives, and her oblivion at l.74 to the poet's own confrontation of death). Although the emotion is finally calmed, it is never in any final sense resolved into acceptance; unrequited loss remains the dominant theme, and above all the tragic forgetfulness which defines the moment and the meaning of death.

One feature of the *Elegy* which emerges most strongly is its structure as a poem of oppositions; varied oppositions are carefully woven into its developing imagery, expressing the dialectic of contradictory values within which the speaker voices his protest. The essence of this conflict could be expressed as a clash between the pagan, 'Roman' ethos invoked by the poet and the rigorous Christian doctrine by which his values (and the Lady's) are refuted, but such a reduction would I think be simplistic. The association of passion with 'nature', with kingliness and with liberty (ll.15-22) is clearly of great importance, and in this the themes of the poem owe much to Ovid; at the same time, as ambition is shown to be 'the glorious fault of Angels and of Gods', so profound love is implicitly shown to be not only the attribute of 'those who greatly think' but also a link with the divine. Lines 67-8 positively suggest that the Lady's self-sacrifice will be uniquely acceptable to a 'pitying' heaven, identified at last with the Christian heaven, while charity is the quality conspicuously lacking in the Lady's guardian and his descendants, 'whose souls the Furies steel'd' and who are therefore cast into darkness. These inversions of the pagan and Christian within the dialectical framework of the *Elegy* are intended to be intellectually suggestive, turning upon the relationships (not the simple polarisation) of 'grace and nature, virtue and passion'. This complexity is deepened still further in *Eloisa to Abelard*, which is based more overtly on an Ovidian model. It would be helpful in assessing the significance of the poem to consider briefly the treatment of Ovid in the hands of contemporary imitators and critics, and to examine more closely the qualities in Ovid which held Pope's interest.

Although Ovid's *Epistolae Heroidum (Heroides)* provided the formal model for Pope's *Eloisa*, his influence in Pope's work as a whole is widely diffused, reflecting Pope's youthful enthusiasm in translating 'above a quarter of the *Metamorphoses*'.[12] Joseph Spence, in the *Anecdotes*, makes note of Pope's early affection for Ovid (disapprovingly, as far as the *Metamorphoses* in particular are concerned) and describes some of his early poetic exercises as 'imitations of the stories that pleased him most in Ovid'.[13] Literary historians who have traced the fortunes of Ovid through the early eighteenth century emphasise the doubtful standing of his reputation, although the terms in which they account for the marked decline in his authority and popularity after about the mid-seventeenth century are inevitably vague and can only be summed up as an evident change of taste linked with Puritan and rationalist outlooks.[14] Louise Vinge, however, in her study of the transformations of the Narcissus myth, stresses the very healthy number of translations of the *Metamorphoses* produced during the eighteenth century (the figures 'exceed those of the previous century'),[15] which should modify the impression that Ovid was altogether a neglected author, and burlesque treatments of Ovid were particularly flourishing. It seems clear than it is more specifically in the field of original serious literature that Ovid's influence pales, so that it becomes necessary to account for a prevalent unwillingness to adapt his work creatively to suit contemporary taste. An indication of one of the grounds of this unwillingness may be found in Addison's *Spectator* essay of 30 October 1712 (no. 523), in which he discusses the acceptability of myth to his age; here he takes a severe attitude to the use of 'fable' in the place of 'Truth', concluding with a mock injunction to any hopeful poets who may be contemplating writing an encomium:

I do hereby strictly require every Person, who shall write on this subject, to remember that he is a Christian, and not to sacrifice his Catechism to his Poetry .... In short, I expect that no Pagan Agent shall be introduced, or any Fact related which a Man cannot give Credit to with a good Conscience.

There was also a prevalent distrust of Ovid's 'immorality', a subject taken up by John Oldmixon in the 'Epistle Dedicatory' to his *Amores Britannici* (1703), an adaption of the *Heroides* to touching episodes in British history; he pleads that 'I have taken Care, not to offend the Modesty of the Fair, and have banish'd those Sentiments, which as beautiful as they are in *Ovid*, wou'd be as dangerous to Manners, as agreeable for their Tenderness and Passion.' In context, it is clear that there is an element of satire in his remarks, since he opens this paragraph with the observation that 'these poems, may perhaps appear too Amorous in so Grave and so Wise an Age as this is', but none the less he is forced on the defensive by public taste, which might question whether 'those Sentiments' are as appropriate to England in 1703 as they were to a pagan culture. Oldmixon does have the assurance to satirise Michael Drayton's adaption of the *Heroides*[16] and Thomas Rymer's version of 'Penelope to Ulysses'[17] for their low style and descent into the burlesque, but he is careful to justify his own adaption of the Ovidian mode (following Drayton's example) to 'our English History ... to vary the Subject, and to instruct, as well as please, by this Variety' ('Epistle Dedicatory').

If we turn to a more unreservedly sympathetic critic in Dryden (the 'Preface' to Jacob Tonson's 1680 edition of *Ovid's Epistles*, the collection to which Pope later added his *Sapho to Phaon*), we again find the charge of lasciviousness levelled at the 'Elegies' (*Amores*) and *Ars Amatoria*, but Dryden does go on to defend Ovid warmly as a poet of love:

yet this may be said in behalf of Ovid, that no man has ever treated the Passion of Love with so much Delicacy of Thought, and of Expression, or search'd into the nature of it more Philosophically than he ... I know no Authour who can justly be compar'd with ours, especially in the Description of the Passions ... His thoughts ... are the Pictures and results of those Passions.

He approves the *Heroides* above all as they are 'tenderly passionate and courtly', that is in so far as they treat of passion in a refined way. This defence is of great importance, and we may be certain that Pope would have read it with attention not only as the contributor of *Sapho to Phaon* but in view of Dryden's standing as a critic whose opinion carried great authority;[18] perhaps the most suggestive claim of Dryden's critique is the view that the passion of love may be treated 'Philosophically' by a writer of perception, which implies that the *analysis* of emotion is as much a merit of Ovid as his power to be evocative.

From these comments, both reserved and commendatory, we can form some idea of the context informing Pope's reception of Ovid, and consider this in charting his steps 'from translation to imitation, from imitation to creation' (TE, I, 329). As the editors of Pope's early translations in the Twickenham Edition point out, his version of the 'Polyphemus and Acis' story from the *Metamorphoses* is marked by a refusal to descend into burlesque distortion and by a more 'courtly' tone; Pope is able to treat Ovid's myth seriously and with sympathetic engagement, and the same sympathy is more fully apparent in his rendering of the mysterious relationship between man and the natural world in the *Vertumnus and Pomona* translation (1712). The opening lines of this version (ll.1-18) convey the idea of nature humanised as an innocent analogue to 'Venus and the Nuptial Joy', and the same consciousness underlies the latent eroticism embodied in natural description (ll.59-62). The delicacy of the man/nature relationship is of course central to the *Metamorphoses*, and Pope's sensitivity in evoking the transformation of Dryope (*The Fable of Dryope*, 1717) is further evidence of his responsiveness to that concept; in an early letter to Henry Cromwell, he gives approval (after some prevarication) to the idea of 'sensitive trees' as 'not only defensible, but beautiful'.[19] These characteristics have some importance when we consider the suggestive effects of natural description in *Eloisa to Abelard* (written in the same year as the *Vertumnus and Pomona* translation). In a wider sense also, Pope finds means of infusing his poem with the imaginative dimension to which he is undoubtedly receptive in Ovid by giving full rein to the flights and range of Eloisa's 'fancy'; hers is the power of the 'visionary maid' (l.162), religious mystery and intensity of passion uniting within the psychological complexity which Pope explores.

It appears also that Pope was not especially perturbed by Ovid's alleged 'lasciviousness', as we may judge from one of his letters to Cromwell (July 1710):

> I give you thanks for the Version you sent me of *Ovid's* Elegy. It is very much an image of that author's writing, who has an agreeableness that charms us without correctness, like a mistress whose faults we see, but love her with them all.[20]

Pope goes on in this letter to single out the eleventh Elegy of Book II, the eighth of Book III and the eleventh of Book III as 'above all my particular favourites, especially the last of these'. The three which he has selected show Ovid developing a variety of modes: the first elegiac, a sustained lament at the pains of separation, the second satiric and cynical, dwelling upon the intrusion of materialism into the realms of free love, and the third a bitter dismissal of love succeeded by a contest of love and hate which is never fully resolved. Despite key differences of mood and attitude, it is this third choice of Pope's which is particularly interesting with relation to *Eloisa to Abelard*; the opening to the second section of this poem shows love's victim struggling vainly against the bewildering, contradictory forces of his own heart, a portrait which takes on some poignancy after the disillusionment expressed in the preceding section:

> Luctantur pectusque leve in contraria tendunt
> hac amor hac odium, sed, puto, vincit amor.
> odero, si potero; si non, invitus amabo.

('Struggling over my fickle heart, love draws it now this way, and now hate that — but love, I think, is winning. I will hate, if I have strength; if not, I shall love unwilling.') (33-5)

> sic ego nec sine te nec tecum vivere possum,
> et videor voti nescius esse mei.

('Thus I can live neither with you nor without, and seem not to know my own heart's prayer'). (39-40)[21]

The poem provides a good example of Ovid's strength in exploring, not simply dominant moods, but the transition from one state of mind to another; Pope remarked upon Ovid's sense of design to Spence (*Anecdotes*, I, 226), probably following Dryden in referring to the principle of psychological movement which is so important in the *Elegy* and *Eloisa*. Further points which attracted his interest are well illustrated by his own translation of *Sapho to Phaon*, in which some of his striking elaborations are original, and a few derived from hints in Sir Carr Scrope's incomplete rendering, which had been first published in the 1680 edition of *Ovid's Epistles*.

The foremost feature of Pope's translation as against Scrope's is his heightening of the emotional tone to something less forced and freer in Ovid's manner, and that sense is reinforced when Pope boldly follows Ovid in making the erotic allusion of ll.17-18 specific (Scrope evades these lines, and one of Cromwell's marginalia to the manuscript of Pope's version suggests that they should be suppressed for reasons of decency).[22] Later Pope chooses to develop Ovid's passage describing sex (Ovid, ll.43-50), in a style of hyperbole:

> In all I pleas'd, but most in what was best;
> And the last Joy was dearer than the rest.
> Then with each Word, each Glance, each Motion fir'd,
> You still enjoy'd, and yet you still desir'd,
> Till all dissolving in the Trance we lay,
> And in tumultuous Raptures dy'd away.
>
> (57-62)

There are hints which link this rendering with Scrope's (cf. TE, I, 342-3), but altogether the effect is more direct than the more highly wrought Scropian manner, particularly in ll.59-60 which attempt to convey a sense of urgency rather than of brooding sensuality. Pope heightens the idea of rapturous intensity far more than Ovid does, adding l.58, emphasising by rhyme 'fir'd' and 'desir'd', and following Scrope in transforming Ovid's 'ubi amborum fuerat confusa voluptas' (49) into "all dissolving .../... in tumultuous Raptures', and it is in this stress on the very highest peaks of physical and emotional experience that there emerges a language closely bordering on the language of the spiritual. It is not incongruous to find Pope in the *Essay on Man* (I.278) setting forth the idea of angelic love as rapturous and consuming rather than serene, and the blending of the two orders of experience is brought out most clearly in comparing ll.95-106 of *Sapho to Phaon* with *Eloisa* ll.61-8, both of which share a language of adulation and hyperbole which embraces the ideas of sexual and spiritual love. For Sapho as for Eloisa this quality of experience is closely linked to the strength of imagination; Eloisa declares that in the first dawning of her love for Abelard 'My fancy form'd thee of Angelick Kind' (61) and in the dream-passage of *Sapho* (ll.145-58), which does of course have vital relevance to the parallel passage of *Eloisa* (ll.223-48), it is by the agency of 'Fancy' that the 'visionary Charms' are called to life in despite of physical absence. Ovid treats the dream more as an externalised apparition which arrives to comfort Sapho and then deserts her (l.125: 'illic te invenio ...'), whereas Pope's interest in 'Fancy' leads him to retain the concept introduced in Scrope's version, ll.64-5: 'The dear deluding Vision to retain / I lay me down, and try to sleep again.' Pope makes more dramatic use of the idea again in *Eloisa* ll.239-41, where although Eloisa finds herself bereft of the power to invoke the 'visionary' her will is striving towards that power and the role of the imagination in achieving the fulfilment of desires denied by the world is selfconsciously understood.

This interest in the psychological complexity of love moves Pope to accentuate its central importance even more (if possible) than Ovid does; in ll.73-80 he omits many of Ovid's details concerning Sapho's lifetime of suffering as an undesirable distraction from the central concern, and likewise at ll.19-20 he abridges Ovid's enumeration of Sapho's former Lesbian loves into two lines:

> All other Loves are lost in only thine,
> Ah Youth ungrateful to a Flame like mine!

This could of course be an evasion for reasons of decorum, but since Pope has already not scrupled to be explicit regarding the 'dear objects of my guilty Love' (l.18), that explanation seems inadequate. Instead we may suppose that Pope does not wish to divert the reader's attention from the overwhelming strength of Sapho's love, a strength of which she herself seems conscious with more assumed dignity than Ovid's reproachful Sapho ('improbe, multarum quod fuit, unus habes', l.20); the force of Pope's 'a Flame like mine' brings to mind Eloisa's claim for pre-eminence in love: '[may] Saints embrace thee with a love like mine' (l.342). Another change in mood is the softer despair conveyed in Pope's 'heav'nly Looks, and dear deluding Eyes' (l.22) in place of Ovid's more fierce 'o facies oculis insidiosa meis!' (l.22). Pope continually exploits the source of pain which lies at the heart of Sapho's complaint, that love has the force to transform the soul irremediably from its former peace and self-sufficiency, preventing any return to former pleasures and comforts; Sapho's heightened lament of ll.51-2 is centrally the source of anguish to Eloisa:

> No time the dear Remembrance can remove,
> For oh! how vast a Memory has Love?

The slightly altered phrase at l.7, translating Ovid's 'flendus amor meus est' (7) as 'Love taught my Tears in sadder Notes to flow', also contains the seeds of the idea that love comes as a form of *knowledge*, and with this concept the presence of 'shame' (central throughout the *Heroides*) assumes great significance. Pope retains Scrope's rearrangement of lines 135-42 to give the full weight to Ovid's 'non veniunt in idem pudor atque amor' (121), 'Such inconsistent things are Love and Shame!'. Equally interesting is Pope's couplet on the 'shame' of Sapho at her erotic vision, in which there seems to be a suggestion that guilt may actually testify to pleasure: 'Then fiercer Joys — I blush to mention these, / Yet while I blush, confess how much they please!' (ll.153-4); by blushing, the 'conscious Morn' is also implicated in her guilt at l.98. The distinction which might be drawn between private 'guilt' and public 'shame' does not in fact present the same acute dilemma for Sapho as for certain other Ovidian heroines (notably Dido, Canace, Phaedra, Deianira and Medea), whose sense of crime has as great a part in their anguish as the pain of loss. Pope's Eloisa shares all the intensity of Sapho's despair, but she shows also the more wilful recklessness which invites destruction as a necessary legacy of love; Oenone begs of Paris that he should 'swiftly come to my undoing' ('ut venias in mea damna celer!', *Oenone Paridi*, 58).

Pope is clearly interested in the force of an absolute commitment to love, and a generous triumph over the false dictates of shame, yet his handling of that concern is remarkable in bringing outbursts of defiant conviction into play beside Eloisa's very active sense of approaching spiritual damnation as well as personal guilt; her very insecurity gives emphasis to her capacity for heroism. The force of her will and her intellectual grasp on the nature of her dilemma are immediately apparent in relation to the conflict of love and honour as experienced by Ovid's Helen, for example, and if we note a further interesting analogy between her imaginary defence of Abelard from his attackers and Acontius' possessive frenzy in Ovid (*Heroides*, XX. 146-7), another distinctive dimension to her heroism is emphasised which will be discussed more fully later, and that is her generosity in love. As with the Lady of the *Elegy*, sheer extremity of emotion can represent the feminine equivalent of valorous action, and the heroines of the *Heroides* undergo the fluctuations of response from high tragic passion to lachrymose despair which are so characteristic of *Eloisa*. Love, for the Ovidian heroine, is a complex force in that it absorbs all loyalties, all passions and all relationships into itself (compare *Briseis Achilli* l.52: 'tu dominus, tu vir, tu mihi frater est', and *Hermione Orestae* l.29: 'vir, precor, uxori, frater succurre sorori!', with Eloisa's 'Come thou, my father, brother, husband, friend' (1.152). Because of this there is a strong emphasis on passions conflicting in varying degrees of violence, and in Pope's *Sapho to Phaon* the syntax is very carefully balanced to stress oppositions of feeling:

> I rave, then weep, I curse, and then complain,
> Now swell to Rage, now melt in Tears again.
> (131-2)

In adapting *Eloisa to Abelard* to the 'heroical epistle' form, however, Pope was introducing two essential deviations from the models of Ovid; he followed the path of Drayton and Oldmixon in treating of a known historical episode, and he introduced a Christian setting and morality in place of the pagan — the personification of Love at ll.73-84 is the only significantly pagan reference of the whole poem. But as Pope gives the fullest possible scope to the range of Eloisa's imagination, so he is able to heighten the very intensity of her passion and mental suffering by stressing the dilemma imposed upon her by Christian faith; this is not to argue that the Christian moral framework is of secondary importance within the poem, but the claims of religion cannot be approached by the reader except through the medium of Eloisa's intense feeling, and the nature of her response remains the focus of attention. Passion and imagination are so active throughout the poem that it becomes impossible to reach an objective vantage point from which to judge Eloisa's position. This greatly exalted interest in an acute moral dilemma clearly owes much to the ethos of the Restoration tragedies,[23] in which love and heroism are closely identified and forge an alliance against the encroachments of a hostile (and sternly moralistic) world. One helpful analogy which can be drawn is suggested by Eric Rothstein in his study *Restoration Tragedy: Form and the Process of Change* (1967), in which he discusses the differences between the 'heroic' ethos of the earlier tragedies and the 'pathetic' of those which were written after the 1680s. With the movement towards pathetic tragedy comes a shift in values away from the high heroic ideals and the firm morality which attends them in favour of what Rothstein (p.118) describes as a complex ethos of Epicureanism; there is a marked self-sufficiency on the part of the tragic hero or heroine which reflects the way in which 'the plays are dominated by love, a refined hedonism' (pp.120-1). The morality thus entails a curious fusion of the Stoic and the Epicurean, emphasising self-reliance, and yet a prescriptive moralising emphasis is strikingly absent in the pathetic tragedies. There is, however, considerable emphasis on moral *dilemma* in the greatest of Otway's tragedies, and it is significant that Pope spoke to Spence with particular approval of his 'two tragedies out of six that are pathetic', observing that "'Tis a talent of nature rather than an effect of judgement to write so movingly' (*Anecdotes*, I, 206).

A further point with important relevance to Pope's poem is that 'pathetic tragedy gives the characters an imaginative, even poetic faculty that heroic heroes do not have' (Rothstein, p.134), and this faculty, which as I have already remarked is greatly intensified in *Eloisa*, is shown in its purest form in the projection of pastoral vision into the very heart of the drama. Rothstein isolates the pastoral ideal (which is always the exclusive province of the victimised protagonists) as again inherently Epicurean, depending upon the 'exercise of the imaginative will' and embracing a form of escape from the hostile environment of 'necessity' (p.124). He relates the combined ideal of retirement and love to a passage of Aphra Behn's (*cit*. p.122) treating of love in the Golden Age when pure reason was synonymous with 'nature' and love unrestrained by the invocation of artificial 'Honour'. These ideals have a very close affinity with Eloisa's two imaginative projections of the ideal states of earthly love ('When love is liberty, and nature, law', ll.92-8)[24] and divine bliss ('How happy is the blameless Vestal's lot!', ll.206-22), and Brower (p.80) points out the close link in phrase and thought between ll.217-20 and Pope's pastoral *Autumn*, ll.24-6. Eloisa's momentary breaking out of her dilemma to the terms of pastoral (she is brought immediately back to earth at l.223) owes nothing to the Hughes translation of her letters[25] and nothing directly to Ovid, but there is a significant allusion in her celebrated line, 'The world forgetting, by the world forgot' (208) to Horace's *Epistle* I.xi.9, on the retirement theme.[26] It would seem that the immediate precedent for the 'blameless Vestal' passage may well be the conventions of the pathetic tragedy, although the 'escape through imagination' which the pastoral idyll offers to the protagonists of the drama is not fulfilled for Eloisa.

It is through the medium of Eloisa's imaginative consciousness that a pattern of suggestion is established which unobtrusively draws together on certain levels the apparently antithetical or disparate values of 'grace and nature, virtue and passion'. By confronting the moral dilemma itself, Pope persuasively implies that such a rigid separation of ideals is by its very nature fraught with inconsistency; both David Morris and Henry Pettit[27] have suggested that the terms of the *Essay on Man*, II. 81-6 have an important relevance to this false opposition, and, as different as the works are, the point is just. In reflecting on the oppositions between the erotic and the spiritual, *eros* and *agape*, the complexity of vision and values which Pope elaborates is deepened by the fact that the material of the *Heroides* and the content of Eloisa's letters from the Paraclete have remarkably close affinities, sometimes extending to very close parallels of detail. Eloisa's dream-vision of Abelard as related to *Sapho to Phaon* ll.145-58 is one striking instance of this, as is the seeming coincidence of l.152 ('Come thou, my father, brother, husband, friend'), taken from the letters but already mentioned as a close echo of lines in Ovid. Both sources inevitably share a stress on lost experience and on importunate desires cruelly denied by circumstance, and although Eloisa's profound concern with salvation so deeply complicates the nature of her spiritual suffering, none the less we are constantly made aware that she, like Ovid's heroines, has been transformed by her experience of love and can only attempt to understand the nature of the world and of the spirit in terms of that overwhelming experience. Throughout the poem, however closely she approaches the resolution offered by divine love, it is never fully accepted as a compensation for the relinquishing of human feeling. Hughes speaks in the 'Preface' to the letters of the 'most extravagant Passion' which is their principal feature, and tempts the reader further with their 'surprising Mixtures of Devotion and Tenderness, of Penitence and remaining Frailty, and a lively Picture of Human Nature in its Contrarieties of Passion and Reason, its Infirmities and its Sufferings'. Pope's drawing together of these observations into the succinct oppositions set forth in his 'Argument' to *Eloisa* subtly suggests a struggle which will take place on a higher idealistic plane; 'grace' and 'virtue' take the place of Hughes' 'Devotion' ... 'Penitence' ... 'Reason' (Pope was probably also thinking of Eloisa's fifth letter in the collection: 'I am sensible of the Motions both of Grace and Passion, and by turns yield to each', p.200), and likewise 'nature' and 'passion' represent much more than 'infirmities' in his hands. The passion of Eloisa and Abelard is for Pope 'unfortunate'; it is cut short by circumstance, and it is the force of irreversible circumstance that is most deeply felt in the convent and its setting. The delicate changes which Pope has made in his emphasis prepare us both for the force of aspiration and the driving intensity of despair to which he is so responsive.

The setting of the convent is used evocatively to express the heightened responsiveness of Eloisa's mind, a sensitivity which is accentuated by the condition of isolation, and which is brought into play from the moment when her memory of Abelard is reawakened. The 'deep solitudes and awful cells' to which she is confined bear an affinity with the Platonic 'cave of the mind', the source of oppressive memories and of the 'lov'd Idea' of sublimity. In its recesses lie the terrors of vacuity and of active nightmare, which are yet bound in with a mystic sense of the divine, and the poem dramatises the anguished fluctuations between these psychological extremes. Eloisa's consciousness is seen as intensely active; from Abelard's name alone, and from her own name inscribed in his letters, their 'long train of calamities' is recalled in all its potency and depth of emotional association, and emotion is transmuted by impulse into action (9-16), that is, the action of utterance in speech and writing, ambiguously distinguished in the poem. At certain key moments of crisis, Eloisa invokes her own name in the third person, which in itself represents a form of self-assertion; at such moments her name is made synonymous with the force of love, and within the rhetoric of the verses love is made synonymous with life itself. The tragic lament of l.37, with its allusion to Dryden's version of *Palamon and Arcite* ('Now warm in love, now with'ring in the grave') associates sexual with physical death, and the elegiac note is restated in the lines which follow (39-40):

> There stern religion quench'd th'unwilling flame,
> There dy'd the best of passions, Love and Fame.

Hence the convent as 'this last retreat' embodies both death and the tomb, a burial in the self where no reciprocity is ossible. Likewise, emotion is presented metaphorically in physical terms as the essential vigour of the body, a conception which is brought out in figures of speech in the earliest lines of the lament: 'What means this tumult in a Vestal's veins?'; 'Nor pray'rs nor fasts its stubborn pulse restrain'.

Like Ovid's Hypermnestra, Eloisa takes comfort and strength from the mysterious power communicated by sympathetic grief, which in confinement can alone compensate for physical separation; Pope intensifies Eloisa's defence of this last remaining power to a degree which is expressed as devotional. This devotion is the more remarkable when we are reminded that Eloisa's incarceration in the convent is itself a sacrifice which she has chosen to make through love: 'Sad proof how well a lover can obey!' (172). The duty done to love is indeed a personal form of piety:

> Tears still are mine, and those I need not spare,
> Love but demands what else were shed in pray'r.
> (45-6)

In this devotion Eloisa is extravagantly magnanimous ('Ah more than share it! Give me all thy grief'), and both the warmth and the constancy of human dedication are in marked contrast to the forced and frozen enactment of Christian devotions; statues '*learn* to weep', tears are '*taught* to flow in vain'. Constriction and deprivation exert an almost unbearable pressure on the mounting force of passion, not merely in the 'gothic' chill of the setting but in the emptiness of prayers unanswered; there is a double significance in Eloisa's outcry:

> Relentless walls! whose darksome round contains
> Repentant sighs, and voluntary pains.

For her at least, the acts of contrition are literally 'contained' in a cycle of futility, achieving no relation to any receptive presence outside the convent, and her confession of ll.23-4 declaring the persistence of 'rebel nature' has something of the defiance of hopelessness (cf. Hughes, p.129: 'O Vows! O Convent! I have not lost my humanity under your inexorable Discipline!'). This sense of futility is above all contrasted to the felicity of human love, the greatest bliss being that of reciprocation:

> All then is full, possessing, and possest,
> No craving Void left aking in the breast:
> (93-4)

It is Eloisa's emotional state, Brendan O'Hehir has argued, which is responsible for the 'pathetic fallacy' taking place at ll.107-17 and again at l.274, rhapsodies which he presents as visual distortions caused by her tears. Yet there is also an extraordinary reversal taking place in Eloisa's consciousness which makes the fallacy boldly double-edged in its implications. Eloisa's inspiration at both these moments is not her Christian piety but her devotion to Abelard and to the force of love:

> Not on the Cross my eyes were fix'd, but you;
> Not grace, or zeal, love only was my call.
> (116-7)

Her avowal that 'Saints with wonder heard the vows I made' hence endows her love with a sanctity of its own in the very moment when it is ostensibly forsworn. Again, there is an underlying dignity and defiance in Eloisa's emphasis on her own passionate and enduring nature which greatly modifies the more confessional, 'pathetic' note which follows her evocation of 'that sad, that solemn day':

> Still on that breast enamour'd let me lie,
> Still drink delicious poison from thy eye,

Pant on thy lip, and to thy heart be prest;
Give all thou canst — and let me dream the rest.
(121-4)

The boldness with which Pope treats the passage extolling the freedom of love might be contrasted with the long discussion which is given to the issue in Hughes' introductory 'History', where he comments upon Eloisa's preference of love to marriage:

> Indeed a Refusal of this Nature is so extraordinary a thing, that perhaps another Instance of it is not to be found in History ... It often happens that the Passion of Love stifles or over-rules the Rebukes of Conscience; but it is unusual for it to extinguish the Sensibility of Honour ... but *Heloise* had a Passion so strong, that she was not at all concern'd for her Honour or Reputation ... An excess of Passion never heard of before, made her chuse to be *Abelard's* Mistress rather than his Wife. (pp.21-2)

Although Tillotson refers to Hughes' tone here as marked by a 'slightly vulgar relish and insistence' (TE, II, 325n.), there is also a feeling of astonished admiration which grows into the recognition that 'Honour' is a concept which appears to be outside the heroine's frame of reference, and Pope elaborates this feeling into assertive dignity. He also adds to the human basis of the argument the poetic evocation of love's divinity; love is spoken of as the 'jealous God', calling to mind the rival God (Exodus 20:5) vying for Eloisa's exceptional soul.

It is through her love for Abelard that Eloisa's first transition from the human sphere to the spiritual is represented, effortlessly and innocently by the agency of imagination ('My Fancy form'd thee of Angelick kind') and there is perhaps a deliberate ambiguity as to whether Abelard's 'truths divine' are in fact his doctrines as her instructor in religion or relate to the precept that ''twas no sin to love' (l.68); but we are made conscious of a certain moral courage in her setting aside of 'Fancy' to encounter the joys of physical reality:

> Back through the paths of pleasing sense I ran,
> Nor wish'd an Angel whom I lov'd a Man.
> Dim and remote the joys of saints I see,
> Nor envy them, that heav'n I lose for thee.
> (69-72)

The telling shift here from past to present tense indicates what is still the direction of her commitment. In this passage there is an awareness that in some way her former 'guiltless' self has been left behind, but that state of innocence becomes pale beside the warmth of love. When Eloisa strives to regain innocence by contrition, it is inverted and condemned by her love as a sin:

> Now turn'd to heav'n, I weep my past offence,
> Now think of thee, and curse my innocence.
>
> (187-8)

These central concepts of humanity and divinity, innocence and sin, are charged with suggestions of paradox throughout the poem. Innocence may be seen as a state of unknowing, undivided consciousness, or instead as the conscious refusal to embrace a false morality and to acknowledge 'shame'. Among the passages which reflect upon guilt and self-expression, there is the interesting transition from the appeal to the artificial language of letters, which express the reciprocal 'soft intercourse' of love without betraying the physical signs of shame, to the ideal state of 'shamelessness' when intuition takes the place of speech, to the dramatically pictured scene of Abelard's castration, when literal speech is overcome in Eloisa and she is reduced to the now impotent language of the body: 'By shame, by rage supprest, / Let tears, and burning blushes speak the rest' (105-6).[28] The powerful later passage on the unfettered violence of guilt (223-48) presents, both in its content and context, further depths; 'conscience' as modesty is set aside to make way for the soul's immersion in a rapture of the subconscious, which positively embraces consciousness of guilt:

> All my loose soul unbounded springs to thee.
> O curst, dear horrors of all-conscious night!
> How glowing guilt exalts the keen delight!

The two meanings of 'loose' (unrestrained, and wanton) are equally apt. Structurally, this whole visionary rhapsody — evolving into nightmare — is strikingly set between two evocative passages on the peace of spiritual purity (207-22, 249-56), superficially variations on a similar theme of retired innocence. In the first, the pastoral and paradisal idyll of the 'blameless Vestal', reciprocity is discovered, desires are reconciled, emotion and imagination find undestructive ends, and finally spiritual marriage is united with unalloyed pleasure. Thus the image of marriage is revitalised after Eloisa's earlier repudiation, and is set against the depiction of her marriage to the convent as a parody of sterile matrimony: ('Sad proof how well a lover can obey! / Death, only death, can break the lasting chain'). By contrast with the imagery of physical consummation as the culminating bliss of the 'vestal', the release from passion which is Abelard's lot cannot fail to strike us with a sense of tragic deprivation, despite its premonition of a 'promis'd heav'n':

> Thy life a long, dead calm of fix'd repose;
> No pulse that riots, and no blood that glows.
> Still as the sea, ere winds were taught to blow,
> Or moving spirit bade the waters flow;
>
> (251-4)

The word 'ordain' of l.249 in context evokes a sense of fatality, of a rigorous and definitive sentence which suggests retribution as much as redemption. The whole passage resembles other lines of Pope's concerning passion as an animating force, in particular the images of still water as a negative metaphor for Stoic detachment within the *Essay on Man*, reinforced by the suggestion here of a regression to the time before Genesis (when 'the spirit of God moved on the face of the waters'). The same metaphor in Hughes does not imply a negative 'gain': 'The Punishment of your Body, has cured the deadly Wounds of your Soul. The Tempest has driven you into the Haven' (p.176). Eloisa herself speaks of Abelard's condition as a living death (251, 257, 261-2), and there is a logical link between the earlier recollection of the physical assault upon Abelard and the succeeding image of Eloisa and Abelard as sacrificial victims to religion (108). Yet ironically it is also Abelard who is the founder or 'Maker' of the Paraclete as a house of religion, and (as Eloisa recalls) the instructor or 'creator' of Eloisa as a lover. If he becomes merged in her consciousness with God, it is perhaps quintessentially as the source of her abiding passion, an emotional awakening into life, which persists even when he is metaphorically dead. The emphasis on faithfulness in the reference to Eloisa's 'hopeless, lasting flames' becomes clearer by analogy with her second letter in the Hughes collection: 'When we love Pleasures, we love the living and not the dead. We leave off burning with Desire, for those who can no longer burn for us' (p.12). The connection of tombs with 'dying lamps' recurs again at ll.303-8, and significantly the lamps fade at the time of Eloisa's taking the veil (112). Gradually fear begins to take precedence over courage, and the desire of flight gains in intensity; this fear for salvation is matched with a more personal sense of relationship in Eloisa's apprehension of God: 'Thy image steals between my God and me' (l.268). Pope makes a rhetorical motif of Eloisa's strangely invoking/repelling call to Abelard to 'Come ... and solicite me to love you' (Hughes p.144) and adds to it the fiercer note of challenge '... if thou dar'st' (281); he also intensifies the opposition between the rival claims on her soul in transferring Abelard's 'Assist the Evil Spirits, and be the Instrument of their Malice' to Eloisa's highly dramatic, 'Snatch me, just mounting, from the blest abode, /Assist the Fiends, and tear me from my God!' (287-8). One might see in this crisis Eloisa's final breaking-point, the point at which the terror of the consequences she is inviting upon herself bears down on her more forcibly than anything else, and her appeal to the powers of redemption immediately afterwards (297-302) is both impassioned and eloquent. In the same impulse, her repudiation of Abelard is still suffused with a spirit of (partly reproachful) generosity:

> Ah come not, write not, think not once of me,
> Nor share one pang of all I felt for thee.
> Thy oaths I quit, thy memory resign.
>
> (291-3)

As at several other points of the poem, Pope has transferred to Eloisa one of Abelard's fairly rare expressions of selflessness. Eloisa's state after this outburst is itself close to death (304), and consistent with her final letter in the Hughes edition in which it is the prospect of death made real during a long illness which acts most persuasively on her sense of her spiritual condition. The 'Christianising' of the spiritual apparitions which are familiar from the *Heroides* (appearing both to Sapho and Dido) is a remarkable stroke, and Pope has brought out a shift from the pagan to the Christian explicitly: 'Love's victim then, tho' now a sainted maid' (312). Yet the undeniable closeness of lines 333-4 to the conclusion of the *Elegy* restates the tragic note which has been present throughout, emphasising the sorrow of a love not only forgotten but lost to the memory of posterity:

> See the last sparkle languish in my eye!
> Till ev'ry motion, pulse, and breath, be o'er;
> And ev'n my *Abelard* be lov'd no more.
> O death all-eloquent! you only prove
> What dust we doat on, when 'tis man we love.
> (332-6)

From fearing that the love of heaven may snatch Abelard from herself, Eloisa now comes to hope that the divine love extended to him may equal her own (342); this, and the concern with posterity and the earthly 'fame' invested in exemplary love, argues again a persistent value for human feeling. Pope elaborates this theme greatly in the final verse-paragraph, which owes nothing to the Hughes letters but which, like the ending of the *Elegy*, dwells upon the sharing of sympathetic grief; the 'mutual pity' and the 'human tear'. The feeling of resistance in ll.355-8, the return to a vision of religion once more in conflict with earthly sentiment, and the more unexpected appeal to 'some future Bard' for solace, all imply a recognition which is made explicit at l.365; that the lover's ghost will still be 'pensive', that memory will disturb spiritual peace even after death.

Subjectivity is thus reasserted even in this final valediction; throughout the poem, the central tension of the earthly and the divine is seen as a subjective experience, with its shifting interchanges of memory, association and imagination. Perhaps the most eloquent lines in *Eloisa* express the irremediable nature of her conflict as rooted in the complexity of the mind:

> How shall I lose the sin, yet keep the sense,
> And love th' offender, yet detest th'offence?
> How the dear object from the crime remove,
> And how distinguish penitence from love?
> (191-4)

Memory presents at once the firmest constancy to her human affections, and the most insuperable barrier between the soul and heaven; in the Hughes edition of the letters (p.174), Eloisa refers to the extinguishing of the memory of pleasures as 'the last violence to our Nature'. Forgetfulness is then a condition of mind which must be actively *achieved* (190), a psychological impossibility. The only countering force which may be invoked is direct intervention by God, portrayed as an act of violence (201-2) which parallels the imagery of physical rupture expressing Eloisa's human love (196). There are many indications that her capacity for love may be rivalled by her capacity for ecstatic religious experience; Joseph Warton appropriately commented on these lines (TE, II, 366n.): 'here is the true doctrine of the Mystics ... There are many such strains in Crashaw.' The mystic quality is a remarkable strength of *Eloisa*, reinforced by the element of 'gothic' gloom and psychological melancholy with which the poem is suffused, and which of course owes much to Milton's minor poems, notably *Comus* and *Il Penseroso*. The 'gothic' strain represents a deepening of that pathetic fallacy of scenes strongly coloured by mental association which Pope developed from Ovid (see Pope's *Sapho to Phaon*, 163-78), and it is brought out at a great many points of the poem. Pope was probably referring in part to the evocative power of setting when he wrote to William Cowper in February 1731/2: 'I should not be sorry if you tryed your hand [as translator] upon Eloisa to Abelard, since it has more of that Descriptive, and, (if I may say so) Enthusiastic Spirit, which is the Character of the Ancient Poets.'[29] The reflection of Eloisa's state of mind in her projection of the scenes around her is developed from the earliest passages on the convent, and is most powerful in the striking personification of 'Melancholy' in ll.161ff.; the full extent of the passage, which effectively begins at l.132, represents a series of settings which variously reflect Eloisa's changing spiritual vision, both of the past and the present. The image of the Paraclete as pastoral retreat, a 'Paradise' of spiritual aspiration amid the desert, gives way in Abelard's absence to the 'noon-day night' cast by its walls, recalling the images of the convent in the opening lines of the poem. The transition which has taken place in her mind is subtly developed and yet profound; in certain respects, Abelard comes to assume a dual role of lover and Christ-figure, although Eloisa is here alert to the distinction between *eros* and *agape* ('Oh pious fraud of am'rous charity'). Her yearning towards the repose of contemplation is also a yearning for the fulfilment which has been lost through him, and is expressed in the delicate, slightly Spenserian lines which evoke an erotic, sensitive natural world:

The darksom pines that o'er yon' rocks reclin'd
Wave high, and murmur to the hollow wind,
The wandring streams that shine between the hills,
The grots that echo to the tinkling rills,
The dying gales that pant upon the trees,
The lakes that quiver to the curling breeze;

(155-60)

The quality of these lines, with their blending of sensuality with
fine delicacy, has been described as 'rococo',[30] and it is in contrast
to this imaginary state of receptive motion that the 'dread repose'
of the spectre Melancholy has such morbid power, a power which
impels Eloisa towards thoughts of her own death and the 'cold
dust' of eternity. This spiritual landscape represents the deepest
point of the suffering and repression forced upon her; set against
it are the moments of greatest emotional and imaginative exaltation, the dimension which is most aptly termed 'mystic'. We are
made aware of Eloisa's facility for high spiritualising of experience in the metaphysical terms of her first image of Abelard: 'My
fancy form'd thee of Angelick kind, / Some emanation of th'all-
beauteous Mind' (61-2), and Eloisa's conception both of the
earthly and divine is throughout coloured by an emphasis on
ecstasy and rapture. Thus her imaginative projection of the
'blameless Vestal's lot' culminates in rapture which seems distinctly sexual by analogy with the 'marriage' metaphor (219-22),
and her first vision of her own death is also sensuous and finally
climactic. Again, Eloisa pictures the death of Abelard in terms of
a rhapsody of the divine (339-42), with the plea, '[May] Saints
embrace thee with a love like mine.' It might be possible to dis-
miss these conceptions as a poignant reminder of the strength of
Eloisa's human bonds; but earlier in the poem her vision of the
intensity of divine communion ('Not touch'd, but rapt; not
waken'd, but inspir'd') has no hint of pathos or self-deception
about it, and the 'hopeless, lasting flames' of human love are ultimately sublimated in a 'firing' of the soul, the 'flames refin'd'
(320) which burn in heaven. The imagery of light and fire
throughout the poem, though conventional, unites the conceptions of human and divine love, and it is significant that the full
force of Eloisa's passion should overwhelm her in the very acts of
Christian devotion. Despite the fact that Pope introduces a few
lines of satire on florid extravagance in religion (135-40) which

anticipate the redundant splendours of Timon's chapel, religious ceremony is used to express something more than external pomp and apparently deeper than the emotional fallacy which plays upon Eloisa's vision at ll.111-14 and 271-6; if human passion is active here in bringing about a state close to divine ecstasy, there is at least an implication through the poetry that divine love has part in the experience:

> Priests, Tapers, Temples, swim before my sight:
> In seas of flame my plunging Soul is drown'd
> While Altars blaze, and Angels tremble round.
>
> (274-6)

Pope seems to have forgotten 'such plain roofs as piety could raise' in his vision of ceremony with its profusion of lamps and altars and incense rising in 'clouds of fragrance'. He clearly has an interest in an exuberant descriptive and experiential dimension which can best be characterised as 'baroque'. In this relation it would however be misleading to identify the baroque tendencies with counter-reformation Catholicism specifically, since Pope's conception of rapturous spiritual experience owes much to the verse of the Nonconformist Isaac Watts, to the point of a close debt in l.275 (TE, II, 304). What is important is that the interest in 'extasy' in *Eloisa* does frequently tend towards the mystic, and this peak of spiritual experience is intimately linked with the quieter meditational note which significantly is much indebted to Crashaw (see lines 270, 300, 328 and the specific allusion of l.212). Although Pope's response to Crashaw was in many respects unsympathetic,[31] he did express his admiration for the 'soft and pleasing' verses of 'The Weeper', including stanzas 16 and 17, which contemplate the 'kind contrarieties' of the Magdalene's redemptive grief.[32] As Austin Warren points out in his study of Crashaw, 'Catholicism has persistently affirmed that, as the body, the senses, the affections and the imagination are integral parts of man, they must all collaborate in God's service';[33] this concern could be seen as dominant in the baroque, and in so far as *Eloisa* expresses the affinity between the earthly and divine in terms of a sublimated but pervasive sensuality, its devotional content seems distinctively to reflect Pope's Catholic sensibilities.

If *Eloisa* might be seen as sharing in part a 'baroque' sensibility, then certain elements in its conception — its complex sensuality, its often extravagant pitch of emotion, and the finally inconclusive nature of its moral emphasis — may seem less disturbing than many critics have found them. The greatest difficulty posed by the poem, it seems, lies in its subjectivity; Patricia Spacks, seeing Eloisa as 'psychotic', is highly critical of the fact that 'the poet's voice ... indicates no awareness of anything wrong with his central figure' (*An Argument of Images*, 1971, p.237). She alleges that Pope shows an inability to analyse the 'imbalance' displayed in *Eloisa*, and observes by a pejorative comparison with *The Rape of the Lock* that 'he appeared unable to replace the complexity of satire with any other real complexity: the alternations of an emotional seesaw involve only shifts of attention, not of perspective' (pp.237-8). This assertion is profoundly misleading, since the complexity of *Eloisa* is on a quite different plane from that of the *Rape*, and lies *within* its subjectivity; it is achieved through the very enclosedness, the submergence of the poet's voice in the imagined experience and consciousness of his protagonist. The evocation of the relationship between 'grace and nature, virtue and passion' in terms of an extreme conflict is thus a means of exploration, and the urgency of the opposition is expressive of a struggle which does not point to mere confusion or capitulation on Eloisa's part, but a sustained moral idealism.

Notes

Unless otherwise stated, all texts listed below bear a London imprint.

1. Reuben A. Brower, *Alexander Pope: the Poetry of Allusion* (Oxford, 1959), 64.
2. Cited by Geoffrey Tillotson, *Twickenham Edition of the Works of Alexander Pope*, II, 301n. — volumes of this edition are hereafter referred to as 'TE'; *see* List of Abbreviations.
3. *Correspondence*, I, 338 (March 1716; the date assigned by Sherburn is conjectural). *See* List of Abbreviations.
4. The representation of emotion in the poem is discussed in the light of contemporary aesthetics by Brewster Rogerson in his article, 'The art of painting the passions', *JHI*, 14 (1953), 68-94.
5. *See* Tillotson, TE, II, 308-11, and Hoyt Trowbridge, 'Pope's *Eloisa* and the *Heroides* of Ovid', in *Studies in Eighteenth Century Culture*, edited by Harold Pagliaro (Cleveland and London, 1973), III, 11-34.

6. Robert P. Kalmey ('Rhetoric, language and structure in *Eloisa to Abelard*', *ECS*, 5 (1971), 315-18) sees the four traditional stages of penance — contrition, confession, absolution and purgation — as enacted in the course of the poem. Stephen J. Ackerman ('The vocation of Pope's Eloisa', *SEL*, 19 (1979), 445-57) argues that the Holy Spirit finally commands Eloisa's soul and enables her fully to distinguish *eros* from *agape*. Brendan O'Hehir ('Virtue and passion: the dialectic of *Eloisa to Abelard*', *Texas Studies in Literature and Language*, 2 (1960), 219-32) similarly concludes that at the close of the poem 'no obstacles remain to the consummation of [Eloisa's] marriage to Christ' (231).

7. Johnson (*Lives of the English Poets*, edited by George Birkbeck Hill (Oxford, 1905), III, 226) refers bitterly to Pope's 'illaudible singularity of treating suicide with respect', and William Roscoe (*The Works of Alexander Pope*, 1824, III, 223) speaks of the poet's sentiments as 'unpardonable'.

8. D.C. Mell, *A Poetics of the Augustan Elegy* (Amsterdam, 1974), 39.

9. Howard D. Weinbrot, 'Pope's *Elegy to the Memory of an Unfortunate Lady*', *MLQ*, 32 (1971), 255-67.

10. Rachel Trickett, *The Honest Muse: A Study in Augustan Verse* (Oxford, 1967), 165.

11. Tillotson (TE, 363n.) points out an important analogue from Dryden's *Absalom and Achitophel* which lends authority to the concept.

12. Spence, *Anecdotes*, I, 14; *see* List of Abbreviations.

13. *ibid.*, 232.

14. *See* L. P. Wilkinson, *Ovid Recalled* (Cambridge, 1955), 439-44 and Douglas Bush, *Mythology and the Romantic Tradition in English Poetry* (Cambridge, Mass. 1937), 3-50.

15. Louise Vinge, *The Narcissus Theme in Western European Literature up to the Early Nineteenth Century* (Lund, 1967), 253.

16. Drayton, *Englands Heroicall Epistles* (1598-9).

17. 'Penelope to Ulysses' was included in the 1680 Tonson edition of *Ovid's Epistles*, and Pope's own translation of *Sapho to Phaon* was added to a later edition of this volume in 1712.

18. *See An Essay on Criticism*, ll.458-65, and 482-3, in which Pope praises Dryden's critical powers.

19. *Correspondence*, I, 97 (August 1710).

20. *Correspondence*, I, 92.

21. *Amores*, III. 11; I have quoted from the Loeb Library edition of *Heroides and Amores*, translated by Grant Showerman (London, 1921), which is used throughout this chapter.

22. The manuscript of the translation is in the Pierpont Morgan Library, New York.

23. The point is brought up by Tillotson, TE, II, 299, and by David B. Morris, ('"The visionary maid": tragic passion and redemptive sympathy in Pope's *Eloisa to Abelard*', *MLQ*, 34 (1973), 247-71).

24. Pope used l.92 once more in *An Essay on Man*, III. 208 to describe the 'Origin of Political Societies', as yet uncorrupted.

25. John Hughes, *Letters of Abelard and Heloise ... Extracted chiefly from Monsieur Bayle*; I have consulted the fourth edition (1722), to accord with the pagination of quotations given in TE, II.
26. Stephen J. Ackerman ('The vocation of Pope's Eloisa') also remarks that 'Pope portrays the life of the nun in terms characteristic of the Happy Man theme of Augustan literature' (454), a life in harmony with nature which Ackerman, in accordance with his reading of the poem, represents as culminating in the apprehension of the 'True Nature' of Eden.
27. Morris, '"The visionary maid"', p.262; Henry Pettit, '*Eloisa to Abelard: an interpretation*', *University of Colorado Studies: Series in Language and Literature*, 4 (1953), 67-74.
28. An excellent article by Gillian Beer ('"Our unnatural no-voice": the heroic epistle, Pope, and women's gothic', *YES*, 12 (1982), 125-51) considers the struggle to make language fill the void as presence, and 'substitute for the potentialities of the whole body' (141).
29. *Correspondence*, III, 269.
30. James E. Wellington, '*Eloisa to Abelard*' (Miami, 1965), 46.
31. *See* Austin Warren, 'The reputation of Crashaw in the seventeenth and eighteenth centuries', *Studies in Philology*, 31 (1934), 385-407. Warren is so puzzled by Pope's apparent hostility to Crashaw that he postulates that he was contriving 'to give an impression which he certainly could not have received,' in order to mask his own Catholic sympathies. This conclusion is open to doubt, however, since Pope would certainly have found Crashaw's metaphysical strain over-ingenious and lacking in taste.
32. *Correspondence*, I, 110 (December 1710).
33. Austin Warren, *Richard Crashaw* (Louisiana, 1939), 66.

CHAPTER TWO

'What stranger Cause':
Pope's *Iliad* and *The Rape of the Lock*

In April 1724, Pope wrote to Lord Bolingbroke thanking him for sending a copy of Voltaire's poem *La Ligue* (1723), and remarking that as his French was imperfect, 'I can only tell my thoughts in Relation to the design and conduct of the Poem, or the sentiments'. As a 'heroic' poem, the first aspect of the work which engages his attention and praise is the conduct of the 'machinery', which he analyses in the following terms:

> I think the forming the Machines upon the Allegorical persons of Virtues and vices very reasonable; it being equally proper to Ancient and Modern subjects, and to all Religions and times: Nor do we look upon them so much as Heathen Divinities as Natural passions. This is not the case when Jupiter, Juno &c. are introduc'd who tho' sometimes consider'd as Physical powers yet that sort of Allegory lies not open enough to the apprehension. (*Correspondence*, II, 228)

The problem here formulated concerning allegory was a subject which had occupied Pope's attention throughout the past decade while he had been preparing his translation and commentary on the *Iliad* and the *Odyssey*. At this point, when the project was nearing its completion, it is interesting to find Pope expressing a summary view on the nature of pagan agents and their apparent unsuitability to the action of a modern poem; the explicitness of his formula as expressed here is, none the less, somewhat misleading. In the context of Homer's epics, Pope had found the relationship between machinery and moral allegory to be more elusive, as his final remark quoted above acknowledges. A more flexible interpretation of the role of the heathen divinities is put forward in the 'General View of the Epic Poem ... Extracted from Bossu' which Pope prefixed to his translation of the *Odyssey* in 1725;[1] here the analysis of the 'Machinery' draws the familiar distinctions between theological, physical and moral agents, representing the latter as 'the Images of Virtue and Vices', and in the terms of this analysis Homer's practice is seen as conforming most fully to the latter type:

> *Homer* and the Ancients have given to their Deities the Manners, Passions and Vices of Men. Their Poems are wholly Allegorical; ... since of our Passions we make so many allegorical Deities; one may attribute to the *Gods* all that is done in the Poem, whether good or evil. (TE, IX, 22-3)

It becomes clear from a study of Pope's notes to the *Iliad* that he was eager to pursue this line of interpretation, and that it does in fact form a crucial part of his understanding of the action and significance of the poem. In this chapter I would like to examine more fully the terms of Pope's approach to Homer, considering firstly the broad fabric of his aesthetic interests, and secondly the way in which these are related to his interpretation of the *Iliad*. Pope's work on the translation from 1713 onwards is of central importance to the cast of his own mock-heroic satires, above all to the conception of the *Rape of the Lock*, published in its five-canto version in 1714; and as William Frost has demonstrated, the process of exchange was often complex, with Pope apparently forging allusive links between the *Rape* and sections of the *Iliad* translation as yet unpublished.[2] For the purposes of the following discussion, I have confined my attention to the commentary on the *Iliad*, partly because by the nature of its action and in point of chronology it bears the closest connection with the *Rape*, and partly because Pope was far less dependent in this first phase of his undertaking on his collaborators Broome and Fenton, who had a large hand in the translation and the compiling of notes for the *Odyssey*.

Throughout the 'Preface' and notes to the *Iliad*, Pope's concern with the powers of Homer's 'Invention' and his persistent discussion of universalised psychological and moral issues assume paramount importance, and although his observations draw for support on a considerable body of earlier critics, he was most acutely conscious of the need to be selective and present a coherent commentary.[3] His instructions to Broome, for example, were to extract from Eustathius 'such notes only as concern the beauties or art of the author ... What are allegorical, if obvious and ingenious, abstract; if far-fetched, omit' (*Correspondence*, I, 270). The notes show Pope declaring war on specious emotive rapture as the great bane of criticism ('Tho' I am a Poet', he remarks in the *Odyssey* postcript, 'I would not be an Enthusiast'), yet the claim which he makes for Homer in an early letter to Ralph Bridges,[4] that 'no man who has a true Poetical spirit is Master of himself, while he reads him' is emphatically repeated in the *Iliad* 'Preface'. Something of this spirit of intensity is conveyed also in the manner of the translation itself, although it is not my purpose here to discuss the style of Pope's rendering in any detail. Two aspects of Pope's text that are striking, however, are the universalising tendency which implicitly heightens its 'sententious' content,[5] and the quality often termed 'baroque', which places considerable emphasis on the emotions and their physical effects. Pope endeavours to render the animation and even the violence of the original wherever possible (see Book XIII, n.191), and to give expression (particularly through rhetoric) to the different emotional keys which he finds in it. Recognising that the role of translator in itself implies the role of critic, he makes the 'Boldness' of Homer's expression his foremost concern, and constantly draws attention to this emphasis in the commentary.

Pope's 'Preface' to the *Iliad* is remarkable for the rhetorical flights and extravagances of its key passages, particularly those in which he celebrates the abundance of 'Fire' and 'Invention' in Homer, the qualities which he sees as animating art to the heights of the sublime. The emphasis on invention as the primary attribute of 'original Genius' is something of a commonplace in early eighteenth-century criticism, and Pope's distinction between this attribute and the 'Judgement' of Virgil is (as he himself points out in the 'Preface') a close imitation of Addison's *Spectator* essay no. 279 (1713). Both essays present these two qualities as having equal weight in the achievement of poetic excellence; yet Pope gives an implicit primacy to invention in treating it almost as an artistic 'ruling passion' in Homer, 'a strong and ruling Faculty' which 'in the violence of its course, drew all things within its Vortex': 'It grows in the Progress both upon himself and others, and becomes on Fire like a Chariot-Wheel, by its own Rapidity' (TE, VII, 4). The reiterated allusions to such concepts as 'Fire', 'Rapture' and 'Sublimity' combine to put forward an aesthetic code celebrating both imaginative freedom and the notion of an irresistible emotional or cathartic force. Pope's idea of the 'sublime' is not finally developed to the point which it had reached by the end of the eighteenth century, embracing an abandonment to intense feeling and 'enthusiastic' response;[6] Mack is right to interpret the general direction of Pope's thought in this area as Longinian,[7] and in the *Iliad* 'Preface' this influence is acknowledged when Pope invokes the authority of Longinus in eulogising the 'Sublimity and Spirit of [Homer's] Thoughts'. None the less, although Mack presents these terms simply as 'stemming from an idea of elevated style as the source of "transport"' (TE, VII, ccxxii), Pope has clearly advanced his apprehension of the reader's response to Homer beyond the field of rhetorical theory and into an area of aesthetics which embraces a fuller emotional empathy, evoked by the total *conception* of the poem. Homer's invention 'exerts itself ... thro' all the main constituent Parts of his Work', taking in 'the whole Compass of Nature to supply his maxims and reflections; all the inward Passions and Affections of Mankind to furnish his Characters, and all the outward Forms and Images of Things for his Descriptions.'

The nature of the emotional force generated by this copiousness and high reach of imagination is resolved by Pope into the Aristotelian formula of 'Pity and Terror', and these terms are developed within the body of the notes into a dominant interest in scenes of pathos and scenes of intense passion. 'Terror' is thus an interest which is implicit in Pope's admiration for violence in Homer; for the battle scenes, each excelling the last in 'Greatness, Horror and Confusion', for the 'dread and horror' conveyed in the shipwreck image in Book XV (n.752), and in his dramatised notion of Homer himself, 'boundless and irresistible as *Achilles* ... like his own *Jupiter* in his Terrors, shaking *Olympus*, scattering the Lightnings, and firing the Heavens' ('Preface', p.12). It is interesting that in this last image Pope implicitly identifies Homer with the jealous and angry God of the Old Testament, while he goes on to compare Virgil with 'the same Power in his Benevolence ... regularly ordering his whole Creation', and he raises this distinction again in a note to Book VIII (n.95). The analogy of Homer to Achilles is also significant, since Pope sees in the anger of Achilles the entire motive force of the *Iliad*, and his comments on the moral scheme and psychological details of the poem are shaped round this interpretation:

> The Plan of this Poem is form'd upon Anger and its ill Effects, the
> Plan of *Virgil's* upon pious Resignation and its Rewards: and thus
> every Passion or Virtue may be the Foundation of the Scheme of
> an Epic Poem. (Book I, introductory note)

In context, the formulation of these remarks suggests that
Homer's gift of invention is closely related to his theme of passion,
and Virgil's judgement with his subject of (somewhat Stoic)
virtue. Pope's observations on the opening invocation of the *Iliad*
show that he sees Homer's immediate concern as being with the
'Source' of Achilles' anger, not merely with its 'Effects', and
although this theme is in the first instance understood in
circumstantial terms (Achilles' loss of Briseis), the question as
Pope paraphrases it ('"But tell me, O Muse, what was the Source
of this destructive Anger?"') is actually developed into a wider
psychological enquiry. The ethical perspective is extremely
important in Pope's analysis, but he is equally interested in the
psychological coherence of Homer's treatment of anger and its
consequences; he points out that Homer's greatest strength as a
poet begins with his departure from the 'morally beautiful', and
that in Achilles' character are mingled the qualities which form
the principal 'Lights and Shades' running through the narrative,
valour and anger (Book I, n.155). He emphasises also that these
contrasts in the character of Achilles are expressive of a persuasive psychological realism in the conception of Homer's
protagonists, that is that virtue and vice are closely allied and that
a fault in character is often accompanied by its nearest merit; this
insight, as he sets out to demonstrate with the authority of
Plutarch, is 'contrary to the Paradoxes and strange Positions of
the Stoicks, who held that no Vice could consist with Virtue nor
the least Virtue with Vice'.

Pope notes in considerable detail how Homer has used
different kinds of passion to distinguish his characters, how they
are made to react distinctively to the same object or event, and
how emotional reactions are conveyed in the rhetoric of
individual speeches (Book IX, n.406; Book III, n.55). The gods
themselves are seen to use men not 'indifferently as their second
Agents, but each according to the Powers he is endu'd with by
Art or Nature' (Book VII, n.120). At the same time, he also
attempts to evaluate Homer's verisimilitude by the measure of
universality, 'quod semper quod ubique ab omnibus creditum

est'; he repudiates the idea that 'great Men differ from the vulgar in their manner of expressing their Passion' (Book I, n.298), appeals to the fair sex to approve the natural conduct of Homer's women, and comments ruefully on the displays of mundane passion and folly which emerge in the course of the games in Book XXIII. Most notably, in analysing the behaviour of Achilles Pope begins to expound psychological themes which are developed beyond the limits of moral commentary, reflecting the contemporary emphasis on the 'poetical' treatment of character.[8] It is conceded that Achilles represents a highly flawed, even immoral protagonist, but Pope none the less argues feelingly against Plato's strictures on Homer's choice of hero (Book XXIV, n.14); instead, he concentrates on the description and exploration of Achilles' passion, observing how in his mixed qualities he remains 'a terrible Enemy, but an amiable Friend'. It is not only Achilles' destructive power but his self-destruction which engages Pope's interest; the strength of his distorting anger is seen metaphorically as 'like a Fire blown by a Wind, that sinks and rises by fits', and which reveals its kinship to madness in its obsessional fixation, 'perpetually breaking out upon the same Injury' (Book IX, n.406, n.481). In Pope's view, Achilles' wrath both exalts and debases him, and this paradox is one which he reflects upon in relation to both action and rhetoric throughout his commentary. One of the most interesting of his observations on the subject is a passage in which he effectively introduces the notion of warring passions and a fundamental drive which here might aptly be glossed as the 'ruling passion':

> That Hero whose very Soul was possessed with Love of Glory, and who prefer'd it to Life itself, lets his Anger prevail over this his darling Passion; He despises even Glory, when he cannot obtain that, and enjoy his Revenge at the same time; and rather than lay this aside, becomes the very Reverse of himself. (Book IX, n.530)

This is an interpretation which is central to Pope's particular emphasis; it is applied not just to its immediate context but to the whole course of Achilles' conduct in the *Iliad*, introducing a paradox on the private, subjective level which anticipates the more fully developed arguments of the *Moral Essays*. It is a way of accounting for Achilles' sustained irrationality which eludes direct moralism and yet lays stress upon the idea of self-defeat and self-reversal, both abiding themes of Pope's work.

Likewise, Pope's interest in character leads him to pursue the interventions of the Gods, not as 'physical powers' alone, but in terms of psychological transformation, although this interest does not lead him to discount their 'literal' status as divinities and he does not attempt to impose allegorical meanings arbitrarily. In Book I, n.261, discussing Achilles' quarrel with Agamemnon, he praises the conceit of Minerva's appearance as an overt piece of moralised fiction:

> The Allegory here may be allow'd by every Reader to be unforc'd; The Prudence of *Achilles* checks him in the rashest Moment of his Anger, it works upon him unseen to others, but does not entirely prevail upon him to desist, 'till he remembers his own Importance.

Concluding an extended discussion of Helen's behaviour and the interventions of Venus in Book III (n. 479 ff.), he writes with equal satisfaction 'that the Goddess of Love has been all the while nothing more than the Passion of it' — an observation which may at first sight appear tautological, but the key point of Pope's formulation resides in the phrase 'nothing more than', and according to his detailed analysis it is shown that this understanding emerges in retrospect.

Correspondingly, Pope shows much interest in the 'humanity' of the depiction of the gods, strenuously defending the dignity of this human dimension from any overtones of burlesque; he points out that it is the anger of Achilles which spreads from earth to heaven and occasions the conflict among the divinities, and while each god may be identified with a dominant passion or faculty of mind, Minerva herself is seen to be subject to conflicts of her wisdom with her anger. The inconsistencies of this apparent discrepancy are troubling to Pope (see Book VIII, n.439), but he concludes that the goddess is ruled ultimately by a hierarchy of powers and interests, and so succeeds finally in preserving her characteristic faculty despite the turbulence of the internal factions (Book IV, n.31).

It is in the light of such dominant passions driving both mortals and gods that Pope approaches the key issues of the narrative, notably the problem of honour; in his account it is the dishonour reflected upon Achilles in being forced to part with Briseis, combined with his naturally 'great and fiery Temper', which precipitates the train of disasters overtaking both himself and the Greeks (Book I, n.458). In the heroic context of the *Iliad*, Pope goes so far as to assert that Achilles' honour is exalted in proportion as his passions are depicted as intense by Homer: 'he makes every Passion of his Hero considerable, his Sorrow as well as Anger is important, and he cannot grieve but that a Goddess attends him, and a whole Army weeps' (Book XXIII, n.18): '*Achilles* is as much a Hero when he weeeps, as when he fights' (Book XXIV, n.14).

While the theme of honour is closely connected with the more violent passions, the secondary concern with love, pleasure and the power of beauty is associated with a strain of sentiment which Pope terms 'Strokes of Tenderness' (Book II, n.871) or 'the Natural and Pathetick', and which he tends to discuss with relation to Helen and the sufferings of the Trojans on her behalf. In his note to Book VI (n.462), Pope makes it clear that this emotional key, though subordinate to what he sees as the main force of the poem, plays a vital part in the creative contrasts exploited by Homer:

> *Homer* undoubtedly shines most upon the great Subjects, in raising our Admiration or Terror: Pity, and the softer Passions, are not so much of the Nature of his Poem, which is formed upon Anger and the Violence of Ambition. But we have cause to think his Genius was no less capable of touching the Heart with Tenderness, than of firing it with Glory, from the few Sketches he has left us of his Excellency in that way too.

The treatment of Helen as the central figure in this drama of pathos is particularly interesting, in so far as she is characterised by a strong emphasis on her divisions of feeling and loyalty; Pope presents her as 'a frail, but not as an abandoned Creature. She has perpetual Struggles of Virtue on the one side, and Softnesses which overcome them on the other' (Book III, n.1). There is certainly an analogy with the 'struggles of ... virtue and passion' in Eloisa, reinforced by the stress on unconscious reactions and desires which are revealed only through the train of associations in Helen's mind; Pope's translation of Book III, 1.488 points to the ambivalence in Helen's response to Paris after his unsuccessful duel with Menelaus ('She scorn'd the Champion, but the Man she lov'd'), and he expands on this psychology in a footnote:

> The first Thought of *Paris's* Beauty overcomes (unawares to her-
> self) the Contempt she had that Moment conceiv'd of him. ...
> When the Affections of a Woman have been thoroughly gained,
> tho' they may be alienated for a while, they soon return upon her.
> Homer *knew* (says Madam *Dacier*) *what a Woman is capable of,*
> *who had once lov'd.*

This depth of susceptibility is expressed, in Pope's exposition of
the allegory, by the continued presence of Venus throughout the
scene, overruling Helen in her contests of 'Shame, Fear and
Anger'; Pope approves of the flexibility of this presentation since
it not only expresses through dialogue the nature of love's sway in
Helen's heart, but also allows the reader to sympathise with her as
though she were literally 'constrained by a superior Power'
(n.479). Though the uppermost forces in Helen are expressed as
her 'Sentiments of Honour and Love', Pope responds with
conviction to the idea of her yielding ultimately to 'the most
dreadful of all Threats, Loss of Beauty and of Reputation' (n.515);
this emphasis contains significant echoes of the mock-heroic
world of the *Rape of the Lock*, as does Pope's passing reference to
'another branch of the Female Character, which is, to be ruled in
their Attaches by *Success*' (cf. *Rape*, II. 33-4). The care of Venus to
protect both Helen's beauty and her reputation is strongly
suggestive (despite obvious discrepancies) of Ariel's custody of
Belinda, as is the ambiguity in the use of the word 'Reputation' in
the context of Pope's note quoted above (presumably denoting
'fame' rather than 'honour' in the deeper sense). Pope has transformed the whole conception of Helen's character, being deeply
engaged in the pursuit of a familiar pattern of feminine psychology, and it is notable too that he extends this pattern of frailty to
embrace Paris, depicted as pre-eminently a man of pleasure. Pope
describes him as wavering between his impulses to shame and
courage, 'the usual Disposition of easy and courteous Minds
which are most subject to the Rule of Fancy and Passion' (Book
III, n.86), and is disposed to see him with Helen as the victim of a
passion which overwhelms his better qualities.

Further 'strokes of tenderness' are brought out in the remarks
on the many scenes of elevated sorrow within the *Iliad* — the
parting of Hector and Andromache, Achilles' lamentations for
the death of Patroclus, Priam's petition to Achilles for Hector's
body — and the latter two scenes in particular are interpreted as

part of a developing and crucial movement in the poem whereby the theme of anger is finally tempered and resolved. From the opening of his commentary, it is apparent how pervasive is Pope's tendency to think in terms of oppositional elements, in moral, psychological and (frequently) pictorial terms. His indebtedness to theory of painting emerges in his references to the 'Lights and Shades' of the narrative, sections of which he evokes in specifically painterly metaphors and analyses as arrested tableaux. The same concern with juxtapositions is extended further to contrasts of character and behaviour, as expressed in the note of Book XVI (n.233) which stresses how 'the *Pathetic* of *Patroclus's* speech is finely contrasted with the *Fierté* of that of *Achilles*'; Pope goes on to moralise this theme by relating the fertile opposition of temperaments which unites the two heroes to the *discordia concors* of Providence. The contrasting threads of the terrible and the pathetic are carefully traced both in details of imagery and action and as part of the wider structure of the poem, summed up in the introductory note to Book XXIII: 'Terror and Pity are here wrought up in perfection'; 'our Passions have been in an Agitation since the opening of the Poem; wherefore the Poet, like some great Master in Musick, softens his Notes, and melts his Readers into Tenderness and Pity'. It is the bringing together of the two strains of pity and terror which signifies the ending of the *Iliad's* great subject of anger, only after the heights of wrath have been reached in Achilles and the heights of grief in Priam (Book XXIV, n.291). Following the scenes of violence in Book XXII, the reader is able to 'look back with a pleasing kind of Horror upon the Anger of Achilles', and in the course of Book XXIV, '*Achilles* is to pass from a State of an almost inexorable Resentment to a State of perfect Tranquillity' (n.141); Pope's remarks indicate that he regards the eventual prevalence of reason over anger in Achilles as completing the total scheme of the *Iliad*, a movement shared by empathy.[9] The tempering of Achilles' resentment is seen as a cathartic resolution, and the reflection of a psychological rather than a moral law ('the only reason he has ever to yield, is that Nature itself cannot support Anger eternally'). Nor does Pope adopt the view that the gods themselves act to promote a higher order of justice; in a significant note to Book VIII (n.95), he censures Madame Dacier for attempting to strain Homer's theology to conform to Christian doctrine, stressing that Jupiter is above all 'a Being subject to Passion, Inequality, and Imperfection'. In the final analysis, Pope interprets Homer's theme of extravagant passion in the light of his contention that pagan 'superstition' was founded on the principle of fear rather than love, a doctrine which was later put forward more elaborately in the *Essay on Man* (III. 257-8):

> Gods partial, changeful, passionate, unjust,
> Whose attributes were Rage, Revenge, or Lust.

Such predominantly amoral, 'pagan' supernatural beings (on an appropriately reduced scale) likewise preside over the microcosm of the *Rape of the Lock*, even within the nominal Christian faith which is Belinda's superstition. Besides the petty tyrannies of the sylphs and the deeper threats of the gnomes, the parodic references to the arbitrary events of the epic (the dispersal of the Baron's prayers by 'the Pow'rs' (II.45) and the intervention of 'Fate and Jove' in steeling his subversive resolve) are consistent with the disordered ethos of the poem. Many frameworks of superstition (from fairy lore to Rosicrucian mysticism) are integrated into a wider pattern of destructive passions, struggles for power and, pre-eminently, 'Fear', which is developed in the action from the level of subdued anxieties, echoed in omens and prophecies, to mounting neurosis and desperation. It is in this fundamental movement, the working out of a central passion enacted in Belinda, that the *Rape* most nearly resembles the *Iliad*, and in the developments building up to Belinda's dire attack of Spleen the agency of the machinery of sylphs and gnomes clearly has a crucial role. In examining the 1714 version of the *Rape*, I will begin by considering the interaction of the machinery with the conduct of what Bossu and other contemporary critics of the epic form termed the 'manners'; that is, the ways in which the characters of the protagonists are expressed and shaped within the action of the poem.

Every epic, Bossu proposes, must be distinguished by 'some *Peculiar Passion*', which will naturally be correspondent to 'the *Character* of the *Hero*';[10] he cites the standard example of Achilles' anger in the *Iliad* (the subject of the very first two words in Pope's translation). It is quite evident that the phrase 'am'rous Causes' in the first line of the *Rape* is intended to occupy the equivalent position in the scheme of the poem; the application of the phrase is ambiguous, however (it might be taken to apply to Belinda or the Baron), and from this point the proposals of Pope's invocation are developed with fuller elaboration:

> Say what strange Motive, Goddess! cou'd compel
> A well-bred *Lord* t'assault a gentle *Belle*?
> Oh say what stranger Cause, yet unexplor'd,
> Cou'd make a gentle *Belle* reject a *Lord*?
> In Tasks so bold, can Little Men engage,
> And in soft Bosoms dwells such mighty Rage?
> (I. 7-12)

Two subjects of enquiry are in fact put forward, the first concerning the cause of the Baron's indecorous attack upon Belinda, the second Belinda's extreme response, and the poet pointedly indicates that the latter 'stranger Cause' is the more mysterious and challenging. The final line of the invocation is an explicit allusion to Virgil's 'Tantaene animis caelestibus irae?' (*Aeneid*, I.11), witty in furthering the mock-heroic discrepancy between the exalted and the diminutive, but significant also in expressing the seeming incongruity of vindictive passion harboured in the breast of a 'divinity'. The wrath of Achilles and the spite of Juno, both of which are recalled by the pattern of the invocation as a whole, are equally appropriate in Belinda's case since they share the same source, injured pride;[11] the injury to Belinda, on the other hand, is not an antecedent cause and does not take place until the action is well advanced, so that through the developing narrative Pope is able to prepare us for it, and to suggest and probe the reasons why it should be so deeply felt.

The evidence of Pope's annotations to John Dennis' hostile remarks on the *Rape* is sufficient to show how carefully he had considered the deeper questions of mock-epic form.[12] In pursuing the psychological subjects of the invocation, it can be seen that Pope was intent on maintaining a certain internal consistency whereby the traits of character and the moral of the poem could be revealed, and perhaps most important to this consideration was the concept of the 'unity of manners'.[13] Dennis himself, with customary shortness, presents the clearest case for the necessity of 'strongly marked' manners within an epic poem: '... for an Action instructing by its Causes, which Causes are the Manners, unless I can be certain, what the Principles of the Agents are, I can never deduce any certain Moral from the Action'.[14]

The identification of the 'Causes' with the 'Manners' here is particularly appropriate in relation to the *Rape's* invocation; the causes of the whole of the poem's action are after all psychological ones, and in this respect 'manners' may be understood in Dryden's sense as signifying 'passions' (see n.13 below) or, as in Pope's 'Poetical Index' to the *Iliad*, as a term which is almost synonymous with 'character' (TE, VIII, 593). The coherence of the manners as 'causes' is in fact exceptionally important to the conception of a mock-heroic poem, since the apparently inconsequential and absurd elements of the bathos have to be justified by a forceful and persuasive moral content.

The fullest and most suggestive discussion of the manners, however, is given in Bossu's *Traité* — I will quote hereafter from the English translation of 1695[15] — which is the most important source for an understanding of Pope's reception of critical theory on the epic,[16] and which offers a helpful perspective on aspects of the *Rape* often regarded as simple parody of conventions or satirical digressions. Bossu's discussion has the merit of being exploratory rather than prescriptive, and for the sake of clarity I will pursue the outline of his distinctions between the various kinds of influence which may be seen as forming the manners: 'external', 'mixed', and 'internal'. The first two of these categories together entail an assessment of the setting, physical and spiritual, in which the protagonists are framed and by which they are moulded, and the third an enquiry into the nature of character itself.

The definition of the 'external' causes is a limited one, resolved as 'God, the Stars and our Native country', although by the first two terms might be comprehended any Theological or Physical deity having a direct role in the action. Regarding the native country, Bossu makes the familiar point that the great classical epics were patriotic works, and that consequently '*Virgil* bestows great commendations on the Country of his Hero, and advances it far above *Greece*' (*Treatise*, p.161); Pope's incidental deflations of Great Britain through the references to Anna's counsels (III.5-8) and the dexterity of justice (21-2) thus represent more than simply an extension of the satire's range (sometimes censured as incongruous with the tone of the poem as a whole), and suggest how-

ever fleetingly a setting of arbitrary values and flagrant self-
interest on a national scale. The same observation might also be
applied to two passages reflecting Bossu's 'mixed' causes, the
effects of parents and of education. Ariel reflects on the careful
training of the belle's 'Infant Thought' in vanities and whimsies
fostered by nurse and priest (I.29-36), implying that by these
means the maid may be kept in a permanent state of childhood;
and as to Belinda's genealogy, the passage on the descent of the
bodkin (V.89-96) supplies a brilliantly reductive parody of the
convention whereby the status of material objects possessed by
the hero bespeaks his lineage and authority. By analogy with this
convention Belinda's line of descent suffers a double degeneracy,
not only because the mutating objects themselves barely attain to
one earthly thing of use, but because Pope uses them to present
directly a high degree of vanity and inanity among the forebears
themselves — the phrase 'infant Grandame' yokes together the
extremes of infantility and senility, and there is a sharper indication of the hypocritical 'mockery of woe' at l.92.

This construction of a morally distorted context framing
Belinda's actions does not, of course, amount to a parable of cause
and effect — Bossu is himself dubious as to how far, beyond the
theoretical level, the manners may be seen to conform to external
and mixed causes — but it is none the less formally apt in establishing an appropriate unity between protagonist and setting, and
in making Belinda's foibles consonant with her world. It is however the catalogue of 'inward' causes, which Bossu defines as 'the
complexion, the Sex, the Passions, and the Actions whereby we
contract these habits', which is the active centre of the poem.
Beyond the generalised notion which Bossu endorses that women
are the 'weaker sex', there is in the *Rape* a whole network of implications reflecting upon the nature and conduct of women in
society which has everything to do with gender and which in many
respects anticipates the wider observations of *Moral Essay II*, on
the characters of women; the subject of power and pleasure might
be considered as the chief concern of the poem. Allied to the
subject of femininity is the seemingly trivial question of 'complexion' or personal appearance; Bossu makes a moral point of its
relevance, on the Platonic assumption that external form expresses inward worth, allowing rather uncertainly that this is a useful
poetic fiction ('Poets place high Characters upon Bodies of the

largest size, and the finest make'; p.164). Belinda's personal beauty is elevated in the *Rape* to a primary influence acting upon both herself and those around her, and it is left to Clarissa to recall the full possibilities of Virgil's ideal ('Gratior et pulchro veniens in corpore virtus', *Aeneid*, V. 744) in canto V.18 — 'Behold the first in Virtue, as in Face' — at which point the metaphor of the belle's divinity is most fully exposed.

Throughout the *Rape* too, 'Actions' and 'Habits' are emphasised in the evocation of serene ritual and all the closely observed details of a lifestyle sustained in perpetual vanities. At every point in the narrative, in the focus on pride in the dressing-table scene and on ambition in the game of ombre, 'one may see the passion prepar'd and kept up by the actions' (Bossu, p.165), and the 'unity of manners' which Pope has so fully maintained within his mock-heroic necessarily goes beyond the idea of unity of character to a pervasive scrutiny of a new 'beau monde' supported in all its minutiae. It has often been observed that the power of this transformation is complete enough to allow empathy on the part of the reader to play an important part in the *Rape*'s total effect; paradoxically, Pope can travesty the pro-prieties, call upon the reader to feel admiration at the insignificant and grief at the nominally trivial, yet still compel a certain concernment in the action. Further than this, though, it would be just to observe that the intensities of feeling in Belinda and her response to an ideal of honour, however ill-defined, are direct (rather than inverted) echoes from the heroic world of the *Iliad*. In a general sense, the contrast set out between the fiery tempera-ments of Belinda's entourage and the equanimity of Clarissa might be viewed as expressing in parody the distinction Pope makes between the attributes of the *Iliad* and *Aeneid*; a scheme of 'Anger and its ill Effects' opposed to 'pious Resignation and its Rewards' (TE, VII, 83). By this compression, the final version of the *Rape of the Lock* is supplied with both a passion and a virtue as its foundation, and its moral is doubly enforced.

Anger, bathetically translated into Spleen, thus remains the dominant passion in the *Rape*, but it is closely associated with a complex of other passions. As Pope observes of Achilles that 'his Sorrow as well as Anger is important, and he cannot grieve but that a Goddess attends him, and a whole Army weeps', so Belinda's passions are elevated in Umbriel's appeal to Spleen:

> Hear me, and touch *Belinda* with Chagrin;
> That single Act gives half the World the Spleen.
> (IV.77-8)

In Pope's commentary on Achilles, it is important not only that the violence of his reaction to the forced parting from Briseis goes deeper than the event itself seems to merit, since 'the Action reflects a Dishonour upon him' (Book I, n.458), but that furthermore Pope views Achilles' very anger as running counter to his 'ruling passion' of the love of glory: 'rather than lay this aside [he] becomes the very Reverse of himself' (Book IX, n.530). The psychological point which is taken up by Pope concerns the way in which an individual may defeat his own highest desires by succumbing to the force of an overwhelming passion. Belinda is of course presented with a comparable 'ruling passion', which wins over even the 'earthly lover lurking at her heart', in her pride; the clear analogy with Achilles' behaviour is that she likewise defeats her own ends, both of 'Glory' and of contentment, by allowing herself to be overruled by the desire of revenge and by an inflexible concept of honour. Her lamentation over the demise of the lock (IV. 147ff.) is a parody of the lament for Patroclus (*Iliad*, XVIII. 107ff.), and this is a moment of extremity at which Achilles addressing Thetis bewails his father's fated aspiration for an immortal bride, reflecting on his own crucial choice of a short and glorious life, and recognising fleetingly the futility of discord:

> Curs'd be that Day, when all the Pow'rs above
> Thy Charms submitted to a mortal Love:
> Oh had'st thou still, a Sister of the Main,
> Pursu'd the Pleasures of the wat'ry Reign;...
> Let me — But oh! ye gracious Pow'rs above!
> Wrath and Revenge from Men and Gods remove:
> Far, far too dear to ev'ry mortal Breast,
> Sweet to the Soul, as Hony to the Taste;
> Gath'ring like Vapours of a noxious kind
> From fiery Blood, and dark'ning all the Mind.
> (*Iliad*, XVIII.107-10, 137-42)

The outburst is poignant in that its insight is seen to be incompatible with the direction of the hero's ruling passion, and furthermore the consequences are past redress; Pope comments that 'nothing can be finer than this sudden Execration against Discord and Revenge, which breaks from the Hero in the deep Sense of the Miseries those Passions had occasion'd' (n.137). Belinda's execrations deflate this insight, echoing only clichés about the injuries bound in with the sophistications of Court life, and her alternative vision of a barren, Stoic and ascetic 'un-admir'd' life is far from convincing; yet there is none the less a certain quality of pathos in the very expression of naïvety, and in the lines with which she briefly confronts her own motives:

> What mov'd my Mind with youthful Lords to rome?
> O had I stay'd, and said my Pray'rs at home!
>
> (IV.159-60)

The 'Sorrows' of this speech are the result of Umbriel's breaking open the vial of Griefs, the secondary stage of his attack which began with rending the bag of Furies (IV.92), and here Pope is able to play in parody upon the 'wonderful Contrast and Opposition of the *Moving* and of the *Terrible*' in Homer. While Belinda's scenes of pathos contain significant echoes of the griefs of Achilles and Helen, however, a more consistent series of allusions establishes a correspondence between her state of despair and that of Virgil's Dido, both in the struggles of her awakening love with her sense of honour (*Aeneid*, IV) and as the victim of Aeneas' later desertion. Dido is a particularly apposite parallel to Belinda in her dark inner conflicts of love and inexorable resentment, highlighted by the placing of the allusions at the opening of cantos IV and V. The catalogue of analogies opening canto IV keeps up the themes of monarchy, tyranny, and the defiance of the rejected. Pope's parody of conflicting passions within the mock-heroic also gives him the opportunity to reflect the manners in various kinds of eloquence; his letter to Bridges (*Correspondence*, I, 44) extols among 'the distinguishing Excellencies of Homer', 'the Manners, (which include all the speeches, as being no other than the Representations of each Person's Manners by his Words)'. As Ian Jack notes, [17] all the categories of 'Speeches, or Orations' listed in Pope's 'Poetical Index' to the *Iliad* are present in the *Rape* (with the reasonable exception of 'Speeches to Horses'); the Exhortatory and Deliberate kinds are imitated in Clarissa and Thalestris, the Vituperative in Sir Plume, the Pathetick in Belinda's lament, the Narrative within this (IV. 161-6), and Irony or Sarcasm in the Baron's rejoinder to Sir Plume (IV. 131ff), which is followed by his Oath. All these various speeches take their spring from the passions and conflicts raging after the lock is severed (i.e. from canto III, l.161 onwards), and it is notable that none of the mortal protagonists actually speaks before this. A direct parody of passionate speech in Homer is made in Sir Plume's blustering outburst, imitating the 'hasty manner of Expression without the Connexion of Particles ... extreamly natural to a Man in Anger' which Pope had noted in Hector (*Iliad*, III, n.55) and again in Priam (Book XXIV, n.291):

> And thus broke out — 'My Lord, why, what the Devil?
> 'Z–ds! damn the Lock! 'fore Gad, you must be civil!
> 'Plague on't! 'tis past a Jest — nay prithee, Pox!
> 'Give her the Hair' — he spoke, and rapp'd his Box.

Besides these painstaking details, the conduct of the passions within the poem was above all deepened by the introduction of the machinery of sylphs and gnomes to the 1714 text, which Pope rightly regarded as the most inspired of his expansions. In this, the mock-heroic model gave him a unique freedom, since not only was much of the rationalist unease about the function of mythology dispelled by the semi-serious context, but it had become more or less accepted as a convention that the mock-heroic machinery should represent 'Moral' agents, or (to quote Pope's term from his letter to Bolingbroke of 1724), 'Natural passions'.[18] A note ascribed to Pope in Warburton's 1751 edition of the *Works* (TE, II, 196, n.141) gives an explicit justification for Umbriel's involvement in the action, that is to 'assign the cause of the different operation of the Passions of the two Ladies' (Thalestris and Belinda).[19] He is able to use the sylphs and gnomes as moral agents, and to give them depth of their own as seeming extensions of the mind. 'Spleen' is also a particularly appropriate deity for his purposes, since the very name of the disease carried pejorative associations of self-absorption and hypochondria (in the modern sense of the word); furthermore she is seen to act on her victims acording to their particular character rather than by coercion (IV. 61ff.; cf. *Iliad*, VII, n.120).

Ariel emphasises in his speech to Belinda that he and the other elemental Rosicrucian spirits owe their powers of communication with the human race to popular credulity; above all Pope designs them as creatures of whimsicality and contradiction, particularly in the sexual concerns which are their professed province. This ambiguity is one which stems from his principal source for the spirits, Montfaucon de Villar's *Le Compte de Gabalis* (translated into English in Bentley's *Modern Novels*, II, 1692), to which he refers in the 'Dedication' of the 1714 *Rape*. Pope's lighthearted play on the idea of 'intimate Familiarities' to be enjoyed on condition of 'an inviolate Preservation of Chastity' follows closely the tenor of *Gabalis*, in which a mixed appeal to mystery, the delights of power and erotic interests are all at work. The Count himself is a paradoxical mixture of slightly lewd confidentiality, calculated appeal to the gratifications of power, and zealous 'puritanical' rigour; like Ariel, convinced of his disciple's fortunate birth, he urges upon him: 'the Supream Intelligences shall esteem it a Glory, to obey your Desires: ... And all the Invisible People, who inhabit the Four Elements, shall account themselves Happy, to be the Ministers of your Pleasures' (pp.22-3). This pronounced anxiety of the Count over his protégé is reflected in the exaggerated state of trepidation which holds the sylphs throughout the *Rape*. As far as nymphs and sylphs themselves are concerned, the Count expatiates on the unassuming servility of the spirits and on the delights of ethereal as against fleshly intercourse ('instead of *Women*, whose fading Beauty pass [*sic*] away in a short time, and are followed with horrible Wrinkles and Uglyness, the *Philosophers* enjoy Beauties which never wax old'; p.36). The sylphs have the misfortune to be unenlightened into the mystic order of things, but at the same time they are 'Enemies to Sots and Ignorants' (p.27) and highly jealous of the fidelity of their mortal partners; the Count warns of the previous desertion of a woman by her sylph because of her lack of devotion and her falling away from 'exemplary innocence' (p.162).

These same confused qualities mark the relationship between Ariel and Belinda; at the beginning, before the 'warm desires' rising in Belinda cause it to end in rupture, it is presented as an intimate one, and gives insights into her preoccupations which are relatively distant in the 1712 version of the *Rape*. Ariel's appearance at I.23ff. as 'A Youth more glitt'ring than a *Birth-night Beau*' is aimed to be mildly seductive, and Belinda accordingly responds with glowing cheek; similarly there is some ambiguity over the nature of the contact offered:

... Whoever fair and chaste
Rejects Mankind, is by some Sylph embrac'd:
For Spirits, freed from mortal Laws, with ease
Assume what Sexes and what Shapes they please.

It is implied, in fact, that the spirits are 'freed from mortal Laws' in more senses than one. Ariel's assertion in the face of scepticism that 'the Fair and Innocent shall still believe' confounds the notion of spiritual purity with childish credulity, and is at odds with his own marked distrust of the chastity of 'melting Maids'. The threats, as he acknowledges, are both external and internal, and this is the obvious reflection on Belinda's purity when her petticoat is singled out for protection by a bastion of 'Fifty chosen Sylphs'.[20] There is thus a lewd knowingness at the heart of Ariel's anxiety over the preservation of chastity, against which Belinda's 'desires' seem comparatively innocent; and Pope does in fact provide a note associating the sylphs with the indecent familiarities of 'the fallen Angels' (I. n.145), a suggestion which had been unguardedly brought forward by the Count in *Gabalis*. The Count slides into further suggestions of indecency while defending his spirits against the suspicions of the narrator:

> The *Sylphs*, seeing themselves taken for *Devils*, when they appear in Human Shape, to diminish this Aversion, which is had against them, take the Shapes of ... Beasts; and so address themselves to the wanton Frailty of *Women*: who are affrighted at a Lovely *Sylphide*, but not at a *Dog*, or *Munkey*. I could tell you many Tales of your little *Bolognian Dogs*, and certain pretty *Ladyes* in the World. (pp. 156-7)

Just as Ariel's salacious apprehensions seem at odds with his guardianship of Belinda's innocence, so he is also a comic amalgam of officiousness and servility; his protection of Belinda implies power, while his ignorance of the nature of the threatened 'dire Event' reminds us that he lacks it. The most transparent contradiction is in point of pride; Ariel's distaste for the gnome-like disposition of the overweening belle is strongly marked, and particularly emphasises the vulgar vice of pretension:

> Some Nymphs there are, too conscious of their Face,
> For Life predestin'd to the *Gnomes'* Embrace.

These swell their Prospects and exalt their Pride,
When Offers are disdain'd, and Love deny'd.
                                            (I. 79-82)

Yet at the same time, his opening exhortation to his charge ('Hear
and believe! thy own Importance know, / Nor bound thy narrow
Views to Things below') could scarcely be more designed to exalt
pride, and Pope notes of the phrase 'distinguish'd Care' as used in
his *Iliad* (Book I, l.229) that it is 'perfectly in the exalted Style of
the Eastern Nations, and correspondent to those Places of holy
Scripture where they [Kings] are call'd *Gods*, and *the Sons of the
Most High*'. Ariel's role thus more nearly resembles that of
Milton's Satan at the ear of the sleeping Eve than that of the
admonisher Raphael; exalting Eve's surpassing beauty as the awe
of the heavens, he then incites her to eat the forbidden fruit and
elevate herself to godhead (*Paradise Lost*, V. 44-7, 77-8):

> ... heaven wakes with all his eyes,
> Whom to behold but thee, nature's desire ...
> Taste this, and be henceforth among the gods
> Thy self a goddess, nor to earth confined.

The *double entendre* in Ariel's version of these lines ('Nor bound
thy narrow Views to Things below') adds to the echo a sexual
nuance; while in his delusory catalogue of 'visions', Belinda is to
picture herself among the hallowed chaste, the 'Virgins visited by
Angel-Pow'rs'. The way in which his advent is depicted ironically
conflates the Temptation and Annunciation, both enticing
Belinda with the appeal to her own innocence and playing upon
her least innocent susceptibilities. Bearing in mind that the sylphs
are former coquettes and the gnomes former prudes, it becomes
apparent that the nominally contrary states of coquetry and
prudery are in many respects closely allied, depending for their
definition only on a difference in the degree of pride and of self-
awareness.[21] In terms of their association with the elements, too
(broadly symbolic or expressive of temperament within the
poem's suggestive framework), the sylphs' activities embrace contradictory functions:

> Some in the Fields of purest *Aether* play, ...
> Or suck the Mists in grosser Air below,

> Or dip their Pinions in the painted Bow,
> Or brew fierce Tempests on the wintry Main,
> Or o'er the Glebe distill the kindly Rain.
>
> (I. 77, 83-6)

While the medium of airy projected desires is the apparently harmless realm of the more exalted sylphs, others are operative more dubiously in the opaque and turbulent elements.

Thus the traits put forward in Ariel and the sylphs indicate an uncertainty of role which is highly relevant to their comic ineffectiveness as guardians, and it is an uncertainty, or ambiguity, which is also of course applied on the psychological level to Belinda herself. The sylphs are zealous to assist her in 'the sacred Rites of Pride' at the dressing-table, which perfectly express the paradoxical blending of 'humility' and self-worship. In canto III, Pope plays on her spirit of emulation as a parody of heroic valour, with strong suggestions of aggressive erotic pleasure:

> *Belinda* now, whom Thirst of Fame invites,
> Burns to encounter two adventrous Knights,
> At *Ombre* singly to decide their Doom;
> And swells her Breast with Conquests yet to come.
>
> (III. 25-8)

The complexities of Belinda's 'Pride' as allied with her apparent innocence developed in the opening of canto II forms a central subject of the poem, which is progressively opened up.[22] In metaphoric terms, Belinda though at the height of her powers is herself presented as a 'painted Vessel', buoyed up by her entourage but (with the incursion of the Baron) only temporarily secure. The account of her triumphant embarkation on the Thames serves a function which is more than simply descriptive; if the expedition is reminiscent of Cleopatra's barge, it is especially so in Pope's emphasis on the sensuality of the elements, which although controlled ('Smooth flow the waves, the Zephyrs gently play'), dissolve away from the boundaries symbolically presided over by the legions of sylphs, gnomes, nymphs and salamanders, and enter into erotic synthesis. The description in its full development (II. 47-68) evokes a melting susceptibility which is implicitly propitious and enticing to love, and is reminiscent of the most sensuous descriptive lines of *Eloisa* (155-60). Within the elemental framework of the poem's 'machinery', the setting of the expedition on the floating tides of the river presents a medium of changeability and yielding (as 'soft yielding Minds to Water glide away', I. 61), and the sylphs themselves enter into myriad, diffuse transformations. It is apt that Pope's images for the sylphs here draw particularly on the 'rainbow' motif by which he expresses the shifts and complexities of the imagination,[23] and with the free play of fancy comes the dissolution of the tenuous moral codes at play in the *Rape*.

Ariel's task in his protection of Belinda is to keep her self-deception at the most delicate, repressed level — 'nor let th' imprison'd Essences exhale' — so that the natural passions for power and gratification may be held in play without souring into the affectation and bitterness of the prude. But, since he shares in many facets of her naivety, he is unable to acknowledge that the seeming control of passions he relies on is at the brink of darker impulses. The cosmetic 'Blush' (I. 143) is barely distinguished from the 'bidden Blush' which Ariel abhors, and the lines first given to Thalestris in the 1712 *Rape* (II. 19-20) are much more effective as an unconscious slip on Belinda's part, given greater prominence by the repositioning at the end of canto IV ('Oh hadst thou, Cruel! been content to seize / Hairs less in sight, or any Hairs but these!'). This is one of the elements in the poem which adds a rakish quality to its wit, but with 'Hairs less in sight' it also raises the more serious matter of reputation. Samuel Garth deals with the subject in much the same terms as Pope in his 'silent Mansion of disastrous love' (*The Dispensary*, sixth edition (1706), canto VI), where the lover meets with the abject figure of his ruined Olivia and delivers an ill-timed piece of moralising concerning the distortion and deflection of women's passions, rounded off with a salacious pun:

> Custom, reply'd the Lover, is your Guide,
> Discretion is but Fear, and Honour, Pride.
> To do nice conduct Right, you Nature wrong;
> Impulses are but weak, where Reason's strong.
> Some want the 'Assurance oft, but Few the Flame;
> They like the Thing, That startle at the Name.
>
> (p.114)

The problems of elevating etiquette above impulse are

developed too in John Gay's *The Fan*, published in 1714, which examines the corruptions of modern luxury and female artifice through a somewhat disordered classical parable, and there are again many similarities in tone and subject between this poem and the *Rape*. Gay's interest in adopting the scheme of a classical fable is to explore the process of metamorphosis by which one culture has given way to another, and in particular the changing relations of the sexes; his 'busie *Cupids*' are employed in manufacturing the newly-devised Fan from their fragmented arrows, and it is added to the battery of 'bright Beauty's Arms' and the 'glitt'ring Implements of Pride' with which the modern woman is furnished (*The Fan*, pp.7-8). Venus presents the new article to the gods on Olympus as a desirable sophistication of feminine charms, but it emerges that the purpose of the fan is above all to preserve impersonality, a point which arouses the hostility of Diana. Minerva, very like Clarissa, makes the attempt by painting scenes on the fan to warn the modern lady to distrust mere material attractions, and to place no faith in the 'transient Good' of beauty (pp.24-9). None the less, the fan and woman remain enshrined in their exalted positions, recipients of the earth's store of material luxuries, and Gay finally sets the scene in universal fraud and vanity:

> While Widows seek once more the Nuptial State,
> And wrinkled Maids repent their Scorn too late,
> As long as youthful Swains shall Nymphs deceive,
> And easie Nymphs these youthful Swains believe,
> While Beaus in Dress consume the tedious Morn,
> So long the *Fan* shall female Hands adorn.
>
> (p.31)

Such a picture is arguably more sombre than anything in the *Rape*, but it does serve to emphasise the mutual deceptions of the sexes examined in both poems. We are reminded that the Baron's deliberations over the use of 'Fraud' or 'Force' (II. 30-2) is a particularly apposite mock-heroic allusion; likewise it is implied in the *Rape* that the mercenary powers may be brought into play to assail Belinda as well as to supply her vanities — in her dismay at the seizure of the Queen of Hearts by the Knave of Diamonds during the game of ombre (III. 87-8), she retaliates with another 'nice *Trick*' (94). An important aspect of Gay's poem is that, for all its stress on female pride and artifice, it ends by suggesting that women have unknowingly become too sophisticated for their own good, accepting seeming benefits which can ultimately only be pernicious to them. Pope's *Epistle to a Lady*, while attributing to women the two ruling passions of 'Love of Pleasure' and 'Love of Sway', observes that while the first is the product of nature, the second is urged upon them by experience:

> ... by Man's oppression curst,
> They seek the second not to lose the first.
> (213-14)

Pope sees several layers of artifice, as it were, imposed on the natural impulse to pleasure, with artifice overwhelming the primary aim, and only a life of deception to follow.

Umbriel's excursion to the Cave of Spleen gives a memorable and bizarre foretaste of the 'merry, miserable Night' awaiting the jaundiced and superannuated coquette, and it is this episode which, more than any other of the 1714 additions, deepens the shadows of the whole poem. Pope's underworld owes its most obvious and significant debts to Ovid's *Metamorphoses* (particularly Books II and IV) and to the seventh book of the *Aeneid*, in which Juno descends to stir the Furies to her purposes. Sandys' commentary on the assaults of the Furies (*Ovid's Metamorphoses*, third edition (1632), p.165) stresses that they are 'but the wicked desires and commotions of the minde', and that 'they afflict with the remembrance of what is past, with the present, and fears of the future', the terms in which the 'fierce *Thalestris* fans the rising Fire' after Umbriel's rending of the bag of Furies (*Rape*, IV.97ff.). The gloomy residence of Spleen herself is most closely identified with the Cave of Envy in Book II, [24] and the general link with the *Metamorphoses* is aptly expressed in the grotesque bodily transformations brought on by the agency of 'pow'rful Fancy' in her victims [25] — an inversion of the process by which, in the mortal and conscious upper world of the *Rape*, personality is defined by the assistance of external objects. Pope reduces the figures attending Spleen to two, identifying Ill-Nature with malicious zeal, scandal and satire, and Affectation with the cultivated airs and hypocrisy of the coquette. The one represents repression as prudery and old-maidish Puritanism (revealed in her dress), concealing susceptibilities which find vent in aggression; the other equally assiduously feigns susceptibility in passive 'sickness' and assumed youthfulness. Together they illustrate Spleen's jurisdiction over the female sex 'to Fifty from Fifteen', a formulation which draws attention specifically to the onset of puberty. Both are of the essence of developing prudery, and Umbriel's speech of IV. 67ff. is particularly focused on scandal as a provocation to 'Chagrin', while the notion of Spleen as the disease of snobbish indolents is a popular butt; we find the goddess prostrate upon her bed, the posture in which Belinda is found in canto I. Spleen is thus the perfect model for a goddess appropriate for Pope's moral perspective, containing both a social and a psychological reference, and keeping the integrity of the sufferer nicely in question; there are close links between the popular conception of the disease ('vapours', 'hypochondria', 'hysteria') and the condition termed 'melancholy' up to the late seventeenth century and analysed in Burton's *Anatomy of Melancholy* (1621).[26] There is perhaps some parody of the mechanistic view of physiology and the operation of the mind at the critical moments in the action of canto III of the *Rape*, where coffee exudes stratagems in 'vapours' ascending to the Baron's brain, and Belinda's improper thoughts are physically seen to rise in her mind, closely observed by Ariel. But it is significant that, with the exception of 'Pain' and 'Megrim' waiting at the side and head of Spleen, Pope's treatment of the disease makes nothing of its many alleged bodily symptoms and processes; instead he dwells on the visionary joy and fear (ll.40-6) experienced by the splenetic, alternating between the two as if to suggest a precarious imbalance, and its association with obsessive 'Wit', religiosity and affected pride (ll.59ff.). This emphasis on the psychological foundation of the distemper in its most fantastical aspects casts some doubt on Lawrence Babb's conclusion that Pope treats it as a genuine physical malady, and the testimony of Politheca, the female patient in Bernard Mandeville's earnest *Treatise of the Hypochondriack and Hysterick Passions* (1711), gives an insight into the popular opinion of the vapours:

> Whenever I discover a quarter part of what I feel, my whole Distemper is counted a whimsey, and I have the mortification into the bargain, of passing for Fantastical in the midst of so many real Evils. I never dare speak of Vapours, the very name is become a

Joke, and the general notion the Men have of them, is, that they are a malicious mood, and contriv'd Sullenness of Willful, Extravagant and Imperious Women, when they are denied, or thwarted in their unreasonable desires (p.199).

Umbriel's attack on Belinda is, as already mentioned, twofold, stirring up both abject grief and violent rage, so that her response to the rape progresses from hysterical outrage (III.156) to melancholic despair and then again to fierce aggression; the whole picture is deepened by the associations of vapours with the life of luxury and tedium, and of hysteria with cravings of the womb most effectively stilled by sexual satiety.[27] Martin Price rather overstates the case in representing the domain of Spleen as 'an erotic nightmare of exploding libidinous drives',[28] but certainly the detail of the 'Maids turn'd Bottels' calling aloud for corks presents a direct metaphor for sexual repression. Strikingly, china, earthenware and glass, those artefacts symbolic of fragility, imbalance and tenuous chastity, overrun the underworld in semi-human form. There are also deeper shadows of death about Pope's Spleen, 'screen'd in Shades from Day's detested Glare' — the line is an echo of Davenant's 'Death's detested Shade' (TE, II, 185 n.22) — and the association of the hollow sham of emotion in the upper world with wretchedness and chaos in the lower recurs in the more sombre representation of the 'Lunar Sphere' in canto V (113-22). Death at the last becomes a serious concern as the poem ends, though not without a play on the familiar cliché of the 'deaths' of lovers which has governed the battle scene.

If Spleen represents the perils of too long a constriction by the demands of sophisticated living, the Baron's assault embodies other threats. When he enters the scene, there is a major formal transition from the descriptive to the active, expressed in verbs which move the narrative on from the past tense to an absorbing present, shifting equally dramatically to the Baron's schemes for the execution of his future plot. The formulation concerning his response has an incisive brevity which echoes the imperious 'veni, vidi, vici'; 'He saw, he wish'd, and to the Prize aspir'd.' The whole subject of the Baron's machinations presents a striking shift from the immediately preceding metaphors of constriction, traps and snares to launch into the counter-attack. By that juxtaposition, the idea of provocation to battle is brought to the fore, and the Baron's scene of sacrifice to the powers of Love becomes in its way the parallel to Belinda's toilette; a scene of preparation for combat, seemingly self-effacing but ardently addressed to a purpose. The more foppish elements of the Baron's indentity are consumed in the sacrificial fires, to which he resigns his 'twelve vast *French* Romances, neatly gilt'. In his rhetoric and actions there is a comic yet revealing blend of the romantic and that 'spirit of cruelty' — the impulse to vaunt over a fallen victim (III. 161ff.) — which Pope finds disturbing in Homer's heroes. Certainly he has more of aggression than the mere fops and witlings who are, according to Addison (*Spectator* no. 128, 1711), particularly attractive to the coquette because 'she would have the Lover a Woman in everything but the Sex'; Pope plays on the idea of sedition within the Baron's servility, his cunning sharpened by coffee in the manner of conniving statesmen (who also plot the fall of 'Nymphs at home'), and his possession of the lock ('Obtain'd with Guilt, and kept with Pain') identified with the pernicious betrayal of Nisus by Scylla (III. 122).[29] The contrast between reverential idol-worship and determined opportunism in the Baron is consistent with the mixed tone of his speech of triumph in canto IV (131ff.); this, in its relation to Achilles' oath (*Iliad*, I. 309ff.), is specifically an emblem of division which is more elegiac than aggressive. This theme and tone introduce a note of regret at the heart of the Baron's triumph; a similar elegiac note is important in Thalestris' inflammatory speech, when she exclaims upon the futility of the sufferings borne in the name of sophistication:

> Was it for this you took such constant Care
> The *Bodkin*, *Comb* and *Essence* to prepare;
> For this your Locks in Paper-Durance bound,
> For this with tort'ring Irons wreath'd around?
> (IV. 97-100)

Her words are highly reminiscent of the more intimate and tender lament in Ovid's *Amores*, in which the lover bewails the loss of his mistress' hair in terms which similarly present a more delicate nature distorted by the strains of artifice:

> heu, male vexatas quanta tulere comae!
> quam se praebuerunt ferro patienter et igni,
> ut fieret torto nexilis orbe sinus!

(alas, what woes were theirs, and what tortures they endured!
With what patience did they yield themselves to iron and fire to
form the close-curling ringlet with its winding orb!)[30]

The verses are explicitly moral, however, as Ovid offers a
reproach to his mistress for her excess of vanity, while Thalestris
would have Belinda see her pains as heroic (ll. 101-2); and while
Ovid finally offers comfort (the hairs will grow again), Thalestris
is determined to represent the loss as irredeemable. Yet it is
important that Clarissa herself acknowledges 'loss' at an
unspecified level (V.30); she is herself numbered among the
legion of Court beauties, and her speech is concerned, as Belinda
is, with the most effective use of 'Pow'r'. The sense of movement
and urgency which underlies the homely tone of the whole speech
partly arises from an emphasis on the providential necessity of
disease and death:

> Oh! if to dance all Night, and dress all Day,
> Charm'd the Small-pox, or chas'd old Age away;
> Who would not scorn what Huswife's Cares produce,
> Or who would learn one earthly Thing of Use?
>
> (V.19-22)

Her position in the action is not merely that of impassive arbitress,
and it is she who in canto III passes the 'two-edg'd Weapon' to
the Baron, as 'Ladies in Romance assist their Knight'; this is
entirely consistent with her rejection of the ideal of chastity in
summarily warning Belinda that 'she who scorns a Man, must die
a Maid' (l.28). The threat refers back to Pope's questioning in the
invocation, 'what stranger Cause ... / Cou'd make a gentle *Belle*
reject a *Lord*?', a question which Clarissa's speech is not designed
to answer, but instead to present an alternative both to uncritical
acceptance and intransigent rejection. However, the insertion of
her speech in the action creates an unnatural pause in the midst of
the fervent recriminations, 'Screams, and Scolding', shortly
bursting into physical strife, which are the keynote of the final
canto. The battle itself, in explicit echo of Homer's (*Iliad*, XX.
91ff), entails the pitting of Mars against Pallas, a reanimation of
the dissonance which is at the centre of the poem, and which
Clarissa's invocation of 'Sense' is inadequate to resolve. It is after
all appropriate to the scheme of the poem that Belinda's wrath

should only be stemmed by the confiscation of the object of contention in the apotheosis of the lock:

> But see how oft Ambitious Aims are cross'd,
> And Chiefs contend 'till all the Prize is lost!
> (V.107-8)

Belinda is thus compensated both for the injury to her reputation and, ultimately, for the discourtesy of death only by an elaborate heroic fiction; Clarissa's sterner emphasis on the incursions of smallpox and decrepitude is (by the indulgence of the poet) tactfully suspended.

The reaffirming of the fiction is none the less consistent with the moral and psychological stress of the poem; what makes the *Rape of the Lock* successful as a mock-heroic is not simply that mock-heroic 'reductiveness' provides a potent medium for satire, but that here there is a real sense in which confinement, the pervasive smallness of the poetic world which mirrors the smallness of Belinda's social world, actually breeds intensity. The relationship between confinement and intensity is brought out equally in *Eloisa*, in many of the portraits of *To a Lady*, and in the rampant reductiveness of Dulness and her entourage in the *Dunciad*. In much of the *Rape*, however, as in many sections of the *Dunciad*, this restrictiveness is felt less as a pressure and more as a form of liberation, the freedom which might be posited in sinking self-consciousness and with it all sense of threats and liabilities. The power of Pope's vision here stems from a vivid imaginative attraction to the hypothetical pleasures of stultification, and for all the complexity of the poem it is this sense of attraction towards its carefully expurgated 'upper world' which finally seems to predominate over the darker sides of the *Rape*.

Notes

1. René Le Bossu, *Traité du poëme épique* (Paris, 1675). Pope described this treatise in the 'Preface' to the *Iliad* as 'admirable' and as giving 'the justest Notion of [Homer's] Design and Conduct' (TE, VII, 23).
2. William Frost, '*The Rape of the Lock* and Pope's Homer', *MLQ*, 8 (1947), 342-54.

3. *See* particularly H-J. Zimmerman, *Alexander Popes Noten zu Homer* (Heidelberg, 1966), and Robert Crossley, 'Pope's *Iliad*: the commentary and the translation', *PQ*, 56 (1977), 339-57.

4. *Correspondence*, I, 44; April 1708.

5. *See* Maynard Mack, TE, VII, lvi-lvii, and Brower, *Alexander Pope*, 127.

6. *See* Samuel H. Monk, *The Sublime* (New York, 1935).

7. Pope's admiration of Longinus is expressed in the *Essay on Criticism*, ll.675-80.

8. For some account of the contemporary approbation of 'poetical' over moral goodness in protagonists of epic and drama, and further references, *see* Steven Shankman, *Pope's 'Iliad': Homer in the Age of Passion* (Princeton, 1983), 19-21.

9. *See also* Felicity Rosslyn, 'Awed by reason: Pope on Achilles' (*Cambridge Quarterly*, 9 (no. 3, 1980) 189-202), which makes a close analysis of the final book of Pope's translation.

10. I quote once more from Pope's redaction of Le Bossu's treatise: TE, IX, 20.

11. Virgil's narrative (*Aeneid*, I.38-40 in Dryden's translation: *Poems*, III, p.1065) explains that Juno's resentment of the Trojans goes back to her rejection in the Judgement of Paris, and is aggravated by Jove's infidelities with Electra and Ganymede.

12. *See* TE, II, appendix D (329-99), and the original annotated copy, BM C 116. b.2(6).

13. Dryden offers one of the most concise definitions of the term: '... the manners; under which name I comprehend the passions, and, in a larger sense, the descriptions of persons, and their very habits' (*Essays*, edited by George Watson (2 vols; 1962); II, 278).

14. John Dennis, 'Remarks on Prince Arthur' (1696), *Critical Works*, edited by E.N. Hooker, I (1939), 71-4.

15. *Monsieur Bossu's Treatise of the Epick Poem*, translated by 'W.J.' (1695). Mack (TE, IX, 3) notes that the phrasing of Pope's redaction follows this translation 'rather closely'. *See* particularly Book III, chapter IX, and Book IV, chapters I and II.

16. *See* note 1 above.

17. Ian Jack, *Augustan Satire: Intention and Idiom in English Poetry, 1660-1750* (Oxford, 1952), p.88.

18. Addison makes the point too in *Spectator* no.273 (January 1712): 'we find in Mock-Heroic Poems, particularly in the *Dispensary* and the *Lutrin*, several allegorical Persons ... which are very beautiful in those Compositions, and may, perhaps, be used as an Argument, that the Authors of them were of Opinion, such Characters might have a Place in an Epic Work.'

19. Another carefully contrived detail of the same kind is inserted at V. 71-4, where Pope represents the balancing of Belinda's hair against the 'Men's Wits', choosing to denote victory to the hairs by the sinking of the scale. This is the same reversal of the Homeric weighing symbolism as in *Paradise Lost*, IV. 996-1004, an alteration which Pope approves since it indicates Satan's moral 'lightness' and thus transfers attention away from the 'primary' issue of life and death to that of moral worth (TE, VII, 400).

20. Compare Pope's *Sober Advice from Horace*, ll.130-2. *See also* John F. Sena, '"The wide circumference around": the context of Belinda's petticoat in *The Rape of the Lock'*, *Papers on Language and Literature*, 16 (1980), 260-7.
21. The same point is made in rather different terms in the *Tatler* no. 126: 'The prude and coquette ... are in reality the same kind of women: the motive of action in both is the affectation of pleasing men ... The prude appears more virtuous, and the coquette more vicious, than she really is.' (*Tatler*, edited by G. A. Aitken, (1899), 67-8.) In a whimsical vision of the Day of Judgement, Pope also proposes that 'We shall then see how the Prudes of this world owed all their fine Figure only to their being a little straiter-lac'd, and that they were naturally as arrant Squabs as those that went more loose, nay as those that never girded their loyns at all' (*Correspondence*, I, 353).
22. Aubrey Williams discusses theses nuances in 'The "fall" of China and *The Rape of the Lock'*, *PQ*, 41 (1962), 412-25.
23. David Fairer, 'Imagination in *The Rape of the Lock'*, *Essays in Criticism*, 29 (1979), 53-74.
24. Spleen's wayward peevishness (ll.79-80) is a parody of Envy's reluctance to grant the demands of Pallas:

> Envie cast after her a wicked eye,
> Mutters, and could for very sorrow die
> That such her power ...
>
> (Sandys, p.62)

25. As Tillotson's notes demonstrate (TE, II, 187-8), imaginary metamorphosis is treated as a familiar symptom of melancholy or spleen.
26. *See* Lawrence Babb, 'The cave of spleen', *RES*, 12 (1936), 165-76.
27. *See* Ilza Veith, *Hysteria: The History of a Disease* (Chicago, 1965), 108; also Burton's *Anatomy of Melancholy* (1621), I, iii, 4. Similar points are discussed by John F. Sena, 'Belinda's hysteria: the medical context of *The Rape of the Lock'*, *Eighteenth Century Life*, vol. 5, no.4 (Summer 1979), 29-42.
28. Price, *To the Palace of Wisdom: Studies in Order and Energy from Dryden to Blake* (Garden City, 1964), 154.
29. Sandys comments on Scylla as the epitome of the Machiavellian opportunist: 'She rejecteth religion, piety, and feare, with this wicked assertion:

> 'Wee to ourselves are Gods: they thrive, who dare;
> And Fortune is a foe to slothfull prai'r.'
>
> (*Metamorphoses* (1632),p.286; Book VIII)

30. Ovid, *Heroides and Amores*, trans. Showerman, pp. 372-75; I.xiv. 24-6.

CHAPTER THREE

'Steering betwixt extremes':
An Essay on Man

In the preceding chapters I have made note of two very generalised but significant anticipations of the *Essay on Man*'s philosophy some years before any detailed plans for the work had been laid down by Pope; the first of these is the emphasis on the terms 'grace and nature, virtue and passion' developed in *Eloisa to Abelard*, and the second the note to Book XVII of the *Iliad* (n.5) which refers the contrasting temperaments of Achilles and Patroclus to the balancing of contrary principles within the scheme of Providence. In either case the links may perhaps appear limited or superficial; in fact, however, they express two facets of Pope's thinking which were developed consistently through his works and which became central to the *Essay on Man* in particular — the striving towards a form of moral idealism, and a strong imaginative interest in the concept of harmony through the reconciliation of opposites, the *discordia concors*. When Pope came to develop his theories on human nature within the optimistic framework of the *Essay*, his philosophy was propounded through a process which he described, characteristically, as 'steering betwixt the extremes of doctrines seemingly opposite' ('Design', ll.21-2); the pursuit of this goal was taken as something of a challenge. The 'doctrines' to which he refers are in particular those concerning the various attributes of Man and their potential for perfection or corruption, and it is the nature of his attempted compromise between them which I wish to examine in this chapter. I am indebted in my discussion of the intellectual context of the poem to the excellent commentary and thorough scholarship of Maynard Mack assimilated in the Twickenham text and (on the passions) to further studies by Bertrand Goldgar and Douglas White;[1] in the light of these studies and my own research I have tried to draw together the chief threads of Pope's system, adding further footnotes and analogues of my own where these seemed enlightening, with as much background reference as is consistent with brevity. Instead of pursuing the approach of White and Goldgar, defining Pope's position on specific philosophical issues, I have chosen to follow the line of argument presented within the *Essay* as a whole, keeping in mind the fact that it is shaped not only dialectically but poetically, and that often Pope's manner of delivery has an important bearing on the tenor of his assetions.

The *Essay* was originally conceived as the centre of a wider ethic scheme which was first alluded to by Bolingbroke in November 1729 (see TE, III (i), xiii), and within this scheme it was particularly closely linked with the four epistles which Warburton later entitled the *'Moral Essays'*.[2] Most of the epistles originally projected for the system (which Pope termed his 'opus magnum') were never completed, and he appears to have grown disenchanted with his plans by around 1735; the process whereby much of the material was assimilated into the *Moral Essays* and *The Dunciad* of 1742 has been meticulously charted in Miriam Leranbaum's study *Alexander Pope's 'Opus Magnum' 1729-1744* (Oxford, 1977). Within its wider framework, the *Essay* itself did not immediately emerge as a coherent unit; epistles I-III were published close together between February and May 1733, and it was not until January 1734 that a fourth epistle completed the work as we now have it. Leranbaum sees the first two epistles as distinctively the most assured and carefully related sections of the whole (pp.59-63), although the two manuscripts of the poem, in the Pierpont Morgan and Houghton libraries, show extensive reworking and revision of individual passages throughout.[3] In the Morgan manuscript (p.1, recto) a particularly interesting set of notes maps out the specific links between the 'exordium' opening Epistle I and some of the projected 'opus magnum' epistles, as follows:

A mighty *Maze*	Inconsistencys of character, ye Subject of Ep.5
Or *Wilde*	Passions, Virtues &c. ye Subject of Ep.2
Or *Orchard*	The Use of [wild?] pleasure, in Lib.2

This scheme demonstrates some of the obvious links in Pope's early plans between the *Essay on Man* and the *Moral Essays*, yet the nature of the works as they eventually emerged was markedly different. Pope's survey of man in the *Essay* keeps close to the central tenet that partial evil is compatible with, and even conducive to, universal good; it might be described in Pope's words to Swift (June 1730: *Correspondence*, III, 117) as 'a book, to make mankind look upon this life with comfort and pleasure, and put morality in good humour'. Although the *Moral Essays* share the terms of this optimism, they emerge as predominantly satiric works, stressing and castigating the wild inconsistencies and viciousness of human nature. This distinction arises principally from the fact that the *Essay* deals in universals rather than the 'finer nerves and vessels' of humanity; the approach (as the 'Design' makes clear) is relatively tentative and comprehensive, moderate and less impassioned, although in tone the *Essay* is highly assertive and often marked by a satiric edge.

Douglas White has emphasised the importance of the *Essay's* intellectual eclecticism, and also the way in which specific contentions as summarised in the 'Argument' prefixed to each epistle seem often to suggest commitment to philosophical tenets which are not in fact accommodated in Pope's scheme. This approach to the work, in terms of the 'manipulation of ideas', stresses the urgency of contemporary counter-arguments to many of Pope's assumptions and deductions, and on this basis White suggests that Pope may at certain points be consciously leading the reader towards mistaken conclusions. While such a strategy does appear to me to underlie the structure of *To Cobham* (discussed in the following chapter), in the *Essay* I would see it as a technique which is exploited only within the rhetorical framework of shorter passages. What we need to be aware of is that Pope is propounding an original thesis on premises which were the subject of extensive and time-honoured debate, and that many of his assertions and demonstrations were certainly designed to be provocative.[4] Most contemporary treatises on the nature of man and the status of the passions similarly cover well-tracked territory, with a marked degree of mutual indebtedness and exploitation of common sources; Pope's *Essay* is typical in this respect, and beyond a certain point it is impossible to gauge with any certainty which works he was best acquainted with, although in general it is in the use of analogy and metaphor that his debts seem to become most apparent.

The poem as a whole is however distinctive for its overriding preoccupation with ethics, and consequently in the argument of the second epistle Pope's interest in defining 'passion', or in delineating the operations of the passions, is strictly limited. Fundamentally the *Essay* is more doctrinal than analytical, although its doctrine is built up from the exploratory terms set out in the 'Design', which contends that 'to examine the perfection or imperfection of any creature whatsoever, it is necessary first to know what *condition* or *relation* it is placed in, and what is the proper *end* and *purpose* of its *being*' (ll.6-9). The scheme of the argument embraces firstly man as a unit in the order of the universe, secondly man as microcosm, and thirdly man in relation to society. In considering what 'condition' man is placed in, Pope sets out to assert that it is in the best of all possible worlds, that both human nature and the ordering of this world are not degenerating in post-lapsarian chaos but continue by their own operations to answer the ends of Providence. He eschews the more strictly theological questions concerning grace and faith, not because such issues are divorced from the tenor of his argument, but because he chooses to set out his vindication chiefly in humanistic terms. Thus on the 'end and purpose' of man's existence, Pope confidently pronounces that the immediate human aim is happiness, that happiness consists in virtue, and that virtue concerns the active love of our kind. These points are assumed *a priori*, on premises which are summarised in a general note in the Morgan manuscript (the opening of Epistle IV); there Pope observes that the desire of happiness and the yearning for immortality are both implanted in man directly by God, and that the passion of hope is the medium of such desires:

> ... As God plainly gave [-?-] Hope [as?] instinct, it is
> plain Man should entertain it. Hence flows his greatest
> Hope v greatest Incentive to Virtue.
> 3. *Hope* his suñu bonum, not Possession. H̲o̲b̲s̲ always for
> s.thing to come. So on to Iñortality.[5]

The questions concerning happiness and virtue lead directly to questions on the nature of man himself, how far he is to be seen as degenerate and in what respects he is capable of virtue; in this context, Pope's vindication of the passions and the motivating force of self-love forms the very foundation of his ethical scheme, and thus Epistle II is the focal point of the *Essay* as a whole. The assertions which are made in that epistle form the ground of all the speculations and developments of Epistles III and IV, a formulation which is particularly clear from the Houghton manuscript notes to Epistle I, ll.6-16 — the lines glossed are the same as those expounded in the Morgan MS exordium:

> The 6th, 7th and 8th lines allude to yᵉ Subjects of This Book; the General Order and Design of Providence; the Constitution of the Human Mind, whose Passions cultivated, are Virtues, neg[lected], Vices; the Temptations of misapplyd Selflove and wrong pursuits of Power, Pleasure and false Happiness.

These notes, instead of referring to the sequence of 'opus magnum' epistles, now appear to embrace the matter of the *Essay* as a coherent unit, although the final phrase certainly evokes the 'ruling passion' argument of *To A Lady* (ll.207-42) as well as the *Essay*'s fourth epistle. The unity of theme, founded on the theory of the passions, which the whole outline proposes is reaffirmed in the eulogy to Bolingbroke which closes Epistle IV:

> And while the Muse now stoops, or now ascends,
> To Man's low passions, or their glorious ends,
> Teach me, like thee, in various nature wise,
> To fall with dignity, with temper rise.
>
> (375-8)

In Pope's theory of the passions, the most significant point is the contention that self-love is not only the root of all passions and the principle of action in Man, but equally the natural spring of virtue and of social love. The first part of this assertion adopts the principle of 'motion' animating the soul through appetitive impulse which reaches back in ethical thought to Aristotle, but Pope's emphasis on its supreme force and his definition of it as self-love strongly suggests a Hobbesian line of thought; the Morgan MS note quoted above (p.67) confirms that it had this association in Pope's mind.[6] On this foundation, there is also a potential affinity with the assumptions of the cynic moralists (La Rochefoucauld in particular)[7] who maintained that if self-interest rules over all personal choice, then virtue, in the rigoristic definition of the term, is either a chimera or else thinly-veiled vice. Bernard de

Mandeville's *Fable of the Bees* (1714) took this argument to the point of directing that private gratifications should be guided to their most useful ends, that is to luxurious fulfilments which would also advance the national economy. Thus although both Hobbes and Mandeville see a potential for social cohesion in the force of self-interest, the perspective on 'benefits' is utilitarian rather than ethical, and social rather than personal. The argument stands in contrast to the more intransigently negative perspective on personal virtue which subsists in the tradition of Augustinian pessimism, viewing man's self-love as a testimony to his post-lapsarian state of corruption, which may only be redeemed by the divine light of reason and the intercession of grace.[8] From this standpoint, virtue consists above all in the suppression of the passions, Stoic 'apathy' being transmuted into the supreme moral good of rationality; Malebranche, Charron and Antoine le Grand are perhaps the most notable exponents of this position, with varying degrees of Stoic rigour.[9] The plea for the supremacy of reason, however, is very far from confident rationalism; in Pierre Nicole's *Moral Essays*, the familiar metaphor of ocean, ship and pilot (also taken up by Pope in the *Essay*) is used to emphasise the fallibility of 'raison humaine' as well as the dangerous potency of the appetitive impulses:

> We are tost on the Sea of this World at the pleasure of our Passions, ... like a Ship without Sail, without Pilot: And it is not Reason which makes use of Passions, but Passions which make use of Reason to compass their ends; and this is all the stead Reason stands us in for the most part (I, 43)

It is rather the power of 'raison divine' to which Charron appeals in defining the wise man as one who 'directs all his Aims and Actions so as that they shall agree with Nature, that is, pure uncorrupted Reason, the Primitive Law and Light inspired by God' (*Of Wisdom*, I, 'Preface'). In Malebranche's *Search After Truth*, the epistemology is strikingly opposed to any kind of empiricism; the evidence of the senses is treated as corrupt delusion, and indeed 'sense' is defined as equivalent to 'passion':

> Thus a Man, who *judges* of all things by his *Senses*; who on all accounts pursues the *Motions* of his *Passions*, who has no other

than *Sensible Perceptions*, and loves only *Flattering Gratifications*,
is in the most wretched state of Mind imaginable ... (I, p.a2)

From a more moderate point of view, the 'Peripatetic' group of
moralists[10] (including Samuel Clarke, Bishop Reynolds, and
William Wollaston) had contrived to reconcile an anti-Stoic
reaction with a defence of the rational faculty, by adopting the
argument that the passions are in effect the strongest incentives to
virtue so long as they are held in check by the regulating power of
reason. From this area of debate, and the contention as to whether
the soul should be regarded as a composition of 'antithetical' elements, arise some particularly interesting issues relating to the
definition of will, the problem of complex or mixed motives, and
the process of reasoning. The great philosophical error of the
Stoics and Epicureans was commonly identified as their over-
emphasis on soul and body respectively, and that error is berated
in James Lowde's *Discourse Concerning the Nature of Man* (1694,
pp.23-4) in much the same terms as in the opening of Pope's
second epistle of the *Essay*. Lowde reacts bitterly against Hobbes,
however, particularly for what he sees as Hobbes' undermining
of all certainty in the faculty of will and in the capacity for self-
knowledge. The discussion of 'Trayne of Imaginations' in
Leviathan (part I. ch.3) does raise an especially contentious point
in proposing that reasoning and therefore ultimately the resolution of will is a process dictated by passion, and that an unguided
sequence of thoughts is one 'wherein there is no Passionate
Thought, to govern and direct those that follow, to it self, as the
end and scope of some desire, or other passion'. When Hume
took up the subject in the *Treatise of Human Nature* (1739-40),
his argument concerning the 'Influencing Motives of the Will'
(Book II, section iii) was again to assert that the dualistic separation of reason and passion offers a false paradigm, and that
'reason alone can never be a motive for any action of the will'.
These are some of the most suggestive and interesting problems
which exercised Pope in the *Essay*, and as I will show they also
entered significantly into the epistles which followed it (*Moral
Essays*). Within the scope of the *Essay on Man* and the philosophy
of the passions which it propounds, Pope is clearly anti-Stoic in
recognising an impulsive spring of virtue, but at the same time (as
Mack observes, TE, III (i), xxxv) the broader frame of the work,

adopting the principle of plenitude and the assurance of personal happiness through the practice of goodness, is distinctively Stoic in origin. And although Pope shares some common ground with the 'benevolist' philosophers (notably Shaftesbury and Francis Hutcheson),[11] he does not postulate an innate moral sense discriminating between good and bad actions, nor attempt any distinction between intrinsically self-regarding and socially-directed ('benevolent') passions; this constitutes an important departure from Shaftesbury, both on the nature of motive and hence on the nature of virtue. Pope's position is in fact not only anti-Stoic but also strongly anti-rationalist; reason is presented merely as a 'weak queen', a defective faculty continually overborne by the superior force of the passions. The weakness is demonstrated most disarmingly in relation to the power of the strongest of these, the 'ruling passion' (II.131ff.), yet in contrast to Montaigne (see chapter 4, below), Pope does not make this recognition the ground of total scepticism. Indeed it is the ruling passion above all which is represented as the most potent agent of providential harmony and of stability in the microcosm of human nature. Having made these general observations on the context and implications of Pope's position, the terms in which he presents his contentions are perhaps best examined through an analysis of the *Essay*'s developing argument.

The first epistle of the *Essay* establishes that emphatic castigation of pride which is a hallmark of the whole, and like *To Cobham* the work attempts both to undermine Man's faith in the validity of his own judgement while defending the propriety of his actual disposition. The 'nosce teipsem' injunction which opens Epistle II is thus central to both the epistles, in directing attention to Pope's humanistic frame of reference, and in establishing a predominantly Sceptic perspective on the subject of reason. His scepticism is expressed as a measured and qualified (though often sharply satirical) attack on the overconfidence of certain schools of philosophical thought, rather than as systematic and assertive doubt; overconfidence, indeed, was the primary charge against the most thoroughgoing school of Sceptics, or Pyrrhonists.[12] Like Bacon, Pope proposes to begin with doubts so that he may end in certainties. The disgruntlement of the idealistic philosopher at the imperfections of man is as it were set up as the object of the *Essay*'s argument and rhetoric, and Pope attempts to demonstrate firstly that pride itself distorts the power to reason in the would-be sage, and secondly that man's imperfections are (*sub specie aeternitatis*) only apparent. Thus Pope's satiric gestures are consistently addressed to the naive rationalism or overweening confidence of such analysts, ranging from the complacency of the Stoic to the presumption of the Cynic; cynicism, as Swift once observed, is a soured version of the idealist's credulity. It is important that the misconceptions of both extremes are represented, in the context of the *Essay*'s theodicy, as more than a venial error of judgement; they constitute a breaking of faith in God's ordering wisdom as well as an elevation of man beyond his proper status, and hence the word 'Pride' occurs as a central term of invective against man together with 'Impiety' and 'Madness' in I. 258.[13] None the less, even the scornful opening passages of the *Essay* acknowledge a contradiction on this head, since the note to verse-paragraph 77-90 (on man's contentment in the face of futurity) concedes that 'his happiness depends upon his *Ignorance* to a certain degree'. The point was one which Pope made again to Spence in 1737 (*Anecdotes*, I, 238): 'if a man saw all at first, it would damp his manner of acting; he would not enjoy himself so much in his youth, nor bustle so much in his manhood'. Similarly in the *Essay* Pope goes on to expatiate on the necessity of hope, as contributing to a vital strain of aspiration in man which is part of the spring of his virtue and which properly renders him restless in this world's confinement. Secure self-knowledge, if there could be such a state, would foster an equanimity which is not compatible with these ends; felicity is thus defined as the perpetual anticipation of felicity, and indeed the image of the lamb skipping its way to slaughter is harsh enough to bring to mind Swift's more acerbic definition, 'a perpetual possession of being well-deceived' (*A Tale of a Tub*; *Prose Writings*, I, 208). Hope in this life is seen as ultimately illusory, yet also (in its theological significance) as directed towards a firmer reality than the world itself can offer. The injunction of l.91, to 'Hope humbly then', emphasises the paradox in specifically Christian terms:[14] to aspire beyond this point is to invoke a disruption of the scale of creation, which has been organised to accommodate man's apparent frailties.

The 'great end' of happiness therefore demands deviation from apparent, absolute 'goodness', just as within the natural world fertility is sustained by the shifting elements:

As much that end a constant course requires
Of show'rs and sun-shine, as of Man's desires;
As much eternal springs and cloudless skies,
As Men for ever temp'rate, calm and wise.
(151-4)

By extension of the metaphor of nature, Pope sets out to justify (in a speculative context) the tempestuous side of human nature, and the havoc of world-destroyers in particular; his conclusion is that even the extremes of malice and tyranny are endorsed by the ultimate justice of God, who is here represented distinctively as the God of the Old Dispensation (TE, III (i) 35n.):

Who heaves old Ocean, and who wings the storms,
Pours fierce Ambition in a Caesar's mind,
Or turns young Ammon loose to scourge mankind.
(158-60)

Dubious as Pope's vindication may appear, his countering lines upon the prospect of perpetual tranquillity (167-8) attempt to convey with some rhetorical emphasis the stagnation of the mind bereft of passions; by contrast to this stasis, the passions are described as 'the elements of life', an argument which refers forward to Epistle II (ll.101-14), and which also evokes the 'humoural' conception of character (TE, III (i), xxxvi). Among Man's innumerable follies, in fact, the most absurd and self-betraying is his desire to be freed from the solicitations of desire; in Swift's words, 'the Stoical Scheme of supplying our Wants, by lopping off our Desires; is like cutting off our Feet when we want Shoes' (*Prose Writings*, I, 244). Pope's stress on the 'thin partitions' dividing the mental and sensual powers, the 'nice barrier' between the semi-rational elephant and man as *animal rationale*, presents an implicit challenge to those who choose to ignore his affinities with the bestial world, and attempt to delineate absolute distinctions on the relative uses and values of his mixed faculties. At the same time, the very delicacy of these distinctions is presented as testimony to 'th' insuperable line' which separates each link within the Chain of Being from the next. The theme of man's middle nature is again exploited by Pope partly to humble his constitutional pride, but predominantly in the optimistic context, repudiating the condemnation which such a theme would imply for the rigoristic Christian moralist or the Cynic. The subject is elaborated most forcefully in the celebrated verse-paragraph opening Epistle II; but here there is a subtle shift in emphasis which actually sways the balance towards man's limitations, perhaps suggestive not only of the diversity and extremes of his position, but also of a dangerously latent 'stalemate' between opposed forces, an incipient inertia born of confusion. It is this confusion in particular which stems from our lack of self-knowledge:

> With too much knowledge for the Sceptic side,
> With too much weakness for the Stoic's pride,
> He hangs between; in doubt to act, or rest,
> In doubt to deem himself a God, or Beast ...
> Chaos of Thought and Passion, all confus'd;
> Still by himself abus'd, or disabus'd.
>
> (5-8, 13-14)

'Nosce teipsem' is thus not only a criterion of wisdom, but also a necessary principle of *action*; abstruse metaphysical speculation serves only to confirm the deep paradoxes of human nature, and the mind remains beyond the scope of objective analysis for the ironic reason that its own powers are too inconstant to conform to pure reasoning. Whereas reason is represented in Epistle I (l.232) as a faculty superseding those lesser faculties possessed in a more acute degree by the animal world, here it is seen perpetually confounded by the conflicts within the whole creature. Pope reduces the term at II. 39-42 to its narrowest definition as a mere intellectual system-builder, constantly deflected from its course by the distorting mirrors of individual passion; 'passion' here probably has a close affinity with the concept of 'prejudice' employed in seventeenth- and eighteenth-century psychologies:[15] — 'what Reason weaves, by Passion is undone' (42). In whatever sense we take 'Reason' at this point, the nature of the assertion is suggestive of scepticism, and is central to the satiric note which marks this section of the epistle.[16] As in Epistle I, however, Pope deploys the satire to probe at the weak foundations of rationalist complacency; his own thesis, which he here presents in full, rests on the assumption that a special kind of synthesis between the operations of reason and the passions is ideally possible, even though the passions are inherently the stronger of the two.

Self-love and reason are defined in Aristotelian terms as the two directing forces in human nature — analogous, as Mack notes, with the Renaissance distinction between the rational and sensitive soul (TE, III (i), 62n.). Within this division, self-love is identified as the spring of all the passions (l.93):

> Two Principles in human nature reign;
> Self-love, to urge, and Reason, to restrain;
> Nor this a good, nor that a bad we call,
> Each works its end, to move or govern all:
> And to their proper operation still,
> Ascribe all Good; to their improper, Ill.
>
> (53-8)

This attitude to motive is important, since Pope is aiming to clarify immediately the ground of his departure from the 'benevolists' who would argue for a dichotomy in the nature of 'good' and 'ill' passions. The operation rather than the origin of the passion is Pope's index to morality; it is also possible that Pope is suggesting that moral good and ill are simply the beneficial or destructive *results* of an action, although this would imply an arbitrary role for reason and the will.[17] The analysis makes it clear that, as the spring of the passions, self-love is at least partially restrained and directed by reason:

> Man, but for that, no action could attend,
> And, but for this, were active to no end; ...
>   Most strength the moving principle requires;
> Active its task, it prompts, impels, inspires.
> Sedate and quiet the comparing lies,
> Form'd but to check, delib'rate, and advise.
> Self-love still stronger, as its objects nigh;
> Reason's at distance, and in prospect lie.
>
> (61-2, 67-72)

This division of labours may seem reassuring enough, but lines 77-80 apparently sound a warning note exhorting vigilance from reason, and suggest that habit will act as an ally to confirm its exercise — this is still more disarming in relation to l.145, in which it is claimed of the ruling passion that (second only to its mother 'Nature'), 'Habit is its nurse'. The problem seems to be that, according to whether the general bent of our actions reflects the dominant sway of self-love or reason, habit will work to confirm either the impulsive or the deliberative side of our nature.[18] In either case, 'experience and habit', as Pope wrote to Fortescue (TE, III (i), 64n.), 'are the two strongest of things' — that is, the strongest secondary forces in our nature.

As we will see in reviewing the *Moral Essays*, these reservations on the potential tyranny of the passions are extremely significant; however, lines 81ff (perhaps the central lines of the epistle, and distinctly acerbic) turn the balance again towards the celebration of synthesis, the *concors discordia rerum* within man's soul. The relevance of this vituperation on scholastic pedantry to the ethical values expressed in *Eloisa to Abelard* has already been noted (p.17 above):

> Let subtle schoolmen teach these friends to fight,
> More studious to divide than to unite,
> And Grace and Virtue, Sense and Reason split,
> With all the rash dexterity of Wit:
> Wits, just like fools, at war about a Name,
> Have full as oft no meaning, or the same.
>
> (81-6)

The reference to 'Grace' of l.83 argues that, in so far as fallen man is susceptible of redemption, the retracing of virtue must take place through the channels of his own nature; the passions are emphatically not retrograde impulses to be stifled by divine aid[19].

The chief point of unity and coherence in the 'aims' of both the impulsive and the restraining faculties lies in the avoidance of pain and the pursuit of pleasure (both the real and the apparent, the immediate and the projected); this part of Pope's argument includes the judging faculty within a definition which was often applied to the passions alone, as for example in the second Discourse of Senault's *The Use of the Passions*,[20] which sets out 'What the Nature of Passions is, and in what Faculty of the Soul they reside': 'Passion then is nothing else, but a motion of the Sensitive Appetite, caused by the Imagination of an appearing or veritable good, or evil, which changeth the Body against the laws of Nature.' None the less, Pope makes the moral point that unadulterated self-love culminates in destroying those objects which supply its gratifications (a corollary to the view that vice is ultimately self-punishing). The figure of the bee and flower of 89-90, almost certainly contrived as a refutation of La Rochefoucauld,[21] is thus designed to illustrate reason's superior power of restraint, not of disinterestedness. Pleasure is shown either to exalt or debase the soul, according to the uses to which it is directed, and in the same way the passions may prove either pernicious or beneficent forces. It is important that, within this dialectic, self-love even in the narrower sense of self-interest is seen as a principle endorsed by reason:

> Since Reason bids us for our own provide;
> Passions, tho' selfish, if their means be fair,
> List under Reason, and deserve her care;
> Those, that imparted, court a nobler aim,
> Exalt their kind, and take some Virtue's name.
>
> (96-100)

The approval of 'exalted selfishness' as *strenuous* virtue is pitted against the negative, defensively rationalist virtue ('lazy apathy') of the Stoics, which has none of the outward, social movement which Pope sees as so vital a function of wants and desires. Reverting to the general argument and imagery governing Epistle I, 141-72, he elaborates the thesis that 'ALL subsists by elemental strife' within the microcosm of human nature, and again the agency of God in this struggle for supremacy is affirmed:

> ... strength of mind is Exercise, not Rest:
> The rising tempest puts in act the soul,
> Parts it may ravage, but preserves the whole.
> On life's vast ocean diversely we sail,
> Reason the card, but Passion is the gale.[22]
>
> (104-8)

Although the tempering of the passions is seen primarily as the work of reason, both 'Nature' and God are also closely identified in the process, a significant departure from Shaftesbury's assumption that only the benevolent passions are 'natural' at all (see p.87 below.) This proposed relationship between nature and reason is interesting, and is closely discussed in White's study (pp.106ff.); the analogy as he presents it lies in the conception of nature as 'active and purposive ... an impulse within matter that is responsible for growth and direction' (p.106). Within this analogy there is also a suggestion of the higher 'artistry' which attains the equilibrium of opposed forces, a shadow of the original act of Creation holding the elements in tension (ll.119-22).

Throughout his argument, Pope concentrates his energies on vindicating 'the passions in general' (as they were generally termed in contemporary treatises);[23] he comes no nearer to categorising 'the passions in particular' than to adopt the Aristotelian distinction between the concupiscible and irascible passions, that is impulses tending towards the pursuit of personal good and the avoidance of personal ill:

> Love, Hope, and Joy, fair pleasure's smiling train,
> Hate, Fear, and Grief, the family of pain.
>
> (117-18)

A note in the Morgan MS of the poem (p.3) glosses these lines, and explicates those which follow (119-20) with the observation that 'The mean between opposite Passions makes Virtue, ye Extremes Vice' — the equilibrium between the passions themselves, in other words, is as crucial as the balance of reason against self-love. Pope takes more interest in the social than the personal implications of this notion, as the *Moral Essays* show, although it is central to the ideal of personal virtue expressed in the closing lines of *To A Lady*. Within the more abstract context of the *Essay*, the varying intensity of different passions is explained in terms of the varying susceptibility of the senses in individuals, a directly physical process which deliberately precludes a moralistic interpretation or an emphasis on will;[24] the Morgan MS shows that Pope heavily reworked the whole verse-paragraph (ll.123ff.), and particularly lines 128-30. It also contains an interesting couplet (excised in the printed editions) to follow l.130, which attempts a fuller explanation of the action of the passions:

> Nor here [?] internal faculties controll
> Nor Soul on body acts but that on Soul,
> And hence one Master Passion in the breast ...
>
> (etc.)

This again implies that the passions are ultimately of a 'mechanical', or physical, operation, and in fact strengthens the suggestion of a 'humoural' conception of character within the 'ruling passion' theory. The disappearance of the manuscript lines from the printed text may indicate that Pope wished to retain a speculative approach to the interaction of the soul and body, but none the less the phrase 'organs of the frame' (l.130) still implies a physical basis for personality differences. The general point leads on, by an explicit, consequential link, to Pope's theory that a single dominant passion, unique to the individual, persists through the whole course of life:[25]

> On diff'rent senses diff'rent objects strike;
> Hence diff'rent Passions more or less inflame,
> As strong or weak, the organs of the frame;
> And hence one master Passion in the breast,
> Like Aaron's serpent, swallows up the rest.
> (128-32)

The following powerful train of description representing the 'master Passion' as 'the Mind's disease' has a disturbingly divided effect; it shows the ruling passion on the one hand as an instrument of God's will controlling the vagaries of individual action, and on the other as a seed of incipient destruction monopolising the growing powers of mind and body. Fixing its roots in the matter of 'nature', it is nurtured by habit and further indulged by the imagination, and is finally only intensified in direct proportion to the capacities of the 'victim': 'Wit, Spirit, Faculties, but make it worse' (l.146). This ambivalence is to a great extent a product of the vivid and varied imagery which Pope employs, connecting as it does with patterns of imagery in the whole *Essay*. A central motif is that of growth; here, that of the body and (negatively) of disease and 'the lurking principle of death'; the ruling passion grows like a cancer:

> Each vital humour which should feed the whole,
> Soon flows to this, in body and in soul.
> Whatever warms the heart, or fills the head,
> As the mind opens, and its functions spread,
> Imagination plies her dang'rous art,
> And pours it all upon the peccant part.
> (139-44)

'Peccant' is a term which charges the whole description with a

suggestion of corruption, and yet the very aspect of the conception which is most sinister — the all-engulfing parasitism of the
ruling passion — is also expressed in language which, from the
rest of the *Essay* as well as in its immediate context, has certain
positive overtones. 'Soon *flows* to this', '*warms* the heart', '*fills*
the head', '*pours* it all' dramatise spontaneity and fluidity, picking
up (however subliminally) the tenor of the 'water in motion'
imagery which is so strong a metaphor in the 'passions' debate,
and as we will see Pope ends Epistle IV forcefully and imaginatively on that same motif.[26] The evocation of growth is also
balanced in positive terms by the notion of the ruling passion
itself as a plant (175-94), with God as gardener 'grafting' the virtues upon this 'savage stock' so that they may be reimbued with
vigour and, above all, bear fruit, a metaphor which is perhaps
strengthened by Christ's parable of the barren and fertile trees.
This emphasis on fertility stands in contrast to the image of veget-
able existence as stasis in II.63 — man without passionate
impulses, 'Fix'd like a plant on his peculiar spot, / To draw nutri-
tion, propagate, and rot' — whereas Epistles III and IV present
man as capable of *social* growth, a being who 'like the gen'rous
vine, supported lives' (III. 312), and happiness as a plant which
will sustain growth only in the right 'culture' (IV. 7-8).

Along with the ambivalence of the imagery applied to the ruling
passion, there are also the alarming political and legalistic terms
of the metaphors which present reason as a 'weak queen', an
unarmed defender of 'wretched subjects', a 'sharp accuser' or
'false pleader' of implausible causes; it is a final blow to the morale
that the ruling passion is seen as positively hastened on its course
by the subordinate power of reason, yet it is at this very point that
'Reason' as a sun acquires distinct connotations of 'raison divine',
'Heav'ns blest beam'. In effect, however, reason is shown to offer
only a more acute consciousness of failure, without having the
power of redressing that failure. The hint of complaint in Pope's
lines is deepened to a sustained lament on the apparent futility of
the rational faculty (149-60), usurped as it is by a seemingly alien
force — but the submission and co-operation of reason is none
the less exhorted so that the work of the ruling passion, in directing individuals to their personal goals and fulfilments, can be
realised:

> 'Tis hers to rectify, not overthrow,
> And treat this passion more as friend than foe:
> A mightier Pow'r the strong direction sends,
> And sev'ral Men impels to sev'ral ends.
> Like varying winds, by other passions tost,
> This drives them constant to a certain coast.
>
> (163-8)

The emphasis is thus on the role of domination which is played by the ruling passion: it does not, in the alarming sense of the metaphor, 'swallow up' the lesser passions, but counteracts their tendency to futile, self-defeating internal warfare. This is its primary active role; on the passive side, as we have seen, it is presented more as a catalyst to virtue than as a virtue in itself — a fundamental wildness, even baseness ('dross') is brought out in Pope's discussion of the passion (179-80), and the integration of the claims of the body with those of the mind (echoing the lost couplet from the Morgan MS) is celebrated. This last point is of course assimilated in the wider thesis of the whole epistle, that virtues are by no means distinct from vices, but disturbingly closely allied:

> The surest Virtues thus from Passions shoot,
> Wild Nature's vigor working at the root...
> Lust, thro' some certain strainers well refin'd,
> Is gentle love, and charms all womankind:
> Envy, to which th'ignoble mind's a slave,
> Is emulation in the learn'd and brave.[27]
>
> (183-4, 189-92)

The ingenuity of Pope's approach lies in the way in which he has reversed the familiar cynic's maxims of La Rochefoucauld on a near-tautological basis; if virtues are masquerading vices, vices are equally masquerading virtues, and a couplet in the Morgan MS explicitly pronounces that '... spite of all the Frenchmans witty lies / Most Vices are but Virtues in disguise' (p.5, verso). The positive bias which Pope now gives to his whole argument also serves to clarify up to a point the ambiguous role of reason, since the metamorphoses of virtues and vices tend towards 'good from ill' under the auspices of reason. At the same time, Pope has presented himself with the crux of another problem, the question of whether vice and virtue are in fact distinct in their operations, if not in their fundamental motivations. Sidestepping the threat of moral chaos, he answers this in utilitarian terms by maintaining that they are at least readily distinguished in their furthest extremes, except that our powers of recognition tend to be dampened by personal pride and the stupor of habituation:

> No creature owns it [vice] in the first degree,
> But thinks his neighbour farther gone than he.
> (225-6)

A mysterious dimension to the power of moral discrimination is also implied in the reference to 'the God within the mind' (1.204), which may again relate to the divine agency of reason, but could perhaps (if identified with the testimony of 'your own heart', 1.215) suggest 'conscience'. White (pp.103-6) prefers the reading of 'conscience', but Pope's first conception of the couplet (Morgan MS, p.2) shows that his original meaning was 'reason': 'This *Light* and *Darkness* in our Chaos join'd / 'Tis Reason's task to sep'rate in the mind.' In either case, Pope assumes that the moral sense can only distinguish between *apparent* vice and virtue, not vicious and virtuous motivation; leaving aside the extremes of either, the individual emerges as a being composed of subtly mixed motives, rarely following a pattern of consistently (rigorously) 'moral' action:

> 'Tis but by parts we follow good or ill
> For, Vice or Virtue, Self directs it still;
> Each individual seeks a sev'ral goal;
> But HEAV'N'S great view is One, and that the Whole; ...
> And build[s] on wants, and on defects of mind,
> The joy, the peace, the glory of Mankind.
> (235-8, 247-8)

The greatest power for harmony endowed by Providence thus consists in the bond of mutual needs and desires; such a picture does of course rest on the premise that man is by nature a social creature, and that the 'state of nature' is not in the Hobbesian sense one of 'nasty, brutish' discord, but of concord dictated by our very self-love:

> Wants, frailties, passions, closer still ally
> The common int'rest, or endear the tie:

> To these we owe true friendship, love sincere,
> Each home-felt joy that life inherits here.[28]
>
> (253-6)

Illusion, pride and aspiration actually foster the desired complacency which keeps mankind in this state of harmony, so that
personal self-sufficiency is balanced against the mutual needs
which keep society closely knit; and in the catalogue of self-con-
gratulating exempla (261-70), among the sots and lunatics, Pope
as poet wryly implicates himself. The familiar motif of man as a
regressive infant wandering his bemused way across the cluttered
stage of life is charged with pathos and a vein of worldly wisdom
which modifies the more affirmatory and exalted tone of much of
this epistle. A mounting strain of satire culminates in a dismaying
picture of Providence working to confirm man in whatever folly
and weakness he may possess, only to secure a tinselled, perpetually self-deluding happiness shored against the morbid perspective of truth:

> Each want of happiness by Hope supply'd,
> And each vacuity of sense by Pride:
> These build as fast as knowledge can destroy;
> In Folly's cup still laughs the bubble, joy.
>
> (285-8)[29]

Building upon the survey of man in the abstract, Epistles III
and IV of the *Essay* detach themselves from the more discomforting aspects of the preceding sections and go on to justify more
fully the role of the passions in relation to man's social capacities
and his desire for ultimate happiness. In this analysis, Pope presents the earth united by a 'chain of love' as it is by the 'chain of
being', in a vast system of mutual dependency: the paradigm
which Pope employs is rooted in science, investing the atoms
themselves with the attributes of human, sociable feeling:

> The single atoms each to other tend,
> Attract, attracted to, the next in place
> Form'd and impell'd its neighbour to embrace.
> See Matter next, with various life endu'd,
> Press to one centre still, the gen'ral Good.
>
> (10-14)

Terms like 'embrace' and 'press' suggest that even material forces like magnetism and gravity are a reflection of an apparently universal volition, passion or love. A model of the social network is also at work in this 'neighbourliness' of the atoms, each reaching out to 'the next in place'. Self-sufficiency in the creatures is expressed, on the other hand, as 'joy', the spontaneous pursuit of pleasure, an exuberance which is raised in Pope's evocation of it to ecstasy:

> Is it for thee the linnet pours his throat?
> Loves of his own and raptures swell the note:
> (33-4)

Man's power of control over these living beings may be that of a tyrant, but the law of nature is evidently on the side of the creatures, the birds who 'vindicate their grain' and the horse which is 'justly' remunerated from the harvest yield. Man is also in a sense (and in the manner of *To Burlington*) exploited as a 'vain Patron', his very extravagance and the scope of his demands serving to support the existence of his animal dependants. It is through the example of man's nurture of domestic animals that Pope illustrates how self-interest may address itself (if only for a time) to the interests of another creature. In this, the theme of animal indifference to futurity and hence to death relates back to the image of the doomed lamb in Epistle I (81-4) — Pope attempts in the one instance to demonstrate the propriety of all things, the justification of apparent suffering, and also the limitations imposed by man's 'superior' faculties. Limitations and benefits exchange their nature as the vices and virtues do; while the foreknowledge of death may seem a dubious benefit and brings its own form of suffering, it also acts as an impetus peculiar to man. 'Hope' through this prospect is bestowed in the promise of redemption, and the passions of hope and fear are themselves unique to man because of his powers of anticipation;[30] yet the 'miracle' of his position is that the certainty of steadily approaching death only endears him more to life and his naive faith in its continuance. This is seen as both necessary, and potentially absurd (ll.75-8).

While self-love motivates all creatures, it is also extended by its own impetus beyond self, towards desire of the opposite sex and finally 'love of self' through love of the whole generation of offspring.[31] Since the physical weakness of man demands longer parental care, the family unit emerges as a smaller model of the wider social framework:

> That longer care contracts more lasting bands:
> Reflection, Reason, still the ties improve,
> At once extend the int'rest, and the love;
> With choice we fix, with sympathy we burn;
> Each Virtue in each Passion takes its turn;
> And still new needs, new helps, new habits rise,
> That graft benevolence on charities.[32]
>
> (132-8)

Pope's account of the growth of social benevolence, which is extended to l.146, gives particular stress to the importance of memory, anticipation and reason in the nature of human love, and the affirmation of 'natural' in 'habitual' love. His meaning on this head, and the importance of gratitude within the framework of mutual indebtedness, is made clearer by his letter to Lord Oxford of November, 1725 (TE, III (i), 107n.):

> It is nature that makes us love, but it is experience that makes us grateful ... The better a man is, the more he expects and hopes from his friend, his child, his fellow-creature; the more he reflects backwards and aggrandises every good he has received.

The general point looks back to the closing lines of Epistle II, demonstrating that self-love is naturally transmuted as 'the scale to measure others wants by thine', which might be deliberately contrasted to Hobbes' observation, 'men measure, not onely other men, but all other things, by themselves' (*Leviathan*, p.87). The 'state of nature' in Pope's scheme inherently unites self-love and social love, and the process of development which links the one to the other is not enforced or acquired but spontaneous. It is significant that Pope's primitivist vision emphasises the absence of pride in the ideal state (pride being the primal human transgression), and particularly that reckless desire of dominion which Pope sees as perverting the modern society from its natural course of benevolent interdependency. The machinery of the state may either be supported by the principle of love, or by fear (another reflection of the concupiscible and irascible passions)[33] and the origin of religious consciousness is located partly in the earliest system of patriarchal government, when man first looked to his ruler and thence to God as a father: 'To Virtue, in the paths of Pleasure, trod, / And own'd a Father, when he own'd a God' (233-4). This implies that the primary impulses to religion are themselves attained through the paths of nature (not by enlightenment from above), and more specifically through the operation of passions. In contrast, the principle of fear is accused of founding tyranny in government and superstition in the place of religion:[34]

> Fear made her Devils, and weak Hope her Gods;
> Gods partial, changeful, passionate, unjust,
> Whose attributes were Rage, Revenge, or Lust;...
> Zeal then, not charity, became the guide,
> And hell was built on spite, and heav'n on pride.[35]
> (256-8, 261-2)

Although tyrannical governments thrive through unrestrained self-love Pope also assumes that the self-love of each subject demands some form of social restraint so that the interests of each individual can be protected; hence the development of the state as Hobbes sees it:

> All join to guard what each desires to gain ...
> Self-love forsook the path it first pursu'd,
> And found the private in the public good.[36]
> (278, 281-2)

The political content of these lines is explicitly a part of the wider thesis which links 'th' according music of a well-mix'd State' to the ideal harmony of all things, the 'jarring int'rests' themselves creating firm bonds of dependency and equally firm bonds of personal generosity. Thus all speculators upon the social and religious duties of man are ideally retracing the paths already indicated by 'Nature' and by God (283-8); and it is to the authority of nature and God that Pope returns in the closing declaration of this epistle, that self-love and social love are demonstrably 'the same'. This assertion ultimately places greater emphasis upon benevolence and charity (280, 300, 307-10) than upon the practical needs and demands of each member of the community. Although in the utilitarian sense we are indeed 'forc'd into Virtue

... by Self-defence' (279), Pope's movement towards the issue of happiness which occupies Epistle IV adopts the benevolist assumptions expressed by Shaftesbury, 'that to have the natural, kindly or generous affections strong and powerful towards the good of the public, is to have the chief means and power of self-enjoyment ... to want them, is certain misery and ill' (*Characteristics*, I, 292). The nature of contentment forms the major theme of Pope's final epistle, which makes an emphatic and markedly Stoic declaration of faith in the possibility of absolute virtue and in the equality of happiness; the final unity of both is of course already implied in the equation of self-love with social, and both are seen as the 'end and aim' of the concupiscible passions. The concept of an 'aim' is particularly important to Pope's argument — happiness is first presented as a potential and prospect, an incentive to the continued process of living as hope and desires in general are seen as the stimulants to action, yet its very elusiveness is taken as a sign that it lies within the grasp of every man. 'Extremes' of hedonistic indulgence or of Stoic restraint, of active engagement or disciplined retirement, all miss the 'obvious' mark of personal fulfilment through the practice of social virtue. Man's status as a social animal thus cannot be evaded, even by the most hardened lovers of self:

> There's not a blessing Individuals find,
> But some way leans and hearkens to the kind.
> No Bandit fierce, no Tyrant mad with pride,
> No cavern'd Hermit, rests self-satisfy'd.
> Who most to shun or hate Mankind pretend,
> Seek an admirer, or would fix a friend.
> (39-44)

Whereas the gifts of fortune are manifestly unequal, they are not to be equated with the possession of felicity; furthermore, Pope argues, the imbalance is redressed by the universal passions of hope and fear, the expectation of a better future or the dread of impending adversity. In this perspective, the prospect of eternal redemption or damnation plays the greatest part, but Pope does not dwell upon matters of faith specifically. Instead, this world itself is shown to confirm the final emptiness and miseries of vice and the perfection of enjoyment in virtue; external ills may assail the virtuous, but not disturb the inward security of contentment

(167-9). Historical exempla fill out a satiric catalogue of all those who sank beneath the pursuit of personal gain, and demonstrate how great men are a prey to the vices and acquisitiveness of others. The presumption that vice is inevitably set on the road to 'Human infelicity' is however a difficult one to uphold, and in Pope's couplet concerning the distresses of virtue ('The broadest Mirth unfeeling Folly wears, / Less pleasing far than Virtue's very tears', 318-19) there is a defensiveness and an ambiguity in the word 'pleasing' (pleasing to God, or to the suffering saint himself?) which is never fully resolved in the *Essay* as a whole. Pope's attempt to settle the problem is ultimately dependent on the conviction that Providence finally redeems the wrongs of this world, and his 'Argument' (319ff.) affirms as a last resort that '*Virtue only* constitutes a Happiness, whose Object is *Universal*, and whose Prospect *Eternal*'.

This two-handed argument is partly reflected in Wollaston's observations, cited by Pope in the Houghton MS,[37] that not only are we blind to the '*inward* stings and secret pains' of the vicious, but even supposing

> the pleasures of some, and the sufferings of some others, to be just as they appear: still we know not the *consequences* of them. The pleasures of those men may lead to miseries greater than those of the latter, and be in reality the greater misfortune: and, again, the sufferings of these may be preludes to succeeding advantages.[38]

Although Wollaston appears to be speaking of worldly 'advantages' in this passage, his distinction between immediate and future good is important. It is after all the natural path of 'enlightened self-interest' to seek for the ultimate personal good of salvation, and as Archbishop King argues, virtue is above all amenable to reason in that it is addressed 'even to the true Principle of all our Actions, our own *Happiness*'[39]. By this process, self-love is raised not only to social love, but 'to divine' (*Essay*, IV, 353); because of the nature of man, and above all because of the operation of the passions, it is impossible for the ultimate end to be gained except through the paths of nature, through gradual but progressive development: 'God loves from Whole to Parts: but human soul / Must rise from Individual to the Whole' (361-2).

Epistle IV ends on a theme which is much more personal and political than philosophical, through the closing address to

Bolingbroke; in fact political meaning is already put forward in its opening (ll. 18-19), where we are told that happiness is a quality,

> ... never to be bought, but always free,
> And fled from Monarchs, ST. JOHN! dwells with thee.

Bolingbroke thus represents the incorruptible, unbribable man nurturing virtue in retirement. It is characteristic that the *Essay*, like so many of Pope's poems, should turn the subject to embrace the poet and addressee; in doing so, Pope explicitly links his vindication of the 'low' yet 'glorious' passions with a dramatisation of the grounds of his adulation of Bolingbroke, uniting it with the theme of Bolingbroke's control over his own temperament, his dignified capacity to rise above circumstance, and still further with his eloquence as speaker and conversationalist. The poet indeed claims Bolingbroke's art of conversation as the model for his own facility in varied styles of writing:

> And while the Muse now stoops, or now ascends,
> To Man's low passions, or their glorious ends,
> Teach me, like thee, in various nature wise,
> To fall with dignity, with temper rise;
> Form'd by thy converse, happily to steer
> From grave to gay, from lively to severe;
>
> (375-80)

Implicitly, this laudatory ending has also been anticipated by the verse-paragraph which precedes it, extolling the type of the 'virtuous mind' which grows first to embrace 'friend, parent, neighbour', and then the wider spirit of patriotism and of universal benevolence. Even Pope's most exalted line, 'And Heav'n beholds its image in his breast' is consistent with Pope's naming his mentor (in a letter to Swift, 15 October 1725; *Correspondence*, II, 332) as 'the most *Improv'd Mind* ... that ever was without shifting into a new body or being Paullo minus ab angelis'. While this passage of verse expresses the ideal growth to beneficence as the rippling of water outwards in circles, 'as the small pebble stirs the peaceful lake', Bolingbroke is associated with the 'stream of Time' and animating gale; it is he who becomes the exemplar of the spirit of motion animating the human and cosmic frames, and this final emphatic demonstration of Pope's friendship and regard for him is made an integral part of the overall argument of the *Essay*, as is the case with many of the satires and the *Moral Essays*.

The note of optimism and assurance on which Epistle IV ends is an attempt to affirm that the potential for perfection in this world may actually be realised; yet the greatest power of the whole poem, and equally the greatest problem which it presents to the analyst, lies in its curious blend of declamation and satire, optimism and reservation. The intellectual liveliness of the *Essay* is realised through these often unexpected shifts in perspective and in rhetorical delivery, and this was indeed Pope's wider aim in 'steering betwixt the extremes of doctrines seemingly opposite'; the effect is of a kind which could only have been achieved through poetry, and although Pope himself avowed that he chose the poetic medium for its conciseness ('Design', 29-31), it becomes apparent that it was also a medium in which the tensions embodied in the *Essay* could be kept alive. Within the terms of Pope's philosophy, however, it is evident that it is not finally possible to smooth out, or fully counterbalance, many of the difficulties and contradictions which pervade his optimistic 'doctrine'. These difficulties are most conspicuous with regard to the 'ruling passion' theory, which it seems Pope is not prepared to rescue from an implied determinism and destructiveness. Discussing the problem of free will, Anne Barbeau has suggested that for Pope as for Dryden freedom is attained only in the subordination of personal desire to the ideal order, but that in the characters of Pope's satires the true drama of self-assertion against that order never really begins.[40] They are 'more often guilty of failing to think and will', and vice is seen to reflect above all the loss of a higher goal, a misdirecting of energies which quickly enters the cycle of repetition and stagnation. It is indeed the pursuit of 'ends' which absorbs Pope's attention consistently, both as moralist and psychologist; as we have seen, hope and happiness as incentive and aim are the fundamental questions on which the *Essay*'s whole scheme is constructed, and the ultimate question in the 'Argument' of the *Epistle to a Lady: Of the Characters of Women* similarly concerns 'the *Aims*, and the *Fate* of the Sex, both as to *Power* and *Pleasure*'. The integration of the 'ruling passion' theory with the content of the *Moral Essays* and the role which it plays in Pope's 'characteristical satire' thus raises particularly interesting questions; as I hope to show in the following chapter, the theory is the focal point of all four epistles, and not simply a pet notion which Pope has foisted onto their diverse subjects. Its pre-eminence within their arguments, however, might also be seen as a sign that Pope's philosophical assurance (or over-assurance) is increasingly undercut by pessimism.

Notes

1. Bertrand A. Goldgar, 'Pope's theory of the passions: the background of Epistle II of the *Essay on Man*', *PQ*, 41 (1962), 730-43; Douglas White, *Pope and the Context of Controversy: The Manipulation of Ideas in 'An Essay on Man'* (Chicago and London, 1970).
2. Pope's title for the *Moral Essays* was *Epistles to Several Persons*, and I agree with Bateson that his own title is more appropriate (TE, III (ii), ix, xxxvii); none the less I have referred to the works collectively as *Moral Essays* to avoid confusion with the various epistles of the 'opus magnum', the *Essay on Man*, and the *Imitations of Horace*.
3. *See* Maynard Mack, *Alexander Pope: An Essay on Man. Reproductions of the Manuscripts in the Pierpont Morgan Library and the Houghton Library with the Printed Text of the Original Edition* (Oxford, 1962), hereafter referred to as Mack, *Reproductions*.
4. *See* particularly Anthony Kenny, *Action, Emotion and Will* (1963), and Anthony Levi, *French Moralists: The Theory of the Passions 1586 to 1649* (Oxford, 1964), who observes that 'the theory of the passions was central to the moral debates of the period' (p.3).
5. Mack (*Reproductions*, p.xviii) takes this sketch to be an outline for the closing sections of Epistle IV.
6. The statement which Pope may well have had in mind occurs in *Leviathan* (1651; ed C. B. MacPherson, 1968), part I, chapter XI: 'Felicity is a continuall progresse of the desire, from one object to another; the attaining of the former, being still but the way to the later [*sic*]' (p.160). Compare Thomas Stanley's *History of Philosophy* (3 vols, 1656-60), vol.I, part 4, on Aristippus: 'That pleasure is our chiefe end is manifest, in that from our first infancy, without any instruction of others, we naturally aime thereat.'
7. La Rochefoucauld, *Moral Maxims and Reflections ... made English*, 1694.
8. *See*, for example, Pierre Nicole's *Moral Essays ... Rendred into English, by a Person of Quality* (3 vols, 1677-80), and Richard Baxter, *A Treatise of Self-Denyall* (1660).
9. *Father Malebranche's Treatise Concerning the Search after Truth*, trans. by T. Taylor (2 vols, Oxford, 1694); Pierre Charron, *Of Wisdom ... Made English by George Stanhope* (2 vols, 1697); Antoine Le Grand, *Man Without Passion, or, the Wise Stoick*, trans. by 'G.R.' (1675).
10. So termed by Goldgar, p.735, after the ancient Peripatetic school of philosophers; see Clarke, *Six Sermons on Several Occasions* (1718); Reynolds, *A Treatise of the Passions and Faculties of the Soule of Man* (1640); Wollaston, *The Religion of Nature Delineated* (1724).
11. Shaftesbury, *Characteristicks of Men, Manners, Opinions, Times* (3 vols,

1711; ed J. M. Robertson, 2 vols, New York, 1900); Francis Hutcheson, *An Essay on the Nature and Conduct of the Passions and Affections* (1728).

12. For a discussion of relations between the Sceptics and Pyrrhonists, see Phillip Harth, *Contexts of Dryden's Thought* (1968), 6-13.

13. Compare Walter Charleton's *Natural History of the Passions* (1674), 94, describing pride as 'a Vice so unreasonable and absurd, that if there were no Adulation to deceive men into a better conceipt of themselves than they really deserve; I should number it among the kinds of *Madness*'.

14. In general terms, this might be compared with the philosophical ideal of 'Mediocrity, betwixt hope and despair of the future', which Thomas Stanley glosses in his *History of Philosophy*, III (part 5), 252-3.

15. On the association of the passions with 'prejudice', see Kathleen Williams, *Jonathan Swift and the Age of Compromise* (Lawrence, Texas, 1955), 56.

16. The line is above all suggestive of Montaigne's emphasis on the defective nature of 'raison'; but the word has a variety of significances for the French moralists, and for Montaigne in particular (see chapter 4 below, and Levi, pp.2, 59-63). Pope refers to 'Reason' with some ambiguity throughout the *Essay*, and its various functions are closely discussed by White, 74-125.

17. Compare *Essay*, II. 99, also on reason and the passions. White (181) makes note of the varying punctuations of this line in successive editions, and argues that it may well contain 'a functional, rather than intentional or rigoristic, definition of virtue'.

18. James Lowde's *Discourse Concerning the Nature of Man* discusses virtue itself as 'an Habit', defining habit as 'not a meer dull in-active thing, but Action is included in the Notion of it' (203).

19. Pierre Nicole, for example, maintains that God has the direct power to destroy self-love by Grace (*Moral Essays*, III, 125).

20. J. F. Senault, *The Use of the Passions ... Put into English by Henry Earl of Monmouth* (1671), 17. Compare Stanley's *History of Philosophy*, III, 202: 'the generall affections of the Soul seem to be these four, Pain and Pleasure, the extream: Aversion and Desire, the intermediate ... the rest are kinds of these ... and may be reduced principally to Desire and Avoidance' (ch. XIX, 'Epicurus').

21. La Rochefoucauld represents the bee's activity as a paradigm of selfishness: 'self-love is the *Love* of a mans own self, and of everything else for his own sake ... and if for a little while it dwell upon some other thing, 'tis only as *Bees* do, when they light upon *Flowers*, with a design to draw all the *Virtue* there to their own advantage' (*Maxims*, no.II, 1-2).

22. The commonplace status of the 'sea and wind' metaphor is one point which casts doubt on Pope's supposed authorship of *Spectator* no.408 (1712); see Donald Bond, 'Pope's contributions to the *Spectator*', MLQ, 5 (1944), 69-78.

23. *See*, for example, Senault, *Use of the Passions* (part II, treatises I-VI), Burton's *Anatomy of Melancholy* (1621; I, ii, 3-15), and Charron's *Of Wisdom* (I, chs 19-33).

24. On the role of the senses, compare Antoine Le Grand, *Man Without Passion*, 91,93.

25. This is the 'new hypothesis' mentioned to Spence in May 1730 (*Anecdotes*, I,

130); see chapter 4 below, especially note 21. Charron makes explicit the possible link between 'humours' and dominant passions in a passage which is closely analogous to Pope's idea of the 'ruling passion': 'L'on vainc et l'on estouffe une passion, par une autre passion plus forte: car jamais les passions ne sont en egale balance. Il y en a tousjours quelqu'une (comme aux humeurs du corps) qui predomine, qui regente et gourmande les autres.' (*De La Sagesse*, Bordeaux, 1601, 304; Stanhope's translation (II, 11) omits the reference to 'humours').

26. *See*, for example, Stanley's *History of Philosophy*, III, 232 ('Epicurus'): 'as we would not have the life of a wise man to be like a torrent or rapid stream, so we would not it should be like a standing dead-pool: but rather like a river gliding on silently and quietly.'

27. With lines 191-2, compare Senault (part I, treatise IV, discourse iii, 'That there are no Passions which may not be changed into Virtues'), 145: 'a good emulation may be framed out of a well-regulated envy.'

28. Jacques Esprit, *The Falshood of Human Virtue. Done out of French* (1691), 40, also argues that friendships 'are like so many Rivulets, that take their rise from the Spring of Self-Love', but with a cynical emphasis quite contrary to Pope's.

29. Line 286 closely resembles one of Pope's *Thoughts Upon Various Subjects* (EC, X, 551), that 'every man has just as much vanity as he wants understanding', a maxim which is very much in the vein of La Rochefoucauld.

30. The Morgan MS notes on hope, virtue and immortality (*see* p.67 above) are important in connection with this passage; compare also Senault, 125: 'There is none but will avow, That Passions are necessary to our soul, and that joy must perfect the Felicity which desire hath begun.' Jacques Abbadie, *The Art of Knowing One-Self* (Oxford and London, 1698), 22, sees the fact of Man's immortality as the only justification of his infinite desires.

31. Irène Simon ('*An Essay on Man* III, 109-146: a footnote'; *English Studies*, 50 (1969), 93-8) points out Pope's indebtedness here to certain of the later Stoic thinkers, citing specifically Cicero's *De Finibus Bonorum et Malorum*, III, xix, 62-3 as a source. As she argues, 'some of the Stoics regarded the ties uniting man to his fellow-beings as arising from the natural affections, and *philanthropia* as an extension of the vital impulse' (95), and Cicero, like Pope, is attempting to steer 'betwixt extremes' philosophically.

32. The contrasting view of the family in a state of Hobbesian faction is put in Pope's *Thoughts* (EC, X, 558): 'A family is but too often a commonwealth of malignants: what we call the charities and ties of affinity, prove but so many separate and clashing interests: ... It is but natural and reasonable to expect all this, and yet we fancy no comfort but in a family.'

33. Compare the subject of Senault's *Use of the Passions*, part I, treatise V, discourse iii: 'That Princes win upon their Subjects either by Love or Fear'.

34. Compare Pope's *Thoughts*, (EC, X, 552): 'Superstition is the spleen of the soul.'

35. James Lowde, in *A Discourse Concerning the Nature of Man*, proposes that the Stoics were among the heathen as 'enthusiasts' among the Christians, who are motivated by 'ill-guided Zeal', and speculate 'as if the Sun of Right-

eousness came only to enlighten the understanding; but not either to regulate the Will, or warm the Affections' (34). Pope's lines (261-2) certainly seem to reflect beyond their immediate context to embrace 'enthusiasts' (see TE, III (i), 119n.).

36. An earlier version of III, 269-72 was designed in the Morgan MS (p.5, verso) to follow Epistle II, 249-54, linking the political implications of the passage to the general argument concerning 'wants, frailties, passions'.

37. Pope refers his whole argument upon rewards to Wollaston, 71, 110, 182, in the Houghton MS (the bottom of p.3, verso).

38. *The Religion of Nature Delineated*, 1724, pp.110-11.

39. *An Essay on the Origin of Evil* (1731), translated by Edmund Law from King's *De Origine Mali* (1702), xiv. King also argues (xxv) that 'the Mistake which some have run into, *viz.* that Merit is inconsistent with acting upon *private Happiness*, as an ultimate End, seems to have arisen from hence, viz. that they have not carefully enough distinguish'd between an inferior and ultimate End; the end of a particular Action, and the end of Action in general.'

40. Anne Barbeau, 'Free will and the passions in Dryden and Pope', *Restoration*, 4 (1980), 2-8.

CHAPTER FOUR

'This clue once found':
The Ruling Passion and the *Moral Essays*

For most readers of Pope, the first acquaintance with the 'ruling passion' theory is probably made through the *Moral Essays*; three of the four epistles invoke the theory directly towards the resolution of their arguments, in concise and emphatic passages which lend themselves to summary quotation. Yet the fact that such expository lines can be so readily taken out of their context in the poems has also helped to foster the doubts which have so often been expressed as to their relevance in each epistle. There has been a marked tendency among critics to lament the introduction of Pope's hypothesis as a reductive intrusion upon the real interests of the poems, a fossilised vestige of the uncompleted 'opus magnum' which contributes little to their intellectual liveliness.[1] It is generally assumed that Pope's theory is not only simplistic and inflexible, but that having drawn it up he ceased to think about it or develop it any further. Miriam Leranbaum's extremely helpful analysis of the way in which the epistles were shaped to relate to one another within the 'opus magnum' scheme has done much to question this prevailing assumption,[2] and here I wish to follow up two important facets of the epistles as connected works. The first is to analyse them as a series of progressive discussions debating the paradoxes of human motivation, and the second to examine the strategies of argument in *To Bathurst, To Cobham* and *To A Lady* which build up to the 'ruling passion' as the focal point of each, considering how far the theory is prepared for and susceptible of development.[3]

The *Moral Essays* emerged as a distinct though varied group of works, altogether more complex than their original position as extensions of the *Essay on Man's* philosophy would imply; Pope wished to view them instead as a framework for the elaboration of his ideas, in which illustration would be as important to the argument as exposition. The 'Design' of the *Essay* (prefixed to editions from 1734) closes with the observation, 'I am here only opening the *fountains*, and clearing the passage. To deduce the *rivers*, to follow them in their course, and to observe their effects, may be a task more agreeable.' In the event, *To Burlington* (1731) and *To Bathurst* (1733) were published before the first three epistles of the *Essay*, while the fourth epistle emerged just one week after *To Cobham* (January 1734), followed by *To A Lady* a year later. It is clear from the format of the 1734 'Index to the Ethic Epistles'[4] that the first two published were tied to the *Essay's* fourth epistle, and the other 'pair' to its second; in other words, according to their perspectives on Man 'with respect to *Happiness*' and 'as an *Individual*'. Later, in the 1735 octavo *Works* (volume II), Pope added a number of cross-referencing footnotes designed to emphasise the unity and consistency of all the *Moral Essays*, particularly by reference to the ruling passion theme — no doubt this was one symptom of his growing awareness that the ambitious 'opus magnum' project was unlikely to see completion. Allowing for their obvious relationships as 'pairs', then, it is also apparent that Pope saw all of the *Moral Essays* as interrelated arguments. The connections within his whole plan are well illustrated in Spence's jottings dated May 1730 (*Anecdotes*, vol.I),[5] from which I quote selectively:

> How wrong ye Greatest men have been in judging of the Cause of Human Actions... (a person fights too soon: *bec*: he is of a Vindicative temper). Montaigne hence concludes Pyrrhonically, That nothing can be known of the Workings of men's minds: I Essay, lib. 2? (The best in his whole book...).
> —— New Hypothesis, That a prevailing passion in ye mind is brought wth it into ye world, & continues till death (illustrated, by ye Seeds of ye Illness y^t is at last to destroy us, being planted in y^e body at our births.)
> We s^d not speak ag^{st} one large Vice, without speaking ag^{st} its contrary. —— As to y^e General Design of Providence y^e two Extremes of a Vice, serve like two opposite biasses to keep up y^e Ballance of things. Avarice, lays up ($w^t w^d$ be hurtful;) Prodigality, scatters abroad (w^t may be useful in other hands:) The middle y^e point for Virtue: ...Sr Balaam: The man of Ross: The Standing jest of Heaven. And sure y^e Gods & We are of a mind.

These notes illustrate how the 'New Hypothesis' evolved from Pope's reflections on two philosophical themes — the first of these is the problem of motive, with the emphasis on human complexity and instability; the second is the question of man's corruptibility and its accommodation within the ideal order of Providence. The most important issue raised in connection with these themes is the distinction between motivational and utilitarian definitions of goodness, and the second paragraph of Spence's notes shows Pope clearly aiming to segregate the two; Providence may be justified in working the ultimate good from man's extremes, but on the personal level the 'point for virtue' must lie in the golden mean. In the context of Spence's condensed notes, it might be inferred that the ruling passion is directly responsible for such 'large Vice(s)' as avarice and prodigality, an implication which raises the problems of motivation and determinism, and the nature of the passion as a 'disease', encountered in the second epistle of *An Essay on Man*. That implication hovers over all four of the *Moral Essays*, and is never finally resolved; but since *To Bathurst* and *To Burlington* are focused on the question of ultimate happiness, the problem of whether the ruling passion represents a 'means' or an 'end' in the mind of the individual becomes a crucial one. The probing of this issue is, however, far more important within the dialectic of *To Bathurst*, whereas *To Burlington* builds upon the conclusion reached in that epistle with more grace and less urgency.[6]

Pope's choice of the avarice/prodigality theme directly reflects this interest in 'means' and 'ends', since money is after all only the medium to enjoyment. Avarice and the miser's disquietudes provide matter for much speculation and satire in contemporary morality books, and a characteristic fascination with paradox is expressed in comments on the subject by Edward Young:

> For who subsists on so Little, who grasps at so much? He mistakes the *Means* for the *End*; *Money* for *Enjoyment*; Nay the means in his Hands make against his End, and the *Power* of *Enjoying* is an *Inducement* to *Self-denial*.[7]

This is precisely the paradox which Pope satirises so feelingly in the epistles *To Bathurst* and *To Burlington*, stressing the real alliance between what he terms the 'Pride' and 'Meanness' of the rich, the drifting of their 'Vanities' into their 'Miseries'. The opening lines of *To Burlington* are clearly designed to refer back to the conclusions of *To Bathurst* on avarice, and to carry forward the line of argument:

> 'Tis strange, the Miser should his Cares employ,
> To gain those Riches he can ne'er enjoy:
> Is it less strange, the Prodigal should waste
> His wealth, to purchase what he ne'er can taste?
> Not for himself he sees, or hears, or eats;
> Artists must chuse his Pictures, Music, Meats:
> (1-6)

The phrase 'not for himself' is particularly ironic, not least in its suggestion of a distorted 'selflessness'; the satire which follows is taken up with the mutation of vanities to miseries, the withering of the power of self-enjoyment among the ostentatious. The passion of extravagance is presented as a scourge of heaven, and Timon's prodigality reflects the same absurdity afflicting *Bathurst's* miser Cotta, 'in plenty starving'. The wealthy Visto is prompted by a 'Daemon' into the affectation of taste, just as the demon Satan seizes Sir Balaam's soul in a deluge of cash; gradually the victims of taste descend into a state of exhausted restlessness, expressed in their cyclical whimsies for construction and demolition, piling up and uprooting again. It transpires that false taste is not in itself so great a curse as their underlying false *motives* for taste, and for Villario (as with 'Papillia' in the *Epistle to A Lady*) the misery of a completed accomplishment is the greatest of all, when he 'finds at last he better likes a Field' (l.88). It is notable that the dissipation of money which is chastised in the earlier sections of the epistle is gradually intensified to embrace hints of a deeper moral dissipation; the description of Timon's villa is taken over increasingly by the grotesque and the perverse, with its squirting Cupids and Tritons which 'spew to wash your face' and the indecent sprawling of the chapel's saints to 'bring all Paradise before your eye' (l.148). Although Pope eventually sets out the utilitarian argument that luxury obliquely confers the social benefits of employment and industry, what is more important to him is that Timon's 'charitable Vanity' is an amoral substitute and a meagre apology for charity in the widely different, Christian sense. The ideals of true 'Taste' and 'Sense' are thought of as 'gift(s) of Heav'n' (l.43), expressed as a balance between the

oppositions of regularity and variety, magnificence and prag-
matism, and in this broad sense the architectural theme is analogous to the theme of virtue in *To Bathurst* (ll.219-28). Similarly, the
ideal progression in public works, from the 'shading' of the country to the 'raising' of a town, reinforces the idea that private and
retired virtue must be established before the task of social beneficence can be undertaken.

Although the Christian frame of reference is not made explicit
in *To Burlington*, it is certainly (as Earl Wasserman has so fully
demonstrated)[8] a central theme of *To Bathurst*. In that epistle,
Pope seems to be treading a more difficult path which wavers
between sceptical satire and moralistic assurance in dealing with
man's absurdities; but ultimately his concern with the values of
happiness and virtue defined in motivational terms comes to over-
shadow the economic argument (superficially analogous to
Mandeville's) that the state can make use of luxury and vice.
Mandeville's *Fable of the Bees*, published in 1714, was chiefly
significant to Pope for expressing in economic terms utilitarian
assumptions already familiar from the writings of other sceptical
thinkers (notably La Rochefoucauld)[9]. What is interesting is that
Mandeville is forced to sustain an uneasy and ethically sceptical
attitude bridging his abstract utilitarian argument and a rigoristic
(broadly Stoic) notion of virtue.[10] As incompatible as these
notions may appear, his is not the only work in which such a
reconciliation is attempted; in Abel Boyer's *Characters of the
Virtues and Vices of the Age* (1695), a moral 'commonplace book'
published some twenty years before Mandeville's *Fable*, avarice is
at once condemned as 'the greatest Evidence of a base ungener-
ous Mind, and ... the highest Injustice in the World', yet distinguished from a second species of hoarding 'not for the Mony's
own sake, but for the pleasure of Refunding it immediately
through all the Channels of Pride and Luxury', and it is confidently asserted that 'that Man who is guilty of this, is in a manner
excusable, since by his Profuseness he makes a kind of Restitu-
tion' (13-14). Pope's theory of a providential and social 'Ballance
of things' as exemplified by avarice and prodigality is certainly
not an original one,[11] but it is interesting to observe the tactics of
persuasion in *To Bathurst*, which draw together the seemingly
contradictory arguments on public benefits and private virtues
through the analysis of motives and happiness.

The Horatian cast of the poem as a form of argument ('sermo') addressed to Bathurst has close affinities with *To Cobham*, in that both epistles put forward the sceptical point of view while attempting to define its proper limits. Bathurst is posed as 'philosopher and rake' against Pope as optimist, but the element of posing in Pope's initial stance should not be overlooked; one suspects at least a measure of irony in his insistence on the dignity of man, which is reinforced by the portentousness of the delivery of lines 7-9. The assurance that 'surely, Heav'n and I are of a mind' seems to convey some conscious extravagance — the phrase emerges in Spence's notes (p.96, above) with very different, Momus-like implications, although of course Spence may have slightly misaligned Pope's remarks. In any case, the divergence of opinions turns out to be of limited significance, since Pope lightly avers that 'we find our tenets just the same at last' (l.16); the point is actually brought home by the deliberate parallelism of lines 5-6 and 13-14, a satire on man as the pawn in a comic and futile cycle of acquisition and dispersal:

> You hold the word, from Jove to Momus giv'n,
> That Man was made the standing jest of Heav'n;
> And Gold but sent to keep the fools in play,
> For some to heap, and some to throw away.
>   But I, who think more highly of our kind,
> (And surely, Heav'n and I are of a mind)
> Opine, that Nature, as in duty bound,
> Deep hid the shining mischief under ground:
> But when by Man's audacious labour won,
> Flam'd forth this rival to, its Sire, the Sun,
> Then careful Heav'n supply'd two sorts of Men,
> To squander these, and those to hide agen.
>
>   (3-14)

Whether heaven provided the gold for men, or the men for the gold, both Bathurst and Pope acknowledge wealth to be a superficial instrument in the ends of human life, cast into the hands of the foolish and the mad as it were in a gesture of disdain. Possibly Pope's source for this passage was the stern Stoic moralising on the same subject by Charron (*Of Wisdom*, I, 192-3):

> Now, is not this the very Extremity of Folly, to fall down and worship That, which Nature has taught us to despise, by casting it

under our Feet, and hiding it in the Bowels and dark Caverns of the Earth; as a thing not fit for publick view; ... there it had remained to all Eternity, had not the Vices of Mankind ransack'd those dark Cells, and with great Difficulty and Violence drawn it up...

[Wealth is] a thing that *Providence* distributes Promiscuously, and with a negligent Hand; scattered in common to all the World, and the greatest Share, very often, permitted to the worst and most scandalous Part of Mankind.

The difference in tone points up how far Pope's argument seems casual, even supercilious, but a strain of greater earnestness comes to inform the 'sermo' in his protest against the alarming flexibility of money; it is money which, above all, reveals the discrepancy between human wants as 'needs' and wants as 'desires' which are limitless, and wealth makes it possible for the desires of some to overtake the needs of others. Ironically, it is the 'naturalistic' argument which endorses the satisfaction of over-sophisticated, or depraved, desires; while man may appear merely a fool in the context of the aims of Providence, he is a wretched piece of corruption in his self-interest:

> What Nature wants (a phrase I much distrust)
> Extends to Luxury, extends to Lust.
>
> (25-6)

With the aid of gold, avarice and profligacy are both intensified and run their courses with unnatural speed. Bathurst's resigned acceptance of this sorry state of affairs is countered by Pope's insistence on the misery of those who look to wealth as a universal panacea. The aggressive interrogation of l.83 ('Is this too little? Would you more than live?') forces Bathurst to acknowledge that man's full potential extends beyond 'what Nature wants', at the same time as it reinforces the irony that the money-rakers, in their attempts to refine on the process of material existence, are effectively *less* than living.

But despite the evident self-punishment stressed by Pope, men invariably *think* they act for a reason, and he therefore enters into ironic conjectures on the motives of the avaricious; the 'Revelation', as we would expect, emerges as self-love in the extreme, capable of infinite permutations and even (in the case of

the 'much-injur'd Blunt') masquerading as social conscience.
Blunt's case is a particularly powerful one for Pope's argument,
since his self-deception is far more profound and baffling than
mere hypocrisy. Venality also conspicuously obtrudes in the place
of nobler and softer passions (125-52), in illustration of Pope's
contention that unadulterated self-love can only turn inwards,
paradoxically, to its opposite, the very antithesis of Christian
charity: 'Each does but hate his neighbour as himself.' Even so
the protest of the 'sober sage' (or the rigoristic moralist) that 'all
this is madness' is effectively silenced by the discomforting assertion that reason has little part in the matter:

> "The ruling Passion, be it what it will,
> "The ruling Passion conquers Reason still."
> Less mad the wildest whimsey we can frame,
> Than ev'n that Passion, if it has no Aim;
> For tho' such motives Folly you may call,
> The Folly's greater to have none at all.
>
> (155-60)

This is a particularly complex passage, above all in confronting
the problem of an 'aim', which is related to the conclusion of
verse-paragraph 109-24 'that Avarice is an absolute Frenzy, without an End or Purpose' ('Argument', 5-6). The verses seem to
qualify the declaration of the 'Argument' and reveal avarice as a
ruling passion which, though it evidently has no final 'purpose' in
terms of achieving happiness, nevertheless comes to represent an
end in itself to the individual; it is only in this way that it can
answer the ends of Providence. Pope later commented on this
section that 'concerning the Extravagant Motives of Avarice, I
meant to show those which were Real were yet as mad or madder
than those which are Imaginary' (citing lines 159-60).[12] His point
(which one must concede is little clearer here than in the verses)
seems to be that the motives for eccentric actions which we delude
ourselves into accepting as 'real', however absurd, still fall short
of the pitch of absurdity represented by a totally *undirected* ruling
passion — such motives do at least serve, like gold, to 'keep the
Fools in play'. The setting of the lines on the ruling passion in
quotation marks is a convention for emphasis, but also stresses
that the argument is presented more fully in the second epistle of
the (as yet unpublished) *Essay on Man*. It is difficult to suppose

that the reader should take in the meaning of the lines without the aid of either this discussion of that of *To Cobham*, which was of course published a good deal later, and the gap between the publication dates of *To Bathurst* (January 1733) and the first three epistles of the *Essay* (February-May 1733) is only a very slight one.

Thus we find that although the effects of the ruling passion have been so heavily satirised and shown closely to resemble madness, in the changing direction of Pope's argument it is adroitly vindicated; we are brought back to the tenet that all extremes are ultimately reconciled and contribute to a wider purpose, a thesis which is illustrated in the 'set piece' portraits of Cotta and son. By using the device of the mock-encomium, Pope effectively approaches the question of motive once more. Amid the self-inflicted doleful shades, sustained by the appropriate diet of nettles, we must suppose that Cotta would indeed persuade himself that parsimony borders on saintliness, yet (like the 'good Bishop') find equally plausible reasons to refrain from depriving Providence of the poor.[13] Similarly, the representation of Cotta's son as 'patriot' touches on an element of dogged fanaticism in which self-destruction seems to have a natural and inevitable part. The ruling passion, like gold, seems rather to act as a catalyst to individual virtues and vices than as an agent which is inherently good or bad. Such benefits as Cotta and son obliquely confer on society are quite fortuitous, and (like Timon's) can scarcely be said to redeem their human failings; Pope's encomium on Bathurst himself firmly restores the emphasis on virtue and the active will of the balanced man to avoid extremes; this verse-paragraph, with its careful poising of oppositions, is the most carefully reworked in the manuscripts. Likewise, the charitable activities of the near-mythic Man of Ross validate his own existence, and live on even after his death; he is 'prov'd, by the ends of being, to have been' (290). By contrast, the 'Balaam' tale treats wealth as a kind of appendage to the soul, enforcing its own momentum in his spiritual degeneration; re-division only takes place at the moment of Balaam's exit, when 'the Devil and the King divide the prize'. The accelerating pace of the story is one of its most powerful features; the patience of Job is inverted to illustrate the impatience of Balaam, fulfilled to the pitch of inevitable and overwhelming collapse. This parable had provided the starting-point of the whole poem in Pope's mind (*Anecdotes*, I, 129) and it answers with facility the 'knotty point' as to whether our conduct in this life has immediate repercussions. As in the character-satires of the other *Moral Essays*, death reveals the ironies and paradoxes that may have been disguised in life, and the sense of wasted potential is intensified.[14]

If one reads *To Bathurst* and *To Burlington* in their intended sequence, then, it is clear that the former is engaged in a more involved and more problematical line of argument than its successor, allowing greater scope for facetious or cynical objections which are eventually deployed to reinforce Pope's moral conclusions. A similar relationship of progressive argument clearly governs the sequence of the other two *Moral Essays*, *To Cobham* and *To A Lady*, the former opening in a profoundly sceptical mood which is unexpectedly resolved into conclusions upon which the latter epistle builds imaginatively.

Spence's table notes of 1730 show that the sceptical content of *To Cobham* directly reflected Pope's reading of Montaigne. His praise for the essay 'Of the Inconstancy of our Actions' ('the best in his whole book') is high, but the succeeding remark ('Montaigne hence concludes *Pyrrhonically*' — my italics) show that he saw the scepticism as bordering on the extreme. The Pyrrhonist's freedom to doubt is certainly highly appealing to Pope, who uses that freedom in the early passages of *To Cobham* with force and eloquence to confound the facile theoreticians who would assess man 'in the gross'; at the same time, equally strenuous attempts are made thoughout the epistle to qualify this doubt and to lead the alert reader to hints of a meaning behind the enigmas. The whole movement of the poem actually constitutes an anti-Pyrrhonic credo, exploiting the subtleties and satiric acumen of the Sceptic view of man, but working towards the surprising reversal of the argument whereby Pope reasserts the powers of Providence even within the microcosm of the chaotic individual character. The nature of Pope's 'New Hypothesis' allows him to expatiate freely not only on the wide inconsistencies of mankind, but equally on the defective nature of human judgement; even at the last, the ruling passion is avowedly a heavily disguised force, often manifesting itself in apparently contradictory actions which are understood neither by the observer nor the author of them. This avowal leaves Pope in a seemingly ambiguous position. Thomas Stumpf (see note 1, below) resolves the contradictions of the epistle by arguing that Pope inherits a mixed attitude of amused tolerance and condemnation of inconstancy from his philosophical mentors, the tolerance giving way to disapproval (including 'denunciation of ... the specious consistency of the ruling passion'; p.355). His approach to the problem, however, leaves us with only a loose idea of the poem's shape, the way in which the succession of 'contradictions' is controlled and organised to give a dialectical structure to the whole.

As Bateson observes (TE, III (ii), 16n.), in the first half of the epistle Montaigne's influence is more strongly felt than that of the more extreme Sceptic La Rochefoucauld; but always Pope retains a sharp eye for latent ironies. Something of his elusiveness emerges in comments to Spence which apparently anticipate the *Essay on Man*'s second epistle, but which are equally relevant to the argument of *To Bathurst*:

> As L'Esprit, Rochefoucauld, and that sort of people prove all virtues are disguised vices, I would engage to prove all vices to be disguised virtues. Neither, indeed, is true, but this would be a more agreeable subject, and would overturn their whole scheme.[15]

Pope's 'neither, indeed, is true' — an appealing disclaimer — does not seem to me expressive of simple nonchalance or intellectual vagueness, but rather of a lively distrust of schematic 'notions', with a sense that the bias towards scepticism might reasonably be redressed.

To Cobham is thus broadly concerned with the two interrelated subjects mentioned to Spence in 1730 — the motives of action, and the status of judgement; the relationship between them lies in their being variants of the 'passions' debate. On the latter question, Pope argues for a compromise between knowledge based on empirical observation, and that which is merely deduced from 'the Abstract'; it is the academic approach to man which is identified with the line of cynical, wholesale denunciation (ll.1-8), while on the other side Pope shows that self-love is too strong a force to allow for truly 'objective' individual judgement:

> To Observations which ourselves we make,
> We grow more partial for th'observer's sake;
> To written Wisdom, as another's, less:
> Maxims are drawn from Notions, these from Guess.
> (11-14)

It seems very probable that these opening lines contain (as Warburton supposed) an oblique hit at La Rochefoucauld in particular; it is curious that Bateson should assign to him the identity of 'man-of-the-world observer' (TE, III (ii), 16n.), passing over his more likely place as the archetypal compiler of 'Maxims' of a distinctly misanthropic bias, founded on the *a priori* 'notion' that all men are pre-eminently selfish.[16] Pope's remarks quoted above certainly seem to show him thinking in these terms, and he would be responsive to the irony that the *Maxims*, once enshrined in print, are more likely to be swallowed as 'written Wisdom' than measured with discrimination against experience.

These distortions of the judgement, subjectivity and prejudice, lead the unwary philosopher astray; man's conduct is presented as the product of perpetual inward turbulence, further complicated by acquired 'Opinion'. In the context of the epistle, the term 'opinion' might be defined by contrast to the Stoic ideal of 'suspension of judgement', in relation to which both passion and opinion are analogous forms of falsehood. Pope allies opinion with the passions of hope and pride in Epistle II of *An Essay on Man* (283-6), and Matthew Prior's essay on the subject similarly observes that 'our Passions change with our Ages, and our Opinion with our Passions'.[17] But to this note of distrust Pope adds a significant stress on the creative, enlivening dimension to the distortions imposed by idiosyncrasy:

> All Manners take a tincture from our own,
> Or come discolour'd thro' our Passions shown.
> Or Fancy's beam enlarges, multiplies,
> Contracts, inverts, and gives ten thousand dyes.
> (25-8)

The metaphor of tincture and colouring here tends to associate the forces of passion and imagination, as again in the *Essay on Man* (ll.143-4).

Over and above these distortions, the judgement is disarmed by the rapid shifting of the mind, so that the 'principle of action' (as yet undefined) moves too swiftly for analysis. The individual will is seemingly lost in 'the Passions' wild rotation', which wears it down to the point of accepting the last of a series of chaotic impulses. This is a very similar picture to Hobbes' account of the 'Deliberation' process and his consequent definition of the will:

In *Deliberation*, the last Appetite, or Aversion, immediately adhaering to the action, or to the omission thereof, is that wee call the WILL; the Act, (not the faculty) of *Willing* ... The Definition of the *Will*, given commonly by the Schooles, that it is a *Rationall Appetite*, is not good. For if it were, then could there be no Voluntary Act against Reason. For a *Voluntary Act* is that, which proceedeth from the *will*, and no other. But if in stead of a Rationall Appetite, we shall say an Appetite resulting from a precedent Deliberation, then the Definition is the same that I have given here. *Will* therefore *is the last Appetite in Deliberating.*[18]

It follows from this that motivation is no more 'conscious' than the intrusion of dreams into sleep:

> Something as dim to our internal view,
> Is thus, perhaps, the cause of most we do.
> (49-50)

Yet the terms in which this hypothesis is cast are actually tentative rather than definitive, just as Pope's later observation, 'not always Actions shew the man' unobtrusively implies that there are limits to this rule also. Often, we may infer, actions *do* bespeak the man; but when we wish to make confident judgements, human deviousness abandons us to insecurity. Pope's rhetorical technique exemplifies what Stanley in his *History of Philosophy* (III, 27-8) calls 'Suspension', 'phrases, which declare the Scepticall affection... as, *no more, Not to be defined*, and the like'. Stanley draws attention also to the Sceptic's use of interrogatives (which Pope employs with mounting ferocity in *To Cobham* up to l.173, when they are as suddenly overborne by affirmatory *statements*), and to the use of terms like 'perhaps': 'These phrases declare an *Aphasia*, for he who saith, *Perhaps it is*, implies its contrary to be as probable.' It is in this manner, I believe, that we should take Pope's set of observations and his contention that benevolence and virtue are not *necessarily* (as Esprit and Rochefoucauld never tired of repeating) the motives of worthy actions:

> Not therefore humble he who seeks retreat,
> Pride guides his steps, and bids him shun the great:
> Who combats bravely is not therefore brave,
> He dreads a death-bed like the meanest slave.
> (65-8)

While the former couplet is an echo of La Rochefoucauld (TE, III (ii), 20n.), the latter clearly reflects Pope's reading of the essay 'Of the Inconstancy of our Actions'. Montaigne's original lines are interesting, and worth quoting in full to convey their context:

> Tho I always intend to speak well of good things, and rather to interpret such things as may fall out, in the best sence, than otherwise, yet such is the strangeness of our condition, that we are sometimes pusht on to do well even by Vice it self, if well doing were not judged by the intention only. One gallant Action therefore ought not to conclude a man Valiant ... there is not one Valour for the Pavement, and another for the Field. [The valiant man] would bear a Sickness in his Bed, as bravely as a Wound in the Field, and no more fear Death in his own house, than at an assault. (*Essays*, translated by Charles Cotton, (3 vols., 1693, II, 9).

These insights are offered in a spirit of tolerant interest rather than dogmatism, and there is indeed an acknowledgement that the motivational definition of virtue and vice may not be adequate; Pope's tone in verse-paragraph 61-70 has much in common with Montaigne's, the exploding of simplistic assumptions being made with more shrewdness than invective irony. The cases which he puts foward are to be read as instances rather than generalisations, and he is careful to keep short of the line dividing scepticism and cynicism.[19] Accordingly, this note merges into a vein of satire which seems deliberately fanciful and outrageous — lines 79-86 share a lively sense of the absurd, with their casual irreverence, slang expressions and 'low' rhymes — and the mockery of credulous analysts takes flight in the verses which follow. The picture of inconstancy and paradox and (often) self-interest as dominant human traits takes over in the portraits of Catius, Patritio, Scoto and the rest; what emerges most forcefully, however, is the suggestion that misunderstood motives govern the most apparently significant actions.

Coming on the heels of this disarming catalogue, one is bound to feel that the flourishing of the 'Ruling Passion' should be qualified by some irony, and so in one sense it is; but the rhetorical emphasis and comprehensiveness of lines 174-9 are designed first of all to make a spirited affirmation, to assert that there *is* a principle whereby incongruous actions become explicable and even consistent. Applying this principle to Wharton, 'the scorn and wonder of our days', seems the ultimate test of its viability, and engages Pope in a portrait of sheer, sustained paradox. It is at once comprehensive and baffling as an analysis.[20] There is an affinity with the celebrated 'Atticus' portrait — both pinpointing the dominant, destructive flaw of defensiveness undermining accomplishment, self-love combined with self-distrust — but here the effort of exposition gradually becomes laboured, and it is disturbing to meet the final pat observation that Wharton's extreme vagaries are actually 'plain'. The intellectual bravado does not convince. What should be recognised, however, is that Pope is clearly interested in allowing *complexity* to the ruling passion theory; in Wharton he shows how the passion emerges by utterly devious, dissembling paths, and he immediately goes on (ll.210-21) to emphasise how 'in this search, the wisest may mistake' since 'second qualities' (means) are apt to masquerade as 'first' (the real ends, or private motives). One must concede that from this point Pope fails to illustrate his potentially interesting development with much skill; Catiline and Caesar are rather peremptorily summoned up to illustrate obliquity of motive, although Pope does bring into this a more interesting suggestion about the response to social mores ('That very Caesar, born in Scipio's days, / Had aim'd, like him, by Chastity at praise'; 216-17). The lines which follow on the work of the ruling passion give a strongly negative picture (echoing the *Essay on Man*, II. 133-8), with a grim emphasis on the vigour with which 'honest Nature' co-operates with the wasting disease, and no great assurance of compensatory virtues. The ruling passion's cultivation of 'our follies and our sins' is well illustrated in the satirically vivid series of vignettes which round off the epistle. Benjamin Boyce, in his study of Pope's character-sketches, is troubled by the fact that Pope has here shifted from the 'complex personality' sketch (a mode which particularly reflects the influence of Descartes) to the simpler Horatian or Theophrastan type of the 'fixed personality', which he sees as a regression (pp.106-13). To use this observation as evidence that the ruling passion theory is itself inflexible and ill-suited to Pope's deepest interests is, however, misleading. It is difficult to isolate Pope's many techniques of character-sketching and to try to arrange them in an order of 'progression'; he went on deploying mixed modes of satire throughout his poetic career, according to their effectiveness in context, and it could fairly be said that his strongest interests drew him towards both the obsessional 'type' character and the character of extreme antitheses. Indeed, as far as the ruling passion theory is concerned, and as the Wharton portrait shows, these can present two sides of the same coin. The same fusion of the 'intricacy' argument with a rule for ultimate clarity is common in other discussions of psychology which seem partially to anticipate the 'ruling passion' idea,[21] and (as we would expect) their influence is echoed in contemporary critical theory on the art of character-writing; Boyce cites a particularly lucid example of this from Henry Gally (Boyce, p.114).

But one serious weakness in Pope's handling of the theory which strikes the reader immediately was pointed out by Cobham himself in his letter on the epistle of November 1733 (*Correspondence*, III, 393):

> I like your Leachour better now 'tis shorter and the Glutton is a very good Epigram but they are both appetites that from nature we indulg as well for her ends as our pleasure ... I mean that a passion or habit that has not a natural foundation falls in better with your subject than any of our natural wants which in some degree we cannot help pursueing to the last.

Pope fails to make any distinction between desires which might (in his original words to Spence) be 'brought with us into the world' and those which are through social interaction 'acquired' (Narcissa's love of fine apparel, or indeed the love of money); one might wish to reverse Cobham's judgement on which of the two kinds is the more plausible as a ruling passion, but the confusion is obviously a considerable limitation on the notion of 'second and first qualities', or means and ends in the pursuit of desires.[22]

Having said this, it is clearly important to Pope's argument that his principle of internal consistency is founded on a kind of struggle for supremacy within the passions themselves, and that it should be proffered as the final stage in a predominantly sceptical discourse. In conceiving of the ruling passion theory, Pope's aim had been to answer the seemingly inevitable conclusion of Montaigne's essay on inconstancy, 'that nothing can be known of the Workings of men's minds', but to counter this without resorting to the rationalist's refuge. The challenge which he throws out to Montaigne and 'more sage Charron' at the height of his most sceptical stage of argument (*To Cobham*, l.146) is crucial, though it might at first be taken for a purely rhetorical gesture demonstrating the common link of all philosophers in their disheartening limitations. The word 'sage' is surely to be taken ironically ('knowing'), in view of what might be termed Charron's 'extravagant rationalism'. With the same confidence, Montaigne is also taken to task, if not for being too knowing, at least for being too resolutely resigned to ignorance; as we have seen, Warburton's pejorative reference to his 'Pyrrhonism' (TE, III (ii), 27n.) is echoed more mildly in Pope's table talk to Spence (p.96, above). In context, then, Pope's quizzical challenge opens the field for a last fling of profoundly sceptical argument which naturally confirms the reader's supposition that he has wholeheartedly committed himself to the Sceptic line; to our surprise, however, this assumption is confounded by the sudden reverse, when the lines on the ruling passion call a necessary halt to the indulgence of stupefaction. Both the context and the theory itself contain their own ironies, but these are more in Pope's control than critics have suggested. Though Stumpf contends that Pope could only have resolved the doubts raised within the epistle comfortably by appealing to the sovereign power of reason as the arbiter of action (especially moral action), it is worth considering the ambivalence of the word *raison* as Montaigne understood it. This ambivalence relates directly to the problem of how the sceptical philosopher can embrace both distrust in the faculties of man and faith in an ideal paradigm of truth which lies within the grasp of men; a distinction is implicit between *raison humaine*, disarmingly fallible and subject to multiple distortions, and *raison divine*, the Stoic ideal invested with overtones of Christian 'grace'.[23] Thus, as Anthony Levi observes, 'the object of Montaigne's disparagement is not reason, but the mind's capacity for knowing truth'.[24] There is an analogy to Pope's position here, in so far as the first two-thirds of *To Cobham* is engaged in challenging 'the mind's capacity for knowing truth' along with every other principle of human consistency; while the tyranny of the ruling passion is at once an attribute of the interior man and an instrument of Providence, an 'Aaron's serpent' swallowing up all resistance in its drive to accommodate men within an ideal order. The problem of how far we can be morally responsible in acting on the promptings of this heaven-directed passion is never answered by Pope.

When Pope came to model the *Epistle to A Lady* to take its place within the 'opus magnum' scheme (after it was first drafted in 1733), the central lines on the ruling passion were directed much more explicitly than in *To Cobham* towards the notion of 'second and first qualities', or closely allied impulses:

> In Men, we various Ruling Passions find,
> In Women, two almost divide the kind;
> Those, only fix'd, they first or last obey,
> The Love of Pleasure, and the Love of Sway.
>   That, Nature gives; and where the lesson taught
> Is still to please, can Pleasure seem a fault?
> Experience, this; by Man's oppression curst,
> They seek the second not to lose the first.
>
> (207-14)

By this stage of the argument, despite the contrast with the variety of men, Pope clearly does not mean to conclude that 'most Women have no Characters at all' — it is, in fact, all too evident that they have alarmingly deep ones. What he wishes to show is how, as Gally puts it, 'the same Affection of the Mind, by exerting itself after a different manner, lay(s) a real Foundation for so many distinct Characters'.[25] But although the analytical verses present a lucid development of some of the problems of motivation expressed in *To Cobham*, they like the rest of the poem have complex links with much earlier sketches by Pope, predating the conception of his 'ethnic scheme'; furthermore, the 1735 text was later expanded with the Atossa, Philomedé and Cloe portraits of the 1744 'death-bed' edition,[26] so that what we have is one of Pope's most intricately 'assembled' works. On these grounds, Bateson expresses some doubts about the epistle's coherence: 'the ruling passion makes a brief appearance in ll.207-10, but the poem cannot really be considered a serious contribution to the philosophical *Opus Magnum* in spite of its title (which seems to claim it as a companion piece to *To Cobham*). It is essentially a satirical portrait gallery in Pope's most accomplished Horatian manner' (TE, III (ii), xxxvii).[27] His comments raise two questions; firstly whether the cast of the poem as 'portrait gallery' is inconsistent with its status within Pope's 'system of ethics in the Horatian way',[28] and secondly whether the 'ruling passion' lines really stand detached from the epistle's character sketches. The answer to the first is surely that all of the *Moral Essays* use the character for exposition of the total argument, and the argument here is *about* character; in fact, as Leranbaum has pointed out, the proportion of lines given over to characters is very nearly the same in *To Cobham* as in *To A Lady*. There are also close parallels in the passages on 'high life' (*Cobham*, ll.87-100, *To A Lady*, ll.181-98) and the position of the 'ruling passion' lines in each, changing the tone and direction of the arguments from scepticism to a qualified assurance. The relationship between the two epistles, as she demonstrates, is altogether closer than might at first be recognised (Leranbaum, pp.70-72, 80).[29]

On the second and most important question — the illustrative function of the portraits themselves — it is worth noting that the 'ruling passion' analysis here was not suddenly conceived, but that Pope had adumbrated his ideas concerning the guiding compulsions of women as early as 1712, in his *Epistle to Miss Blount, with the Works of Voiture*. The central lines of that epistle (31-42) are not only closely allied to *To A Lady* in dwelling on the incompatibilities of the inborn and acquired propensities (desire itself and the desire of 'honour'), but also share the distinctive tone of 'sympathetic satire' which characterises the parallel section of the later poem:

> Too much *your Sex* is by their Forms confin'd,
> Severe to all, but most to Womankind;
> Custom, grown blind with Age, must be your Guide
> Your Pleasure is a Vice, but not your Pride;
> By nature yielding, stubborn but for Fame;
> Made Slaves by Honour, and made Fools by Shame.
> Marriage may all those petty Tyrants chace,
> But sets up One, a greater, in their Place;
> Well might you wish for Change, by those accurst,
> But the last Tyrant ever proves the worst.
> Still in Constraint your suff'ring Sex remains,
> Or bound in formal, or in real Chains.
> (*Epistle to Miss Blount*, ll.31-42).

The motif of 'tyranny' and subservience which both epistles share directs attention to their common concern with power-seeking as well as fulfilment through pleasure, and both reflect on the contradictions in the public and private mores. If, as Pope argues, the world and its custom rule that 'your Pleasure is a Vice, but not your Pride', it follows that the veterans of such a world will find themselves at the last incapable of pleasure and vainly seeking to 'be Queen for life' (*To A Lady*, l.218);[30] women are 'accurst' by honour and shame, as they are 'by Man's oppression curst' in *To A Lady*. The central lines on their predicament from the section quoted above (i.e. ll.35-6) echo the couplet which was adapted for 'Narcissa' (*To A Lady*, ll.61-2) from the much earlier portrait 'Sylvia' (published in 1727):

> Affronting all, yet fond of a good Name,
> A Fool to Pleasure, yet a slave to Fame.
> (9-10)

The continuity of ideas which draws these three passages together is surely significant, and it is strengthened further by the series of epigrammatic verses found in one of Pope's early manuscripts, a version of the Earl of Peterborough's song 'I said to my heart'.[31] These include, in stanzas 3, 5 and 6, the various prototypes of the 'Sylvia' portrait, and hence of the later 'Narcissa' and 'Calypso', while the conduct of 'Prudentia' is in effect a more extended reflection on 'her, whose life the Church and Scandal share' (*To A Lady*, ll.105-6):

> Prudentia the pure one still walk'd the right way,
> Yet, like a true Just one, fell Sev'n times a Day.

The arrangement of the verses — showing mounting voracity of lust and passion breaking through the shell of specious worldly 'virtue' — parallels the first half of *To A Lady*, both illustrating the overthrow of 'acquired' propensities by primary impulses. The sham modesty of 'Celia' (stanza 2) becomes the lasciviousness and feigned devotion of 'Prudentia' and 'Daphne', moving finally to the brink of madness in 'Cornelia'; without explicit analysis or summary, a consistent view of women's conduct is put forward. In these verses, however, there is little sympathy for the 'victims'; the satirist simply pierces the charade of feminine behaviour to expose the real distinction between modesty and self-love, imperceptible to the myopic eye of high society. *To A Lady* takes this further in showing the moral ambiguity to be grounded in a confusion of means with ends among women themselves:

> Bred to disguise, in Public 'tis you hide;
> There, none distinguish 'twixt your Shame or Pride,
> Weakness or Delicacy; all so nice,
> That each may seem a Virtue, or a Vice.
> (*To A Lady*, ll.203-6)

The fact that these lines were almost certainly followed by the portraits of Philomedé, Atossa and the Queen in the 1735 folio edition of Pope's *Works*[32] shows another distinct train of development in that poem's structure, illustrating the 'ruling passions' hypothesis; Philomedé takes the cult of pleasure to one extreme, while Atossa provides a grotesque exhibition of 'Love of Sway', and the Queen the supreme sham. Considerable depth is given to 'Atossa' by Pope's emphasis on self-defeat, the undefined aim unconsciously sought:

> Strange! by the Means defeated of the Ends,
> By Spirit robb'd of Pow'r, by Warmth of Friends,
> By Wealth of Follow'rs! without one distress
> Sick of herself thro' very selfishness!
> (143-6)

Atossa's childlessness becomes a paradigm of selfishness; on a much more extreme level than 'Papillia' she is 'curs'd with ev'ry granted pray'r', and with all her intensity of will finally becomes a pawn of Providence like Timon or Cotta. The same paradoxes are uppermost in the 'witty' Flavia, endowed with so strong an appetite for living that it becomes reversed by the most trivial springs to its opposite, 'Death, that Opiate of the soul'. Whereas death provides the perspective of truth in the character sketches *To Cobham* and *To Bathurst*, the point at which the ruling passion most conspicuously asserts itself and reveals the direction of the whole life, *To A Lady* presents death as the enviable losing of the self and an escape from the whirlwind of passions to stupor or suspension of the will. The drift from 'killing time' to 'killing thought' (l.112) represents the easy bridge between mere aimlessness and a harsher self-destruction. Contradiction of this order goes far beyond the folly of a 'Silia' or of the other opening portraits which are reminiscent of Young's decidedly less disturbing women; yet it is merely an intensification of the inherent instability ascribed to the female sex in the closing lines of the earlier 'Sylvia', whisking through the vicissitudes of lust and false pride, atheism, superstition and piety, self-delusion and calculated recklessness. The stress on self-destruction is especially strong in the 'ruling passion' section of ll.207ff., and it is vital to realise how the apparently 'brief appearance' of the theory at this point embraces not only the rather static four lines of 207-10 but also the brilliant developments of ll.215-42, the 'moral' of ll.243-8 and the final compliment to Martha Blount. From the 'Nature' and 'Experience' theme of lines 211-14, the analysis of the '*Aims*, and the *Fate* of the Sex' takes us to the defeated 'Love of Sway' — the fading beauty as ageing tyrant — and the exhausted and futile pursuit of 'Pleasure':

> Pleasures the sex, as children Birds, pursue,
> Still out of reach, yet never out of view.
>
> (231-2)

The picture developed in these passages is much more suggestive than the 'dissolute/despotic' view of women put forward in lines 215-18.[33] All the parables are finally linked to illustrate the perfection of the 'estimable woman', and in this portrait Pope celebrates not the suppression of impulses but their restraint within a harmonious balance; 'love of Pleasure' held in check by 'desire of Rest', and the power of sway affirmed in the art of 'submitting'.[34] With this change of context, 'charm' is redefined to lose its associations with frippery and superstition (38, 108), and becomes an attribute of the personality which gains force over others, above all through *shared* pleasure. The question of power and liberty is one which again enters Pope's reference to Martha's freedom from 'the Pelf / Which buys your sex a Tyrant o'er itself'; despite the fictitious details of a married state introduced into the portrait, it seems to me that here as in the *Epistle to Miss Blount*, l.38, Pope is alluding to money-seeking husbands as the tyrants, rather than money itself. The drawing together of the 'Poet' and the virtues of Martha Blount in the closing lines of the epistle thus becomes a form of affectionate gallantry which is substituted for the threatening power-struggles and jealousies of marriage already exposed, and her most conspicuous virtue is finally her self-sufficiency.

It is thus in this epistle that Pope endorses a more individualistic notion of excellence which gives free rein to the contradictions of character and yet attains a delicate internal balance. The most challenging passage of Pope's final compliment (ll.273-80) is in fact a close parallel to the eulogy of *To Bathurst* (ll.219-28), and in keeping with the pattern of 'praise and blame' which characterises the formal verse satire. But the effect of each passage is strikingly different; while the latter adopts a tone of loftiness (to which the natural counterpart is its servility), the former succeeds in uniting a sense of intimacy with that of 'wonder', an affectionate raillery which qualifies the satire of the epistle. Whereas Bathurst is represented as having the gift of virtue, here the 'golden mean' is established within the shifting oppositions of the personality itself; it is not promoted by the force of an individual ruling passion (as with Cobham), and it is notable that *To A Lady* is the only one of the *Moral Essays* in which Pope makes no attempt to justify the ultimate balance of Providence through the vices and follies exposed. The whole epistle might in fact be taken to illustrate the contention of *To Bathurst* that the strangest motives dictated by the ruling passion are not as baffling and self-destructive as truly aimless passions:

> For tho' such motives Folly you may call,
> The Folly's greater to have none at all.
> (159-60)

Hence 'true No-meaning puzzles more than Wit' (*To A Lady*, l.114). The pursuit of this 'No-meaning', however, leads Pope into a more complex and deeply considered elaboration of his ruling passion theory than he had encompassed before; although the *Epistle to A Lady* was the last of the *Moral Essays* to be published, and had its roots outside the 'opus magnum', it might be argued that Pope applied the theory more fully and consistently here than in any of the other epistles. For all its limitations, within the final ordering of the *Moral Essays* the development of the 'New Hypothesis' is both progressive and steadily more assured.

Notes

1. F.W. Bateson places emphasis on their status as Horatian satires (TE, III (ii), xx, xxxvii). The same distinction is made by Brower (*Alexander Pope*, 260). *See also* Benjamin Boyce, *The Character-Sketches in Pope's Poems* (Durham, N.C., 1962), 108-9, 116-18; and Thomas Stumpf, 'Pope's *To Cobham, To A Lady*, and the traditions of inconstancy', *Studies in Philology*, 67 (1970), 339-58.

2. Leranbaum, *Alexander Pope's 'Opus Magnum'*, 64-81.

3. More recently, Howard D. Weinbrot's study *Alexander Pope and the Traditions of Formal Verse Satire* (1982) has emphasised with Leranbaum that the epistles are vitally linked to the *Essay on Man* through the 'shared belief that the world was created and is held together by God's gift of a ruling passion and by his felicitous *discordia concors*' (180). Weinbrot acknowledges that although 'this concept has often been used and abused ... it remains essential for our understanding of Pope's several epistles and their consistently optimistic conclusions'; his valuable discussion of the poems, however, concentrates on overall patterns of dialectic and thematic structuring, rather than on the emergence and shaping of the ruling passion theory as such.

4. This is the 'Index' which was prefixed to some volumes of the 1734 quarto edition of the *Essay on Man*, setting out the projected 'opus magnum'; the copies were later recalled and destroyed , and only one appears to be still extant. It is reproduced by Leranbaum (28) from the Scholar Press facsimile of that edition. A less reliable and more ambiguous version is given in Spence's *Anecdotes* (I, 132) — *see also* James Osborn's note, *ibid.*, II, 720.

5. A transcript of the whole set of notes is given by Bateson, TE, III (ii), xx-xxii; in Osborn's edition of Spence's *Anecdotes*, it is dispersed over pages 142, 130, 138 and 141 of vol. I.

6. Details of the evidence supporting the sequence of these epistles are set out by Frederick Keener (*An Essay on Pope* (New York, 1974), 71n.). The intended relationship is equally clear from the 'Argument' of *To Burlington*, ll.15-16, where the verses on the distribution of wealth are referred back to the lines on the ruling passion in *To Bathurst* (159ff.), and to the second epistle of the *Essay on Man*.

7. Young, *A Vindication of Providence* (1728), 46.

8. Wasserman, *Pope's 'Epistle to Bathurst': A Critical Reading with an Edition of the Manuscripts* (Baltimore, 1960).

9. *See Moral Maxims and Reflections ... made English*, 163: 'It is much better that great Persons should thirst after Honour; nay, that they should even be vain upon the account of doing well, than that they should be wholly clear of this *Passion*; for though the good they do, proceeds not from a principle of *Vertue*, yet the World however hath this Advantage, that their Vanity makes them do, what, if they were not vain, they would not have done.'

10. *See* Paul Alpers, 'Pope's *To Bathurst* and the Mandevillian State', *ELH*, 25 (1958), 23-42.

11. *See* Swift's *Intelligencer* no. 9 (1728), in *Prose Writings*, ed Herbert Davies (12 vols, Oxford 1939-55), IX, 53; and Bacon, *Essays* (1597), no.15 (in *Essays and the Advancement of Learning*, ed A. W. Pollard (1900), 35-6).

12. TE, III (ii), 106n.

13. Pope's treatment of Cotta may well reflect Boileau's miserly couple from his tenth satire (*Works ... Made English By Several Hands* (3 vols, 1711-13), I, 272):

> This Pair, well-mated, now are left alone,
> No Children come, and all the Servants gone;
> Triumphant in their House they live, and free,
> In all their greedy griping ways agree.
> No Limits to their Av'rice now they put,
> The Cellar's now condemn'd, the Kitchin shut.

14. *See* Christopher Fox, '"Gone as soon as found": Pope's *Epistle to Cobham* and the death-day as moment of truth', *SEL*, 20 (1980), 431-8. Fox draws attention to 'the revelatory and confirmatory function accorded the death-day by Pope's ancient and Renaissance predecessors', and specifically the connection 'between death and knowledge of the characters of men' (437). The Stoic ideal of dying exalts rationality in the last moments, while the Peripatetics (and, later, Montaigne) emphasise the revelation of dominant passions.

15. The date '1728' entered in Osborn's edition of the *Anecdotes* (I, 219) appears to be uncertain.

16. Pope uses the term 'maxims' in his letter to Swift of October 1725 (*Correspondence*, II, 333) on writing 'a set of Maximes in opposition to all Rochefoucaults Principles'.

17. Prior, 'Opinion', in *Literary Works*, ed H. B. Wright and M. K. Spears, 2 vols, (Oxford, 1959), I, 587. Pope seems to have been influenced by this essay, and his close examination of Prior's unpublished MSS after his death in 1721 is documented in Spence (*Anecdotes*, I, 91-2).

18. *Leviathan*, 127-8. Compare La Rochefoucauld, *Maxims*, 178: 'It is but very seldom, that *Reason* cures our *Passions* but one *Passion* is commonly cured by another. *Reason* indeed often strikes in with the strongest side. And there is no *Passion* so Extravagant, but hath its *Reason* ready to keep it in Countenance.'

19. Compare Pope's letter to Allen of November 1723 (*Correspondence*, IV, 479): 'indeed, no true Judgment can be made, here, of any Man or any Thing, with certainty; further, than that we *think* another man means well, and that we *know* we ourselves mean well. It is in this Situation that every honest man stands with respect to another, and upon which all well-princi-pled Friendships depend.'

20. Boyce observes (*Character-Sketches*, 108), 'one might even suggest that the trouble with Wharton was that, driven by a restless mind and strong passions, he unluckily had no *ruling* passion'.

21. Some references are given in Bernhard Fabian, 'Pope's konzeption der 'Ruling Passion': eine quellenuntersuchung', *Archiv für das Studium der neueren Sprachen*, 195 (1959), 290-301. *See* Montaigne's *Essays* (trans.

Cotton), I, 366-71 and II, 492-549, Prior's 'Opinion' (*Literary Works*, I, 588), and Dryden's 'Preface' to *Troilus and Cressida* ('*Of Dramatic Poesy' and Other Critical Essays*, ed. George Watson (2 vols, 1962), I, 249-50).

22. Compare Dr Johnson's strictures in his 'Life of Pope': 'It must be at least allowed that this 'ruling Passion', antecedent to reason and observation, must have an object independent of human contrivance, for there can be no natural desire of artificial good ... Pope has formed his theory with so little skill that, in the examples by which he illustrates and confirms it, he has confounded passions, appetites, and habits' (*Lives of the English Poets*, ed George Birkbeck Hill, 3 vols (Oxford, 1905), III, 174-5). The same point might be made about the thesis of Edward Young's influential satires *Love of Fame, the Universal Passion* (published collectively in 1728). Charron meets some difficulty in attempting to define 'Natural' desires (those which we share in common with beasts): 'strictly speaking, they are not Passions' (*Of Wisdom*, I, 202).

23. *See* Montaigne's 'Of Custom' (Cotton, II, 151). Compare also Swift, 'On the Trinity' (*Prose Writings*, IX, 166): '*Reason* itself is true and just, but the *Reason* of every particular Man is weak and wavering, perpetually swayed and turned by his Interests, his Passions, and his Vices.'

24. Levi, *French Moralists*, 60.

25. Henry Gally, 'Critical essay on characteristic-writings' (prefixed to *The Moral Characters of Theophrastus*, 1725, 34); *cit*. Boyce, *Character-Sketches*, 114.

26. 'Atossa' and 'Philomedé' were incorporated in the 'Prince of Wales' text of 1738, and 'Cloe' was published separately in that year; *see* Vinton A. Dearing, 'The Prince of Wales's set of Pope's Works', *Harvard Library Bulletin*, 4 (1950), 320-38. Frank Brady ('The history and structure of Pope's *To A Lady'*, *SEL*, 9 (1969), 439-62) is convinced of Warburton's responsibility for the arrangement of the portraits in the 1744 'death-bed' text, and prefers the 'Prince of Wales' text (which he terms '1738a' in his textual apparatus). The principal variations in this text from that of 1744 (from which the Twickenham text is taken) are that 'Philomedé' should directly precede 'Atossa', and 'Cloe' should be omitted.

27. Stumpf also observes (*op. cit.*, 340) 'in the *Epistle to A Lady*, it is perfectly evident that the lines about the ruling passion (207-10) are somewhat extraneous, a last obeisance, perhaps, to the larger philosophical design [of the 'opus magnum']'.

28. Pope's description of the 'opus magnum' in his letter to Swift of November 1729 (*Correspondence*, III, 81).

29. The evidence concerning the compositional order of the 'pair' of poems is very complex (*see* Leranbaum, *Alexander Pope's 'Opus Magnum'*, 64-81). *To A Lady* was drafted in some form in February 1733 and Pope seems then to have composed *To Cobham* to 'create a link between it and Epistle II of *An Essay on Man*' (77) and thus incorporate the poem in the 'opus magnum'. In their final forms, however, Leranbaum concludes that 'Just as the *Epistle to Cobham* assumes a reading of *An Essay on Man*, Epistle II, for an understanding of the general theory of the Ruling Passion, so the *Epistle to a Lady* assumes a reading of the *Epistle to Cobham* for a justification of

the utility of the hypothesis'; when read together, 'The movement from the *Epistle to Cobham* to the *Epistle to a Lady* is a progressive one' (80).

30. In Hobbes's *Leviathan* (part I, ch. 11; 161), a similar set of observations on the pursuit of pleasure and power is applied to the question of why kings should perennially seek conquests: 'in the first place, I put for a generall inclination of all mankind, a perpetuall and restlesse desire of Power after power, that ceaseth only in Death. And the cause of this, is not alwayes that a man hopes for a more intensive delight, than he has already attained to; or that he cannot be content with a moderate power: but because he cannot assure the power and means to live well, which he hath present, without the acquisition of more.'

31. *See* Robert M. Schmitz, 'Peterborough's and Pope's nymphs: Pope at work', *PQ*, 48 (1969), 192-200; and Isobel Grundy, 'Pope, Peterborough and the *Characters of Women*', *RES* (n.s.), 20 (1969), 461-8.

32. The characters seem to have been suppressed at a later stage of the printing, until they were reinstated in different positions in the 'death-bed' edition. *See also* Frank Brady (note 26, above).

33. For the passage of 221-4, Pope probably had in mind the poem 'To a Coquet Beauty' in the *Works of John Sheffield... Duke of Buckingham*, which he himself had edited (2 vols, 1723: I, 55):

> Like a restless Monarch, thou
> Would'st rather force Mankind to bow,
> And venture round the World to roam,
> Than govern peaceably at Home.

34. Pope was no doubt recalling Prior's 'Jinny the Just' (*Works*, I, 302):

> Declining all power She found means to persuade
> Was then most regarded, when most she obey'd,
> The Mistresse in truth when She seem'd but the Maid.

Pope had attempted to print this poem in the Swift/Pope *Miscellanies* of 1727, but permission was refused by Lord Oxford (Spence, *Anecdotes*, I, 92).

CHAPTER FIVE

'Th'unbalanc'd Mind':

The *Imitations of Horace*

Pope's anecdote to Spence, relating how he was prompted by Bolingbroke to attempt the first of his Horatian *Imitations* (*To Fortescue*, written in the wake of the 'Timon's villa' controversy) is suggestive of certain questions which are raised by the group of poems as a whole: 'he observed', says Pope, 'how well that would hit my case, if I were to imitate it in English'.[1] The decision to proceed in the same manner with adaptations of further pieces from the *Satires* and *Epistles* in itself testifies that Pope's interest in possible affinities with Horace went on developing, but the direction of that development has since been a point of much critical debate. The political motive behind the poems (particularly the later pieces) has naturally been a focus of attention, which has emphasised the mounting intensity of Pope's protest against public corruption in the 1730s,[2] culminating in what Howard Weinbrot sees as the rejection of Horace with more than a measure of contempt in the *Epilogue to the Satires* (1738).[3] Likewise in the background to the *Imitations*, the active contemporary critical debate over the relative merits of Horatian and Juvenalian satire (ironic raillery versus vehement attack) undoubtedly has an important place, and it is chiefly in reflection of these tensions that recent critical interpretations of the relationship between Pope and Horace present such a variety of viewpoints. Thomas Maresca has argued for a heavily Christianised Horace invested with 'an authority ... that was little short of canonical', while it has also been argued that the *Imitations* 'are in no sense genuinely or intrinsically "Horatian"',[4] and that Pope used Horace's works merely 'as a ploy to smuggle through Juvenalian matter'.[5] In pursuing these lines of emphasis, however, it is possible to lose sight of the force and coherence of the *Imitations* as free adaptations of the Horatian originals, and the success with

122

which Pope was able to build on many of their themes. In all the editions after 1735, Pope's 'Advertisement' (attached to *To Fortescue*, but also making reference to the whole group) retains the assertion that 'an Answer from *Horace* was both more full, and of more Dignity, than any I cou'd have made in my own person' — a claim which, while it requires careful examination, would be odd in the context of serious retrospective disenchantment with Horace.

It is therefore worth considering how far, despite those areas of tension which are particularly related to the political content of the two sets of poems, Pope was able to find answering echoes in Horace which he could develop with conviction; indeed, his tendency to sharpen and elaborate Horace's text to achieve a distinctively personal expression often seems to affirm this conviction rather than suggest incompatibility. Horace offered Pope a base for exploring two problems fundamental to the moralist which were developed very fully in his original works, and which will form the focus of my discussion in this chapter. The first of these is the psychological analysis of vices and follies, a theme which for Pope entails a close link with the issues of the *Essay on Man* and the *Moral Essays* (published in the same years as the earlier *Imitations*); pride, self-love, and the inconsistencies of human nature. The second concerns the proper response of a satirist to these provocations; whether his aim should be to give offence to the offenders at a directly personal level, and whether (as Edward Young voiced the problem in his 'Preface' to *Love of Fame*) his 'Judgement' or his 'Passion' should be most in evidence as assurance of his integrity. This question is of course central to the *Epistle to Dr. Arbuthnot*, on which Pope had been working for several years before its publication in 1735.

While he speaks of the dignity of Horace in the 'Advertisement' to *To Fortescue* (*Satire II i*), Pope adds qualifying remarks which are important in marking what he sees as the chief ground of his departure from the Roman satirist: 'The Example of much greater Freedom in so eminent a Divine as Dr. *Donne*, seem'd a proof with what Indignation and Contempt a Christian may treat Vice or Folly, in ever so low, or ever so high, a Station.' The phrase 'Indignation and Contempt' carries most weight here (particularly as boldly reconciled with the moral duty of a Christian), and its place within Pope's own satiric theory will be discussed more fully later, but the key terms 'Vice' and 'Folly' to cover the objects of attack also merit consideration. The theoretical distinction between the two is common in contemporary discussions of satire, and the paired words recur throughout the *Imitations* and Pope's correspondence. It was frequently observed of Horace that his chief quarry lay in the follies rather than the vices of mankind; Walter Harte calls him 'the Foe of Fools not Vice' (though not pejoratively — he is still capable of 'rage'),[6] while Dryden observes that 'Folly was the proper quarry of Horace, and not vice; ... the defects of human understanding, or at most the pecadillos of life, rather than the tragical vices, to which men are hurried by their unruly passions and exhorbitant desires' (*Discourse Concerning ... Satire*, pp. 128-9).[7] It is worth noting, however, that Dryden takes the Augustan reign to have been freer of these 'enormous vices' than the times of the more savage Domitian: 'they were better for the man, but worse for the satirist' (p.132). Pope would seem to acquiesce in the latter judgement when he observes to Arbuthnot (July 1734; *Correspondence*, III, 420) that 'under the greatest Princes and best Ministers ... Poets exercised the same jurisdiction over the Follies, as Historians did over the Vices of men' (giving as an instance the reign of Augustus, when Horace was 'protected and caress'd'), and at the same time implies that his own field is a wider one than Horace's. Not only this, but Pope's terms in the 'Advertisement' quoted above maintain that 'Contempt' is the proper reward even of 'Folly', rather than the 'laughter', 'fine raillery' and 'tickling' assigned rather opprobriously to Horace by Dryden. Within Pope's satires, of course, this nominal distinction between vices and follies is frequently overborne; R. W. Rogers has justly observed that in the *Imitations* 'the key to moral character is the state of the passions',[8] and through these subversive forces the slide from mere inanity to deeper depravity is constantly threatening, an assertion of the irrational self in which the will is overwhelmed.

The works which Pope chose to imitate are concerned in a variety of ways with the themes of indulgence and restraint, and he is responsive to the (often ironic) reflections which they make upon Epicurean and Stoic doctrines, above all as these philosophical influences were very much alive in his own time. At the centre of Pope's response is the Stoic view of Horace put forward by André Dacier in the 'Preface' to his highly influential edition of the

Satires and *Epistles*; here the works are presented as pre-eminently guides to self-knowledge and aids in the purgation of extravagant desires:

> Horace veut nous apprendre à combatre nos vices, à regler nos passions, à suivre la Nature, pour donner des bornes à nos desirs; ... à revenir de nos prejugez; à bien connoistre les principes et les motifs de toutes nos actions.[9]

Pope studied Dacier's commentaries on Horace carefully and commended him warmly for his 'good Sense, Penetration and ... Taste of his author';[10] the stress on 'moderation in all things' is essentially congenial to his own interests as a satirist, and of course the *Moral Essays* themselves are heavily indebted to Horace, particularly the two epistles on the 'Use of Riches' with their exposures of avarice and its attendant miseries. In these works and in his imitations of the Horatian satires on temperance, however, Pope treats the subject of 'mediocritas' with an exaggerated urgency, often heightening the frenzy and farce but conveying also a deeply sardonic sense of perplexity. His tendency is to sharpen and particularise Horace's attacks on human extremes, taking up political themes which are more specific and topical, and dwelling on the idea of self-abasement more insistently.

The imitation of *Satire II ii* (*To Bethel*) is a particularly interesting case in point, since its complexity in handling the theme of temperance reflects a degree of self-mockery or elusiveness in Horace's text. In his edition of the latin text, E. P. Morris asserts that 'the whole satire is a parody of a Stoic sermon',[11] and an intention to parody seems also implied in Pope's letter to Hugh Bethel on the imitation: 'Have you seen the last Satire of Horace in which You are so ill treated?'[12] Pope's manner of treatment has been aptly presented by Peter Dixon as a delicate exercise in raillery, which serves to dissipate the potential embarrassment of Bethel's sententious sermon itself;[13] thus in the opening lines 'the doctrine of frugality is urbanely admitted to be a wise one even while it is disowned' (p.35), and finally it can be reasserted as 'soundly moral'. There is a winning delicacy and obliquity in Pope's strategy which makes the moralising more palatable, and altogether the play of irony is more complex here than in the original; yet what is most striking is that this very obliquity draws Pope's version towards a more earnest moral conclusion, an effect

which chiefly depends on Pope's taking over the last section of
the lecture himself. Horace uses the persona of Ofellus in a more
consistently playful way, and the ending of his satire seems therefore more apologetic. Dacier is at first unclear as to how far
Horace may be satirising the zealous excesses of his spokesman,
presenting 'Ofellus rusticus' as the type of a plain good man steering a middle path between Stoic and Epicurean doctrines, but he
takes note of the element of self-mockery in line 2 ('nec meus hic
sermo').[14] The satiric diatribe which pours forth in the 'sermo'
itself is certainly in some danger of being undercut by its very
extravagance, especially in the obsessive detail with which physical grossness is pilloried. Pope, however, has created a more
comfortable licence for 'Bethel's' satire, and ushers it in with a
certain authority by making the first attack on intoxicating
luxuriance himself (ll. 5-8). He goes on to exploit this opportunity
to probe more sharply and disarmingly into moral faults; between
lines 10 and 24, the latin text is considerably contracted to shift
the weight emphatically onto the strenuous exhortation of the
speech:

> Go work, hunt, exercise (he thus began)
> Then scorn a homely dinner, if you can.
> (11-12)

Although there is still a parody of preaching in the passage on
subsiding souls (77-80), the direct address to the wastrel later is
invested with some sardonic bitterness, a sense of waste which is
also very much alive in the *Moral Essays* and which modifies the
comedy with an emphasis on self-destruction and self-contempt:

> When Luxury has lick'd up all thy pelf,
> Curs'd by thy neighbours, thy Trustees, thy self,
> To friends, to fortune, to mankind a shame,
> Think how Posterity will treat thy name;
> (105-8)

Pope's depiction of the dissipated glutton is similarly sharpened
from Horace's more general observations (Horace, 26-8), bringing out the irony of what Dacier translates as 'une malheureuse
abondance'; significantly, Pope italicises in his latin text the key
words 'Putet ... recens, / sollicitat ... rapula / ... acidas ... omnis / ...

Pauperies', all of which he has either rendered more forcefully or transformed for his own effect:[15]

> When the tir'd Glutton labours thro' a Treat,
> He finds no relish in the sweetest Meat;
> He calls for something bitter, something sour,
> And the rich feast concludes extremely poor.
>
> (31-4)

Paradox is uppermost in this rendering, in which the feast has become much more of a metaphor for life itself, with a heightened interest in the painfulness, effort and tedium of excess — the spiritual self-punishment implied in line 33 is characteristic, and clearly a studied refinement on Horace's radishes and pickles. The same traits are pronounced in the joint portrait of 'Avidien and his wife' (line 50 prepares us for some special savagery) who with an additional gesture of grotesque meanness are made to 'sell their presented partridges, and Fruits' to live on the fruits of 'grubbing' (rabbits and roots), the most glaring inversion of the laws of largesse exalted at the end of the poem. Again Pope's latin text is revealing;[16] the use of 'mutatum ... vinum' goes one stage further, 'and is at once their vinegar and wine'[54], and the free dispersal of this 'old vinegar' is seen as morally appropriate to a peculiarly nasty pair of festive occasions, quite unprecedented in Horace's innocuous 'repotia, natales':

> But on some lucky day (as when they found
> A lost Bank-bill, or heard their Son was drown'd)
> At such a feast old vinegar to spare,
> Is what two souls so gen'rous cannot bear.
>
> (55-8)

Pope's attack on mercenary greed in lines 115-22 is likewise pointedly set against the ideal of charity (as in *To Bathurst*), not simply public works of construction, and there is a characteristic emphasis on pride, 'that spreads and swells in puff'd Prosperity'.

As a balance to all this invective Pope's appropriation of the last section of Ofellus' lecture, making specific virtues of his own circumstances and his own friends, becomes the more necessary; it sustains a balance of the positive and the negative which is marked within the series of *Imitations* as a whole (the *Epistle to*

Dr. Arbuthnot is of course the fullest of these apologias, combining affection and indignation within the pose of a 'manly' inner fortitude, a readiness to assign praise and blame where they are strictly due). Despite the deliberate casualness of the closing section of *To Bethel* ('Content with little, I can piddle here'), Pope's stress on expansive generosity is aimed at something more energetic than conviviality, homeliness or simple self-sufficiency; there is an added strain of the protective (139-40), echoed in the friendly concern of 'Swift' (161-4), and a line of defiance which for Pope has specifically political import (151-80). Even on the level of personal enjoyments, the profusion of figs and 'show'r' of walnuts express Dacier's paradoxical exposition of the pleasures of temperance, 'De sorte que la frugalité pourroit estre appellée justement *un reservoir de volupté*', (VII, 84-5; italics as in the original). Perhaps the most important point here is that like Horace Pope has contrived to end his poem on a noticeably Stoic declaration of self-reliance — 'Let us be fix'd, and our own Masters still' — but in a context which has emphatically brought home the altered meaning of that statement; not crabbed retreat but active and sociable engagement, entailing the full exploitation of the Twickenham property and its grounds, and a spirited ideal of friendship. We find Pope elaborating the theme of sociability with similar freedom and energy in completing Swift's imitation of *Satire II vi* (the town and country mouse):

> My Friends above, my Folks below,
> Chatting and laughing all-a-row, ...
> Each willing to be pleas'd, and please,
> And even the very Dogs at ease!
> (135-6, 139-40)

Pope's rendering in this imitation makes the prating of the fashionable the more effete and malicious (141-4), the relationship between Court mouse and rustic more pointedly one of officious patronage matched with awed servility. As we would expect, in reflection of these blatant oppositions, Pope's expression of Horace's philosophical debate on friendship becomes less of a series of open questions and more of an open satire:

> Which is the happier, or the wiser,
> A man of Merit, or a Miser?

Whether we ought to chuse our Friends,
For their own Worth, or our own Ends?[17]
(147-50)

The sanctity of friendship is for Pope self-evident, and is a theme united with the anti-Walpolean stroke on which he ends the tale.

The title of Pope's lively imitation of *Satire I ii* on the virtues of sexual restraint, *Sober Advice from Horace*, suggests another exercise in parody of the sermon, and in this instance the impression is fully appropriate. John Aden has moralised the song by reference to the *Essay on Man* and the *Moral Essays*, treating of lust as a 'ruling passion',[18] and although it is not a work which should be over-solemnised, specific thematic links with the latter group of epistles are certainly apparent. The moral point of the satire is expressed succinctly in Horace's line 'dum vitant stulti vitia, in contraria currunt', and Pope reinforces this indictment by accentuating with much sprightliness the perilous extremes and absurdities to which uncontrolled lusts entice their victims. Sex is taken up by Horace specifically as an Epicurean theme, a prime instance of the seeking of pleasure irrationally, and *Satire I ii* 'shows us ironically that the real cause of our sexual difficulties resides not in our sexual instincts, but rather in our inability to subject them to rational inspection or control',[19] a point which Pope's translation elaborates with some force:

> Hath not indulgent Nature spread a Feast,
> And giv'n enough for Man, enough for Beast?
> But Man corrupt, perverse in all his ways,
> In search of Vanities from Nature strays:
> Yea, tho' the Blessing's more than he can use,
> Shuns the permitted, the forbid pursues!
> (96-101)

If there is something of the libertine in this 'naturalistic' view of a permissive, free-for-all Nature, it actually serves to lend force to the sense of inane frenzy which is accentuated in the rest of the satire.[20] The sermon is delivered with all the robustness and acumen of the 'plain Man, whose Maxim is profest, / "The Thing at hand is of all Things the *best*"'. With the Restoration allusions which keep surfacing in the poem, the term 'Maxim' here is perhaps designed to suggest the voice of a 'cynic philosopher' like

La Rochefoucauld, sharply and jibingly incredulous of the lengths to which others will go in their relentless pursuit of the inaccessible, the woes of the 'Men of Pleasure still in Pain'. Pope concentrates on women in place of Horace's male exempla in the introductory section, and his opening vividly links sexual lust and the lust for money rather than preserving Horace's transition from the one subject to the other as comparable examples of inconsistency; thus there is altogether a tighter thematic unity in his work. The same equation is implicit in his version of *Epistle I i* (ll. 124-31), and lines 13-4 of *Sober Advice* brilliantly evoke a grotesque frenzy in which desire surges on from libido to avarice in gargantuan proportions:

> "Treat on, treat on," is her eternal Note,
> And Lands and Tenements go down her Throat.

The voracity here becomes more alarming than ridiculous, and Horace's opening catalogue of opposite eccentric types (wastrels/misers) is transformed in Pope's hands to a vision of pervasive insanity and disorder, embracing 'all the Court ... and half the Town'. 'Benignus' as applied to Horace's harmless Tigellius has immediately become subject to heavy irony, and the perversity that this implies is upheld in Pope's tendency to fuse Horace's diverse types into bafflingly self-contradictory characters. The effect is to plumb new depths of recklessness and meanness together (7-10), of hypocrisy and inconsistency (31-4). Women become the unconscious predators, fools their willing victims, and Pope is particularly taken up with satirising the paradoxes of 'empty Pride', a pride which seems bent on inverting itself to abasement. There are more concentrated references to dirt and disease (the sewer and 'sluttishness' of ll.29 and 111, the pox in ll.17, 36 and 94-5), which go beyond the warnings about the circumstantial dangers of wife-hunting and suggest perils or corruptions which are more latent. For all the deftness and liveliness of the adaptation, Pope has rendered *Satire I ii* more unsettling, and by no means less serious; the problems of its alleged 'obscenity' are deftly deflected through the busily obsessive and pedantic 'Notae Bentleianae',[21] and *Sober Advice* represents a particularly vivid and penetrating satire on the universal human drive towards irrational indulgence. The ideal solution which is jocularly but ingenuously put forward in the closing lines is not so much one of reticence as of recognising one's own immediate interests and acting straightforwardly to gratify them, a doctrine which restores a welcome sense of sanity.

It is significant, however, that these satires on the theme of temperance, dealing with the restraint of physical desires, are among the earliest in the sequence of Pope's *Imitations*. The deepening of the theme in Horace's *Epistles* entails the elusive pursuit of spiritual self-knowledge and equanimity, and while that subject is problematic for Horace it appears still more problematic for Pope. The imitations of *Epistles I i* and *I vi* ('nil admirari') occur very late in Pope's sequence and were published within two months of one another in 1738; both are mature and complex philosophical reflections in which the significance of Horace's texts is deeply considered and, in some sections, intriguingly redirected. A major source of difficulty certainly concerns the role of the passions, an issue relating directly to the second epistle of *An Essay on Man*. For Horace, the search for self-knowledge and happiness means that one must as far as possible come to terms with the disturbances of the soul caused by the passions and attempt to subdue them; in so far as these reflections tend towards Stoic thinking, they must inevitably raise a measure of unease and a consciousness of presumption in Pope, for whom happiness (as the *Essay on Man* argues) depends upon faith and an appropriate fulfilment of the 'heav'n-directed' passions.[22] Horace's ideal of wisdom relates above all to the full understanding of the self, while Pope's refers beyond this to the harmonising of the self with the dispositions of Providence. A tension between these attitudes is apparent in the two imitations, both of which endeavour to inculcate the Horatian pursuit of equanimity with a more strenuous idealism.

Horace's plea in *Epistle I i* for peace in which to pursue the goal of moral enlightenment is, however, explicitly not an exercise in Stoic retreat, as the eclecticism expressed in lines 13-19 makes clear. It is also a discussion which pointedly acknowledges the limited motions which can be made towards the desired end of assured and active virtue (20-32), and this strain is expressly deepened in Pope's rendering. Most prominent in his imitation is a heightened awareness of the external and internal threats which beset the hard-won emotional balance, and he introduces a corresponding stress on moral urgency. The poem is opened with a sharper sense of despair, of persecution by disturbing human forces ('Now sick alike of Envy and of Praise'), whose wearisome intrusions are less comic than in the opening of the *Epistle to Dr. Arbuthnot*, and are emphasised by the wording of his plea, 'Why will you break the Sabbath of my days?' This last phrase hints at a Christian perspective, and this is reinforced as Horace's 'disinterested' approach to moral enquiry is given a more precise and dramatic personal aim;

> Let this be all my care — for this is All:
> To lay this harvest up, and hoard with haste
> What ev'ry day will want, and most, the last.
> (20-2)

The harvest metaphor as an allusion to Luke 12: 19-21 is pointed out by Maresca,[23] and the association of the 'last' day with the Day of Judgement is immediately felt; but a concern with personal and active virtue as the foundation of this spiritual harvest becomes all the more apparent in the close parallel between these lines and one of Pope's letters to Bethel (July 1723): 'Humanity and sociable virtues are what every creature wants every day, and still wants more the longer he lives, and most the very moment he dies.'[24] The task of attaining to wisdom through self-knowledge does not represent the complete fulfilment of this impulse towards positive virtue; although the declaration of philosophical independence which follows this passage (23-34) begins with something of Horace's cavalier mood, Pope does not lay himself so open to the charge of relaxed hedonism or sheer intellectual confusion as Horace does. The avowals that he makes are deepened and complicated by the meaning they would have held for Pope's addressee, Bolingbroke, a dimension which is illustrated most fully in a recent enlightening study by Brean Hammond.[25] Hammond believes that the terms in which Pope declares his eclecticism contain private references designed to provoke, even somewhat to 'affront' Bolingbroke, who had particular views on the excessive scepticism of Montaigne and the credulity of Locke in religious matters, and who favoured the philosophy of Aristippus and execrated the authoritarian influence of St Paul. In a number of ways the imitation can be seen as 'a rebuke to Bolingbroke's facile philosophising', reflecting on the influence he had once had as Pope's mentor and the fact that 'Horace's *Epistle I i* was one of Bolingbroke's favourite poems, and while in exile in France, he had made a couplet translation of its most Stoic passage' (p.119). Pope's rather casual declarations of 'yielding to the tyde', 'as drives the storm' echo Horace's dubious 'furtim', and seem to repudiate the stance of moral purism which Bolingbroke assumed within his Opposition role. None the less, it appears to me that in this passage there are equally positive signs that Pope is at the same time *responding* to Bolingbroke in just these terms, that is as a man of political action, high-principled, 'active in debate'; even though the cloak of public benefactor constitutes only one of Pope's shifting 'identities', the Patriot cause is still very strikingly animated in contrast to Horace's deliberately portentous 'rigidusque satelles' (translated by Dacier, 'comme un Stoïcien rigide et severe'; VIII, 44). Most striking of all is Pope's key line 'Still warm to Virtue, and as warm as true' (30), which marks the difference emphatically. In this section at least, the passage gains depth from being engaged in serious irony rather than adopting a tone which is more casually wry or disingenuous. Even in the allusion of lines 31-2, one could argue that Pope contrives to present his principles in an unexpectedly positive light:

> Sometimes, with Aristippus, or St. Paul,
> Indulge my Candor, and grow all to all;

In this context, 'Candor' may mean quite the opposite of 'impartiality' (TE, IV, 281n.), but rather 'purity of mind; openness; ingenuity' (Johnson's definition) so that 'indulge' and 'Candor' placed in close proximity make a witty play, confounding the reader's expectation of a confession of narrow self-interest and expressing instead a kind of spontaneity or self-revealing artlessness. Significantly, this is not the point at which Pope concedes the 'slipping' of which Horace speaks, but instead he invokes a 'slide' to 'my native Moderation', certainly a less culpable trait than the mere capitulation which Horace admits to, and even arguably a virtue, in both political and religious terms. Altogether there are more suggestive implications and more positive possibilities here than in Horace's playful ironies, even though Pope is conscious of 'some weakening of principle, some invertebracy about this state of mind' (Hammond, p.121); the question of principle *concerns* him much more, and this is reflected in the deeper insecurity of the whole epistle, both in the challenge and also in the avowal of admiration and indebtedness which he delivers to Bolingbroke. The seriousness of the passage in which Pope evokes the frustration of the soul blocked from its clear purpose is so deep as to become the high point of the epistle, a meditation of moving poignancy and lyricism (35-46):

> So slow th' unprofitable Moments roll,
> That lock up all the Functions of my soul;
> That keep me from Myself; and still delay
> Life's instant business to a future day.
>
> (39-42)

To counterbalance this, however, there is more direct, wry self-mockery in the succeeding lines (47-52). As the analysis proceeds, Horace's irony on the prospect of exorcising the passions is much reinforced in Pope's hands, 'Love' being slyly introduced to transform the seven deadly sins to eight universal passions (55-64), and hopes of purgation decisively qualified. The tone is one of dramatic parody, harassing the reader:

> Say, does thy blood rebel, thy bosom move
> With wretched Av'rice, or as wretched Love?
> Know, there are Words, and Spells, which can controll
> (Between the Fits) this fever of the soul:
> Know, there are Rhymes, which (fresh and fresh apply'd)
> Will cure the arrant'st Puppy of his Pride.
>
> (55-60)

The aggression of line 60 leads one to suppose that the 'Rhymes' in question are specifically the purgative medicine of satire, the great leveller; the ensuing assault on the moral and spiritual blind alleys into which the rest of the world is compulsively driving itself shows that the human soul is replete with insane inconsistencies, 'that Dev'l within / Which guides all those who know not what they mean' (144). The parable of 'Sir Job' (echoing the briefer sketches of 'Papillia' in *To A Lady* and 'Villario' in *To Burlington*) elevates this restlessness to a major vice, an irresistible provocation to satire. When finally the parody turns to the figure of the 'Demi-god' Stoic in his 'painful preheminence', he is deflated very appropriately by a 'Fit of Vapours' — a temperamental disorder which is rather less arbitrary than the physical collapse jibed at by Horace — just as 'Spleen' has already attacked the whimsical knight and his lady (145). However, there is more in this closing passage than a jest against presumption, self-aggrandisement and vulnerability; there is also a genuine feeling for the appeal of idealistic endeavour and resilience which is explicitly allied to Pope's own stance as moral poet (179-84), and Horace's exclamatory extravagance has lost its sense of the ludicrous. Whereas the Horatian 'sapiens' is endowed with manifestly unconvincing perfections ('Dives! ... honoratus! pulcher!'), Pope is addressing the idea of a strenuous inner fortitude which, while its goals have been shown to lie beyond man's fallen nature, still demands our attention as the antithesis of the low interests and insatiable desires perturbing rich and poor alike. Pope's catalogue of virtues has also an unmistakable political relevance to Bolingbroke's own position as a former exile and member of the Opposition:

> Rich ev'n when plunder'd, honour'd while oppress'd,
> Lov'd without youth, and follow'd without power,
> At home tho' exil'd, free, tho' in the Tower.
>
> (182-4)

This is a passage which strikingly expresses, in Frank Stack's words, an 'emotionally demanding' friendship, 'the intensity of his feelings for Bolingbroke and his desire that Bolingbroke should make *him* into the Stoic wise man';[26] it is in fact the very warmth of the reproach, as well as the warmth of admiration, which contradicts Stoic 'detachment', and the complexity of its feelings is achieved because in an important sense the 'man divine' represents both Bolingbroke and Pope as he would wish to be. That the description is in some measure apposite to Pope can be seen by setting it alongside the final 'heroic/domestic' portrait in *To Bethel*, and in both cases the change in application brings about a significant revision of meaning. In *Epistle I i*, Horace's capacity for enriching his philosophical enquiry with a feeling for irony has been developed by Pope into a sharp and challenging sense of latent contradiction, a tension between idealism and disillusionment, the yearning for moral progress and the sense of its inaccessibility.

These traits are again dominant in the rendering of *Epistle I vi* ('nil admirari'), which, while its adage has often been taken to epitomise the spirit of the English 'Augustan' age, is in fact the most complex and ambiguous of the *Imitations*. Horace's somewhat over-energetic satire in parts of the epistle, and his characteristically cryptic closing lines, do to a significant extent inform Pope's sense of irony; but more important than this is an ambiguity which certainly did not constrain Horace, concerning the meaning of 'admiration' itself and its relationship to Christian faith.

The doctrine of *Epistle I vi* is summed up in straightforward terms by Dacier in his 'Remarques' (VIII, 290): 'pour guerir les hommes de leurs passions .. il vaut mieux tâcher, s'il est possible, de les reduire toutes à un seul et même principe', that is a principle which is the ideal of equanimity. Admiration, or the susceptibility of the soul to sensations of fear, desire or astonishment, is 'entierement opposée à la vertu, qui consiste à avoir son esprit dans une assiete ferme et tranquille, sans qu'il puisse estre surpris, ému, ni étonné de quoy que ce soit' (291). Put in these terms, the doctrine has strong overtones of Stoic assurance and self-reliance; it transpires, however, that Dacier himself sees a need to qualify these terms in order to reassert a Christian conception of virtue, unpresumptuous yet vigilant against all forms of apathy, 'Car les Epicuriens le poussoient à un excés tres-pernicieux'. He resolves this moral difficulty by drawing a distinction between two kinds of admiration, the first of which is a laudable response 'raisonnable et intelligente, qui porte les hommes à la vertu'; it is not this admiration which Horace is attacking, but 'l'admiration vicieuse et folle qui naist de l'ignorance' (291), against the ill effects of which, Dacier is at pains to assert, 'il faut avoir une ame grande et genereuse, ... une ame intrepide' (292). Peter Dixon (p.164) has drawn attention to the fact that 'admiration' gradually changed its meaning between the late seventeenth and mid-eighteenth century from the pejorative 'stupefaction' to 'rational approbation', and it is interesting to find that Dacier's commentary is effectively attempting to define both by reference to the ideal of virtue. Another writer who takes considerable interest in the idea of admiration is Shaftesbury, who likewise sees 'the air of the Epicurean discipline and Lucretian style' in the opening of this epistle as apparent only, and takes Dacier's argument one step further in asserting that admiration in the best sense is a proper expression of the awe of God: 'if there be naturally such a passion, 'tis evident that religion itself is of the kind, and must therefore be natural to man.'[27] He is careful however to distinguish this from the extremes of 'enthusiasm':

> Now as all affections have their excess, and require judgment and discretion to moderate and govern them, so this high and noble affection which raises man to action ... requires a steady rein and strict hand over it ... in religious concerns particularly, the habit of admiration and contemplative delight would, by over indulgence, too easily mount into high fanaticism or degenerate into abject superstition. (*Characteristics*, II, 178)

These expositions, and the semantic change in the word 'admiration' itself, are interesting in that they almost encapsulate a major tension in Pope's own thinking about the passions — a distrust of their extremes, allied with a benevolist defence of their necessary importance. While Pope is inclined to cling to the pejorative sense of 'admiration', his treatment of the theme in his imitation of *Epistle I vi* (*To Murray*) shows that he is concerned to define its range of meaning by relating it to the problems of Christian virtue and faith.

The opening lines of the imitation (1-4) give an apparently unqualified authority to the Horatian precept, which accords with Pope's private remark to Spence that '*Nil admirari* is as true in relation to our opinion of authors as it is in morality.'[28] But his following verse-paragraph (5-10) enforces the view that unperturbed contemplation of the wonders of the universe is upheld not simply by inward serenity but by positive faith:

> There are, my Friend! whose philosophic eyes
> Look thro', and trust the Ruler with his Skies,
> To him commit the hour, the day, the year,
> And view this dreadful All without a fear.
>
> (7-10)

The shifts of emphasis in the passage are subtle, but significant; there is the assumption that God has the disposal of his own creation ('Presume not God to scan'), which includes what appears to be a reference to the hour of death. But at the same time, there is a deeper feeling than in Horace's text for the awesomeness of the Newtonian universe, 'This Vault of Air, this congregated Ball, ... this dreadful All', a fusion of reverence and resignation which strikes the reader in a distinctive way. Indeed, this kind of admiration is presented as a *reasonable* response; it is interesting to compare this with one of Pope's early letters to Caryll (August 1713; *Correspondence*, I, 186), in which he speaks of man as a grain of dust or a mite in the perspective of eternity, but objects that such meditations would leave one 'stupefied in a poise of inaction, void of all desires, of all designs, of all friendships', and that 'we must return (thro' our very condition of being) to our narrow selves, and those things that affect ourselves. Our passions, our interests, flow in upon us, and unphilosophise us into mere mortals.' The argument in the letter associates admiration with abstract contemplation and unresponsiveness, passion with an empirical, day-to-day concernment with life. Pope's lines of verse, however, reflect more closely on Dacier's response to Horace's third line, where he comments that absolute indifference to the heavens themselves would be impious: 'dans le mesme temps qu'ils refusent nostre admiration, ils nous crient de la donner à celuy qui les gouverne, et de ne la donner qu'à luy' (VIII, 295). The concern with faith is of course readily extrapolated from Horace's 'formidine nulla / Imbuti', probably the line which inspired Shaftesbury's warning on 'abject superstition'. In Pope's version, this perspective condemns the 'idolatrous' worship of the mortal rich:

> Say with what eyes we ought at Courts to gaze,
> And pay the Great our homage of Amaze?
>
> (16-17)

The other extreme of 'high fanaticism' is elaborated from Horace's ll.15-16 with little violence to the original:

> Thus good, or bad, to one extreme betray
> Th' unbalanc'd Mind, and snatch the Man away;
> For Vertue's self may too much Zeal be had;
> The worst of Madmen is a Saint run mad.
>
> (24-7)

Here admiration is presented as a passion of violence, which is seemingly in contradiction to the lines opening the verse-paragraph which describe the 'weak' impressions the soul receives from superficial desires and fears. At that point Pope has taken the notion of stupefaction ('defixis oculis, animoque et corpore torpet') into the realm of moral failing, a lethargy which is a direct contrast to the strength of 'trust' evoked at the beginning:[29]

> If weak the pleasure that from these can spring,
> The fear to want them is as weak a thing:
> Whether we dread, or whether we desire,
> In either case, believe me, we admire.
>
> (18-21)

The implication that more strenuous satisfactions are to be had is brought out clearly by the time Pope translates Horace's lines 'Si Virtus hoc una potest dare, fortis omissis / Hoc age deliciis' (30-1), from which he has italicised the words 'una ... omissis ... deliciis':

> Would ye be blest? despise low Joys, low Gains;
> Disdain whatever CORNBURY disdains;
> Be Virtuous, and be happy for your pains.
>
> (60-2)

This is highly characteristic of Pope's most consciously 'exalted' manner, and in the use of the triplet, and the citing of an exemplary public figure, gives the greatest possible emphasis to the notion of happiness gained through renunciation; the attitude of vigorous fortitude and contempt is reflected also in the vituperative tone of the satire throughout the epistle, and in the moralising tendencies which are so marked in the other *Imitations*. There are obvious puns and allusions in the passage on disease and self-martyrdom (54-5), the mock-injunctions endorsing greed (67-96) are more savagely sarcastic and fantastical (1.73, 'Advance thy golden Mountain to the skies', conjuring up the impudence of the Tower of Babel), and the meaning of the latin at 1.46 is turned to overt sententiousness ('which it much becomes you to forget', 1.94), probably upon a hint from Dacier: 'Qu'y a-t-il donc de plus ridicule que de faire consister son bonheur dans des biens dont on ne doit faire aucun usage, et que l'on doit mesme ignorer?' (VIII, 328). The name of Ulysses is picked up by Pope to suggest the abasement of Circe's victims, 'transform'd to Beasts' (123), and the fable of the sham hunter Gargilius, which in Horace's text seems to be of limited relevance, is adapted for the highly moral tale of Lord Russel, defeating his own appetites in an exemplary way by pure over-indulgence; there could be no better paradigm of selfishness than the one this story offered for Pope's purposes. Finally, and by way of contrast, the invoking of Swift in the final lines as the spokesman of the lighthearted view of life adds greater weight to the doctrine of the rakish Rochester, and modifies the immediate irony and nonchalance of the valediction. Pope ends the epistle, like Horace, on an ambiguous note; but 'the Cordial Drop of Life' none the less seems to represent something of an antidote to the fevers and tribulations of the world at large, and in its own terms helps to define the sociable idea of happiness through the practice of virtue promoted more earnestly within the main body of the imitation.

In my discussion of the *Imitations* so far, I have concentrated on Pope's manner in adopting the satirist's didactic role, that of 'instruction' and philosophical enquiry (although of course this function is a part of the manner of attack). It is equally apparent that Pope's more vigorous moral idealism and his more acute concern with the paradoxes and perversities of human behaviour is reflected in his sense of the other traditional role of the satirist, that of 'purger' through the aggressive weapon of ridicule. 'Purging' as a medicinal concept is of course central to the *Epistle to Dr. Arbuthnot*, and Pope's choice of *Satire II i* as the first of the *Imitations*, and above all the *Epilogue to the Satires*, also show him questioning actively the problems concerning the morality and effectiveness of satire. Dacier, adopting the metaphor of weeding and sowing, presents purgation as the necessary preparation for instruction, and hence regards Horace's first and second books of satires as pursuing those functions according to such a plan (VI: 'Preface sur les Satires'); his terms, familiar ones in satiric theory, are correlative to Young's 'Passion' and 'Judgement', and as we will see Pope adopts analogous terms also in defending his satire.

One of Pope's key themes in this debate is the notion of the insensibility (whether innate or acquired) of his quarry, and throughout the *Imitations* we are continually confronted with his marked emphasis on pride as a near-impermeable barrier to self-knowledge or self-improvement. The reassuring, 'Providential' notion that vice entails its own punishment, upheld with seeming confidence in the *Essay on Man*, is often accentuated within the satiric portraits, yet it is equally characteristic of Pope to treat the idea with irony in his more general observations on satire. In *Epistle II ii*, for example, Pope has significantly added a couplet repudiating Horace's proposal that we might learn to treat the diseases of the soul as directly as those of the body:

> The Heart resolves this matter in a trice,
> "Men only feel the Smart, but not the Vice."
> (216-17)

There are also those who are entirely insensible of 'the Smart'— fools are endowed with miraculous self-conceit, knaves with 'the happy quality of *Want of Shame*'. Pope's lines satirising 'fierce champion Fortitude' among the dunces (*Dunciad* A, I. 45-6) are, with double irony, adapted from Horace's line on the Stoic posture as described by Davus: 'quem neq; pauperies, neq; mors, neq; vincula terrent' (*Satire II vii*, 84). The advice of the provoking *adversarius* 'Friend' in the *Epilogue, Dialogue I* (53-4) sums up the bane of the satirist's mission:

> Laugh then at any, but at Fools or Foes;
> These you but anger, and you mend not those.

In support of Pope's earliest concerted attack, the 1728 *Dunciad*, there appeared in 1730 Young's *Two Epistles to Mr. Pope, Concerning the Authors of the Age* and Walter Harte's *Essay on Satire*, both of which almost certainly had an influence on Pope's later works. Harte's *Essay* enforces a point which is vital to Pope's apologia, representing the dunces as by no means obtuse unfortunates, but as malicious agents, endowed with a power for injury which inverts all the codes of charitableness ('The Learn'd they wound, the Virtuous, and the Fair, / No fault they cancel, no reproach they spare'; p.24). Young concentrates on the breed of hack who is equally insidiously subversive in unleashing base instincts, the pornographic scribbler whose 'Verse immoral kindles loose Desires' (*Epistle I*, l.66), but also adds to licentiousness the passions of rage and envy, to a degree of 'raving' and 'frenzy' which is equated with madness or inebriation. Pope's *To Arbuthnot* animates further the drama envisaged by Young, particularly in its opening sections where the theme of assault and persecution is uppermost, united with its animal imagery (as Pope writes to Ralph Allen in April 1736: 'They let in a Poet upon me at dinner'). Indeed, passion as appetite in the most literal sense is conveyed in his many references to empty-stomached, ill-fed hacks driven to biting or (in the case of Sporus) uselessly slobbering whatever he cannot taste or 'dare not bite', while the hour of dining for the true poet (Pope) is treated as sacrosanct because, as again with the close of *To Bethel*, it is a kind of index of his ordinary human needs, his well-fed balance and sociability. Against this model, the irascible John Dennis provides the most cogent example of an angry critic who has lost all power of self-control (as Bentley does in *Sober Advice* and the *Dunciad*), analogous to the malice of the rejected hacks. The whole poem crucially enacts a process of provocation, both of Pope and on Pope's part; beginning with the comparatively innocent frenzy of the poetic fit — 'mad or vain' — the next stage of provocation is one of intrusive impudence (45-8) which builds up to unrestrained bombastic venom when the would-be poet's ambitions are punctured ('If I dislike it, "Furies, death and rage!"'). On his side, Pope presents himself as 'glad of a quarrel', preferring open warfare to covert assaults, and open contempt to prevarication, which (it is implied) is one of the repressions leading to 'honest anguish, and an aking head' (38). Indeed it is the sheer difficulty of self-suppression which becomes united with the 'torture' imagery of 31-8, with the poet as a figure of temperamental openness, 'Who can't be silent, and who will not lye'. Part of Pope's satire on the hacks consists in taking a serious, even compassionate dictum from the *Essay on Man* — that pride is 'bestow'd on all, a common Friend' — and turning it to aggressive ridicule:

> That Casting-weight Pride adds to Emptiness,
> This, who can gratify? for who can *guess*?[30]
>
> (176-7)

In the imitation of Horace's *Epistle II ii*, likewise, there is the ironic acknowledgement that all poets are more or less vain and unbalanced in their compulsion to write,[31] but Pope's tone in self-defence, like the retort of his soldier to the General (450), is decidedly more defiant. The vein of satire here on conceited poets and their impotence is still more aggressive, and the phrases which are picked out in the latin text (ll. 81-3, 102-12,[32] 127) echo the themes which are most prominent in Pope's original satires.

From their initial role as active oppressors in *To Arbuthnot*, the dunces are turned into passive fodder for the pride of the world at large, and particularly that of patrons. The quality of passivity, of reprehensible pusillanimity to which they subside is likewise the cornerstone of the satire on Addison as a flawed critic (no longer the idealised Addison of *Epistle II i*, who actively 'sets the Passions on the side of Truth'; 218). 'Atticus' is undermined by the very inverting of his own passions; consumed with the envy of excellence, 'willing to wound' and yet, unlike the more intrepid hacks, 'afraid to strike'. Pope's most damning reflection upon him — 'Alike reserv'd to blame, or to commend / A tim'rous foe, and a suspicious friend' — stands framed by the recklessness of the hacks on the one hand, and Pope's freedom towards his friend Arbuthnot on the other: his own dignity resides in this balance, 'not proud, nor servile'. Servility is the attribute which unites the pacified poetasters with the Court, the 'hireling Scribler' with the 'hireling Peer' (364), and Pope's version of *Epistle II ii* again echoes this line of satire. The worthless slave humorously equated with the indolent and conceited poet by Horace is here the son of a foppish Frenchman presented as 'Mere Wax' to the hands of a Lord, for which his evident effeminacy (5,11) makes him eminently suitable. The pleasing life of delusion enjoyed by Horace's bad poets is applied by Pope to 'no small Fool, a Lord' (twisting the sense of 'haud ignobilis'), and his illusion of watching great tragic drama to less forgivable delusions of power.

These developing motifs in Pope's satire on hacks and courtiers are most brilliantly drawn together in the attack on Lord Hervey as Sporus, Hervey being consistently represented as the epitome of the malicious poetaster and fawning, corrupt seeker of power together (see *Satire II i*, 5-6 and *Sober Advice*, 91-2). The paradoxes of Sporus as flimsy butterfly and stinging bug, manipulated 'Puppet' and manipulator, 'familiar' of evil, are reflected in the generic chaos of his literary output; above all, his moral and physical ambivalence is (by rhetorical extension) seen as a characteristic of his wit:

> ... all see-saw between *that* and *this*
> Now high, now low, now Master up, now Miss,
> And he himself one vile Antithesis.
>
> (323-5)

This concern with bisexuality as in some sense a property of his writing is almost obsessively elaborated in Pope's vitriolic *Letter to a Noble Lord* (1733): 'indeed I think *both sexes* had a share in it, but which was *uppermost*, I know not: I pretend not to determine the exact method of this *Witty Fornication*' ... 'No Critic can have a perfect taste of your Lordship's Works, who does not understand both your *Male Phrase* and your *Female Phrase*.'[33] It is not only of his personal virtues, but of his literary talents, that Pope maintains that 'if he pleas'd, he pleas'd by manly ways' (337); Hervey presents instead a contorted fawning self-abasement, 'Pride that licks the dust'. Many of the features of the portrait may well have been suggested by those of the 'secret libellers' in Walter Harte's *Essay on Satire*,[34] in particular the promiscuity in mixed vices, and Pope uses this theme of indiscriminate evil-doing to emphasise also Sporus' imperviousness to moral correction: 'Satire or Sense alas! Can *Sporus* feel?'

In Pope's apocalyptic vision of rampant vice in the *Epilogue* (*Dialogue I*), a special place is reserved outside the flurry of the active, City world for the inverted, emotionless 'Paradise' of the screened and compromised Court; a state remarkably close to the blissful inanity of the dunce, lulled to a sleep resembling death:

> Silent and soft, as Saints remove to Heav'n,
> All Tyes dissolv'd, and ev'ry Sin forgiv'n,...
> There, where no Passion, Pride, or Shame transport,
> Lull'd with the sweet *Nepenthe* of a Court;
> There, where no Father's, Brother's, Friend's Disgrace
> Once break their Rest, or stir them from their place;
> But past the Sense of human Miseries,
> All Tears are wip'd for ever from all Eyes;
> No Cheek is known to Blush, no Heart to throb,
> Save when they lose a Question, or a Job.
>
> (93-4, 97-104)

Pope's powers of damning with ironical terms of innocence are perhaps most perfectly realised here; the comforting moralistic assumption that 'Virtue alone brings Happiness below' has been satirically turned on its head, with all the redeeming passions, loyalties and social energies banished in favour of anaesthetised contentment and satiety. The question of whether human ties and relationships would in fact be 'dissolved' on the soul's entry to heaven was one which did interest Pope, as one of his early letters to Martha Blount shows (1715; *Correspondence*, I, 319).

Pope's vivid evocation of these double evils, mounting depravity and corresponding shamelessness and incorrigibility, is wrought to a pitch in the two brilliant *Dialogues* of the *Epilogue to the Satires*, and constrains him to question more and more sharply the ideal of moral, instructive 'delicacy' in satire. This key word 'delicacy' was repeatedly applied to characterise the urbanity of Horace's satire, generally with approval;[35] none the less, the value of 'moderate' satire was also the subject of active critical debate. In this debate, the state of the passions (both in the satirist and his quarry) was a focus of attention, and this issue is taken up by Pope with sharp interest. One of the most forceful points in Pope's observations on satire is the conviction with which he focuses on satire as a *personal* calling, even a compulsion; but the framework of ideas through which he presents his practice is indebted to several works on the subject which he would certainly have read with attention, foremost among them Dryden's celebrated *Discourse Concerning ... Satire* (1693),[36] Shaftesbury's *Advice to an Author* (1710; *Characteristics*, 103-234), and Young's 'Preface' to the collected satires of *Love of Fame* (1728).

The theoretical balance to which the satirist is said to aspire lies between two obvious extremes; on the one hand, he must by definition aim to wound, and few critics would quibble with Young's exclamation in his third satire,

> How terrible it were to common sense,
> To write a *satire*, which gave none *offence*?
> (*Love of Fame*, p.58)

On the other hand, the impulse to wound renders him vulnerable to the charge of mere malice: 'if we are angry with [the world], they say we are ill-natured' (Pope to Caryll, June 1715; *Correspondence*, I, 344). The cause of satire must be firmly allied to that of 'Virtue's better end' if it is to be acceptable, but this without having its teeth drawn; these platitudes are restated from Horace in Pope's *Epistle to Augustus* (*II i*), 241-62, and inform the whole body of his satiric work. In his rendering of this passage, Pope shows more interest in the ideological progress of satire and its moral foundation than in the historical account which Horace gives; he also implies a significant distrust of the control of satire through censorship and legal restraints, as a result of which he declares 'The Poets learn'd to please, and not to wound', and 'Most warp'd to Flatt'ry's side' (258-9). There is no basis in the latin for the direct condemnation of this second phrase (which makes Pope's 'wholesom dread of statutes' appear retrospectively ironic), and no mention of the ideal 'medium' of Pope's definition of satire, which 'heals with Morals what it hurts with Wit' (262).

In his willingness to embrace the virtues of intensity and attack, Pope is far removed from the approach of Edward Young, who endorses the 'delicacy' of Horace without reservation in his 'Preface':

> He appears in good humour while he censures; and therefore his censure has the more weight, as supposed to proceed from Judgment, not from Passion. *Juvenal* is ever in a passion; he has little valuable but his Eloquence, and Morality.

Absurd as Young's final statement appears, the grounds of his valuation are sifted in his theory of the passions engaged in satire, where it is argued that the degeneracy of the world must always provoke 'some passion', but that as a response laughter is less painful to ourselves than grief or anger, and most offensive to those ridiculed because it wounds their pride most keenly.[37] It is taken for granted, within his rather contorted formulation of his thesis, that the purgation of one passion by another is inherently necessary:

> Laughing at the misconduct of the world, will, in a great measure, ease us of any more disagreeable passion about it. One passion is more effectually driven out by another, than by reason; whatever some may teach. For to reason we owe our passions; had we not reason, we should not be offended at what we find amiss. And the *cause* seems not to be the natural cure of any *effect*.

Both Young and Dryden represent the chastising of vice as salutary and heroic, but Dryden denies the full height of heroism to Horace, endorsing Scaliger's censure on his characteristic lack of vehemence,[38] in conscious opposition to the judgements of Heinsius[39] and Dacier; the objection (restated from Barten Holyday) that 'a perpetual grin, like that of Horace, rather angers than amends a man' (p.136) anticipates the provoking remark of 'Friend' in Pope's *Epilogue*, quoted earlier. Dryden's defence of Juvenal in Horace's stead is vigorous and brilliant, concentrating on the emotional charge which is conveyed from writer to reader:

> He treats his subject home; his spleen is raised, and he raises mine; I have the pleasure of concernment in all he says; he drives his reader along with him ... and the greater the soul of him who reads, his transports are the greater. (p.130)[40]

But it is important to observe too that Dryden's denigration of Horace (which reachs its peak of disdain in the memorable phrase 'ever decent, because he is naturally servile'; p.132) is throughout the *Discourse* expressed in extraordinarily defensive terms, with many backtrackings to propitiatory and even rather contradictory remarks (see pp. 113, 117, 125, 128-9, 136). In sum, he avers that vice had reached more desperate heights in Juvenal's time, and that 'indignation' was therefore a more justified response (p.138); Horace is to be praised for his 'instruction', and has a valid place if it is allowed that 'the end and scope of satire is to purge the passions', rather than to raise them (p.143).

In Pope's prose, the most extensive discussion of the grounds of satire is in the interesting letter addressed to Arbuthnot of 26 July 1734 (*Correspondence*, III, 418-20); in Sherburn's opinion it is most probably a 'forgery' concocted by Pope out of salient points in his other letters, and recurrent in his verses, and for that very reason it is the more full and coherent. The central section of this letter needs to be quoted in full to show the clarity and scope with which Pope outlines his principles:

> What you recommend to me with the solemnity of a Last Request, shall have its due weight with me. That disdain and indignation against Vice, is (I thank God) the only disdain and indignation I have : It is sincere, and it will be a lasting one. But sure it is as impossible to have a just abhorrence of Vice, without hating the

Vicious, as to bear a true love for Virtue, without loving the Good. To reform and not to chastise, I am afraid is impossible, and that the best precepts, as well as the best Laws, would prove of small use, if there were no Examples to inforce them. To attack Vices in the abstract, without touching Persons, may be safe fighting indeed, but it is fighting with Shadows. General propositions are obscure, misty, and uncertain, compar'd with plain, full, and home examples: Precepts only apply to our Reason, which in most men is but weak: Examples are pictures, and strike the Senses, nay raise the Passions, and call in those (the strongest and most general of all motives) to the aid of reformation. Every vicious man makes the case his own; and that is the only way by which such men can be affected, much less deterr'd. So that to chastise is to reform. The only sign by which I found my writings ever did any good, or had any weight, has been that they rais'd the anger of bad men. And my greatest comfort, and encouragement to proceed, has been to see, that those who have no shame, and no fear, of any thing else. have appear'd touch'd by my Satires.[41]

As an extended, 'public' statement, this account is very important and very fully considered; the final remarks quoted anticipate the central claim of the *Epilogue* (*Dialogue II*, 208-9) that 'I must be proud to see / Men not afraid of God, afraid of me', and in its total range it embraces most of the vital points of debate on satire, including the question of personal versus pseudonymous, 'type' satire. Pope's practice over the years was to move more and more toward direct attacks on individuals; here, however, his meaning in 'touching Persons' is not apparently attack on named individuals — in fact the observation that 'every vicious man makes the case his own' argues rather the opposite — but refers to the forcefulness of 'characteristical satire', *based* on specific cases, which is one of Pope's most successful modes. John Butt ('Pope's poetical manuscripts', p.36) observes that the *Arbuthnot* manuscript shows corrections tending (unexpectedly, perhaps) to tone down personal allusions into 'Theophrastan' character-types; in *Satire II i* this is presented as the most effective means of attack, not necessarily with irony since 'Friend' is reporting two observed cases in point:

> A hundred smart in *Timon* and in *Balaam*:
> The fewer still you name, you wound the more;
> *Bond* is but one, but *Harpax* is a Score.
>
> (42-4)

But given the terms in which Pope advocates this practice in his letter — the use of 'plain, full and home examples' which will rouse an emotional response — the movement towards naming individuals is an inevitable development of his satiric theory and of his determination to act as the aggressor, to 'chastise' in order to 'reform'. His choice of the dialogue form (the manner of Horace's second book of satires) for his original Horatian poems, the *Epistle to Dr. Arbuthnot* and the *Epilogue to the Satires*, is also made to give himself licence for powerful vituperative irony and impassioned declamation. As I have argued, Horace as 'instructor' does have a very important, though carefully examined, role in Pope's *Imitations*, and his techniques as a satirist are equally influential; but in giving satire its fullest dignity and power, Pope is compelled to use much greater freedom.

Pope's impulse towards self-dramatisation and outspokenness emerges clearly in the first of the *Imitations*, *Satire II i (To Fortescue)*, the subject of G. K. Hunter's now classic essay 'The "Romanticism" of Pope's Horace'.[42] For both Horace and Pope, the poem represents a defence of satires already written, but in contrast to Horace's lighter spirit, Pope has a more concerted attack to make on the outside world. The rendering is very free, and his most striking gesture is to adapt the lines originally applied to Lucillius to his own case (105-32), with marked stress on independence and defiance; Pope adds his sardonic 'Tim'rous by nature, of the Rich in awe' to emphasise his contempt for fear or prudential considerations, and the self-parodying lines of Horace are made serious in the passage of 51-68. What is most significant here, as a reflection of Pope's view of satire, is that the compulsion to compose satire is represented as a spontaneous emotional force — 'My Head and Heart thus flowing thro' my Quill' — and also again as a distinctively masculine form of energy. This last point is subtly intimated in the sexual innuendo introduced by Pope in the opening exchanges (16-18), and in the rejection of the effete verse recommended ironically at 29-32. This is certainly the freest of all the *Imitations*, and the effect which Pope was aiming at is stated in Aaron Hill's response to his first perusal of the poem, referring to 'the honest vivacity of that piece', and lauding the 'man' above the 'poet'.[43] This animation anticipates the spirit of the two dialogues making up the *Epilogues*, where irony and defiance are again intensified, and by this stage freedom of expression for the satirist is seen as dependent on the power to attack specific individuals (I, 63-5). Pope pointedly redefines 'pride' and even 'impudence' in the celebrated lines justifying the morality and necessity of his compulsion (II, 205-9); his remarks on 'indignation and contempt' which preface the whole collection of satires are most fully expressed in these final works, showing that 'The strong Antipathy of Good to Bad' is as personal and as little abstract as the retaliatory attack should be: 'Th' Affront is mine, my Friend, and should be yours' (II, 197-204). The concern with virtue, driven home with the emphatic capitalised motto of *Satire II i* 'Uni aequus Virtuti atque ejus Amicis', is also presented as highly personal and spontaneous:

> Fond to spread Friendships, but to cover Heats,
> To help who want, to forward who excel;
> This, all who know me, know; who love me, tell.
> (*Satire II i*, 136-8)

The abstract 'friendship' to virtue is linked with the warmth of personal friendship which is celebrated in lines 125-32, and indeed throughout the *Imitations*, above all in *To Arbuthnot* where it is merged into filial piety and tenderness. This is described as 'no unpleasing Melancholy', a particularly solicitous and protective care which is associated with the waning of life rather than the engendering of it — 'Domestick Bliss' belongs to Arbuthnot, since Pope has no progeny but his writings, and this is accentuated by his reference to his duty 'To rock the Cradle of reposing Age' (409). In acting as nurse to his parent, Pope re-enacts the concerned care of Arbuthnot towards himself as a patient (one who among other infirmities may need protecting from his own dangerous humours), and himself practises the 'lenient Arts' which are by definition the very antithesis of satire. He pointedly identifies his own imputed virtues, of long-suffering patience in the face of attack and forgiveness of distressed or repentant antagonists, with the innocuous simplicity of both his parents, whose attributes likewise are pre-eminently neighbourly virtues. While they do indeed appear incongruous progenitors of a satirist, Pope's citing his line of descent from such harmless, uncontentious figures is in a manner to validate the origin of his own writing in 'innocent', well-natured beginnings, when 'The Muse but serv'd to ease some Friend' and when his writings were received 'with open arms' by good-natured men (125-42). The consciousness of Christian benevolence, however obliquely expressed, is a significant dimension in Pope's satire, and is expressed in a variety of contexts.[44] The final lines of the satire on Addison present the laughter of the satirist as a compulsion, but unite it with an avowal of regret which is the response of a more controlled magnanimity:

> Who but must laugh, if such a man there be?
> Who would not weep, if *Atticus* were he!

The verbs here are unobtrusive, but Pope's successive revisions of this couplet show how carefully they were weighed (see Johnson, *Lives*, III, 178). Throughout the *Imitations*, Pope builds on the central concerns in Horace's defence of his satire, but with an emphasis on high moral purpose and dignity which is distinctive; while the portrait of Addison is a complex masterpiece of 'sympathetic satire', at the other end of the scale there are the celebrated lines of *Dialogue II* which exalt and indeed transform the concept of 'Ridicule', presenting it as a 'sacred weapon' and the 'Sole Dread of Folly, Vice and Insolence' (212-19). R. L. Brett persuasively represents this as an expression of Shaftesbury's 'doctrine of ridicule', the conviction that satire is a valid medium for religion itself (*Characteristics*, II, 217),[45] and a vigorous means of attack which lies between the extremes of innocuous, laughing raillery and vindictive malice: 'with Pope ridicule knows no bounds; it is not something intrinsic to particular topics. Its object is vice, and the whole of evil is something to be ridiculed' (p.177). Ridicule becomes Pope's controlled power of 'Indignation and Contempt', ideally vituperative but not vindictive.

Almost all critics who have surveyed the *Imitations* as a whole have observed that Pope is in a marked degree more passionate and personal than his Roman model, and it is clear that, like Dryden, he is highly conscious of the inadequacies of Horace. It is worth asking what has become of the Horatian virtue of 'delicacy' in Pope's developing perspective. There are clear accusations of insipidity and hypocrisy on the part of Horace in the words given to 'Friend' in *Dialogue I*, 11-12, 19-22:

> But *Horace*, Sir, was delicate, was nice;
> *Bubo* observes, he lash'd no sort of *Vice*:....
> His sly, polite, insinuating stile
> Could please at Court, and make AUGUSTUS smile:
> An artful Manager, that crept between
> His Friend and Shame, and was a kind of *Screen*.

The irony against Horace here is certainly damning enough; Pope, however, has deliberately preserved an ambiguous attitude towards the lines by placing them in the mouth of the naive and self-condemning 'Friend', and there is almost certainly a double irony at work. 'Bubo' (Bubb Dodington, the lampoonist of *To Arbuthnot*, l.280, and flowery rhetorician of the *Dialogue*, l.68) is scarcely the best authority for judgement, and a note to his name reading 'Some guilty person very fond of making such an observation', is assigned to Pope in Warburton's text of 1751. The famous lines of Persius (*Satire I*, 116) are cited in a footnote as the source of the opprobrious line 22 — 'omne vafer vitium ridenti Flaccus amico / Tangit, et admissus circum praecordia ludit' — and as Weinbrot observes, Pope 'has the Friend employ only the most ambiguous part of Persius' description of Horace — his "sly insinuating Grace" — and ignore the affirmative lines immediately thereafter'.[46] This fact is open to diverse interpretations, but it does not argue critical depth in 'Friend', any more than in 'Bubo'. In one of Spence's entries for 1739 — one year after this *Dialogue* was published — Pope quotes these same lines with the observation that 'the best time for telling a friend of any fault he has is while you are commending him, that it may have the more influence upon him. And this I take to be the true meaning of the character which Persius gives of Horace'; he repeats this observation in April 1742, complaining that 'I scarce meet with anybody that understands delicacy.'[47] Both these remarks surely sound, if anything, like a defence of Horace from obtuse or hostile commentators; even Dacier, in his preliminary 'Preface' to the satires, makes the point that Horace could at first reading be taken for a superficial poet, and that his primary task as editor is to bring out the philosophical depth and lasting relevance of the works. We should also bear in mind that, as Shaftesbury observed, Horace's career was made up of mixed phases — the first as follower of Brutus and liberty, the second a 'debauched, slavish, courtly state', and the third a 'returning, recovering state' of moral rigour and introspection.[48] These distinctions need to be borne in mind in considering the range of Pope's responses to Horace as moralist and satirist. For Pope, the Horatian gifts of tact and sensitive irony appear as virtues which need not in themselves be demeaning, above all in the context of affection which he values highly. On the other hand, it need hardly be said that in the satires as a whole Pope is emphatically not engaged in persuading his friends of their foibles. The Horatian virtues are inadequate to his own satiric bent, and he makes a point of drawing this to the reader's attention — hence the complex irony of *Dialogue I*, 11-22. Such an independent and flexible attitude is indeed characteristic of many central discussions of Horace (Dryden's *Discourse* being a case in point); none the less, the first *Dialogue* is pointedly cast as a poem 'Something like Horace' in its first edition of May 1738. Given this choice of subtitle, it may well be true that Pope gained a certain freedom from the very differences which stood between himself and Horace which he could not have reached as imitator of the more intractably impassioned work of Juvenal.

Notes

1. *Anecdotes*, I, 143.
2. *See* particularly Weinbrot (note 3 below); and John Aden's *Something Like Horace* (Kingsport, Tennessee, 1969) and *Pope's Once and Future Kings; Satire and Politics in the Early Career* (Knoxville, Tennessee, 1978).
3. Weinbrot, 'History, Horace and Augustus Caesar', *ECS*, 7 (1974), 391-414, and *Augustus Caesar in 'Augustan' England* (Princeton, 1978); in the latter work (182-213), Weinbrot argues that Pope's 'Epistle to Augustus' (*Epistle II ii*) is as much engaged in irony at the expense of Augustus Caesar and his minion Horace as it is critical of England's George Augustus. *See also* his *Alexander Pope and the Traditions of Formal Verse Satire* (Princeton, 1982).
4. G. S. Rousseau, reviewing Maresca's *Pope's Horatian Poems* (Ohio, 1966); *PQ*, 47 (1968), 409.
5. Allan Rodway, in *The Times Literary Supplement*, 24 December 1982, 15.
6. Harte, *An Essay on Satire, Particularly on the 'Dunciad'* (1730), 15.
7. Dryden, *A Discourse Concerning the Original and Progress of Satire* (1693); in *Essays*, II (1962), 71-155.
8. Rogers, *The Major Satires of Alexander Pope* (Urbana, 1955), 85-6.
9. Dacier, *Remarques Critiques sur les Oeuvres d'Horace, Avec une nouvelle Traduction*, 10 vols (Paris, 1697); VI, 'Préface sur les Satires d'Horace'.

Weinbrot, in *The Formal Strain* (60) observes that 'Dacier's essay on Roman satire supplied both a title and much information for Dryden's "Discourse"', and documents the high reputation and influence of Dacier's edition. *See also* his 'André Dacier in 'Augustan' England: towards the reclamation of his *Horace*', *Romance Notes*, 7 (1966), 155-60.

10. Pope to Bolingbroke, September 1718; *Correspondence*, I, 492.

11. Morris, *Horace: Satires and Epistles* (Oklahoma, 1939; 1968 reprint), 156. *See also* W. S. Anderson, 'The Roman Socrates: Horace and his Satires', in *Critical Essays on Roman Literature: Satire*, ed, J. P. Sullivan (1963), 1-37.

12. Pope to Bethel, August 1734; *Correspondence*, III, 427.

13. Dixon, *The World of Pope's Satires* (1968), 34-8.

14. Dacier, *Oeuvres d'Horace*, VII, 86-7; 'Il ne veut pas que l'on croye que c'est luy qui parle: car il sentoit bien que cela seroit ridicule dans sa bouche, et qu'on se moqueroit de ses preceptes; parce qu'il estoit connu pour un homme qui aimoit la bonne chere.'

15. Pope's practice of printing the latin text beside his own version, with the key words and phrases picked out in bolder type, is an important index to the attentiveness with which he has responded to Horace.

16. Pope has accented the latin words 'mutatum ... vinum, / repotia, natales, / ... veteris non parcus aceti'.

17. Dacier observes that 'les Stoïciens et les Epicuriens estoient de different avis sur cette matiere', but he resolves the debate readily: 'l'amitié est une chose si sainte, que Platon n'a pas fait difficulté de dire, que Dieu en est l'Auteur. Il fait voir mesme, que les méchants ne sont pas capable de ce sentiment' (VII, 478). *See also* L. L. Davidow, 'Pope's verse epistles: friendship and the private sphere of life', *HLQ*, 40 (1977), 151-70, where it is observed that 'to an even greater extent than Cicero, Pope associates the abuse of friendship with political corruption' (151).

18. Aden, *Something Like Horace*, 47-68.

19. W. S. Anderson, 'The Roman Socrates' (see note 11, above), 26.

20. *See* G. D. Atkins, 'Strategy and purpose in Pope's *Sober Advice from Horace*', *Papers on Language and Literature*, 15 (1979), 159-74. By reference to this passage in particular (ll.96-105), Atkins proposes that Pope has developed a persona as spokesman who is more of an 'insinuating and arousing' rake and a pontificating moralist pleading for sexual licence than a truly moral satirist. Consequently there is a complicity and sympathy with the adulterers, and overall 'no contempt or ridicule is felt' (p.170). There is much that is valid and convincing in his reading, but it must be said also that Horace's *Satire I ii* is permissive in attitude, and I disagree with Atkins as to the total effect of Pope's version.

21. Thomas Creech complains of modern commentators in the 'Preface' to his translation of *The Odes, Satyrs and Epistles of Horace* (1684): 'all is permitted to every Eye, and laid open to the dullest sight by the most shameful Notes that can be pen'd: You may see a Grammarian with a demure mouth cry out, *O Foedum*! at a loose expression, and yet presently fill a Page with a more fulsom explication; and the design of all his pains is only to indulge a petulant Humor, or assist the lazy Ignorance of the common Instructors of our Youth.' Pope manages to draw attention to the relative discretion of his

version, as against the crudity and obvious *double entendres* of 'Bentley's' remarks (see for example TE, IV, 80n.).

22. *See also* Dixon's discussion, *The World of Pope's Satires*, 163-6.
23. Maresca, *Pope's Horatian Poems*, 176.
24. *Correspondence*, II, 179.
25. Brean Hammond, *Pope and Bolingbroke: A Study of Friendship and Influence* (Columbia, 1984), 110-25. See also Frank Stack's essay 'Pope's *Epistle to Bolingbroke and Epistle I i*' in *The Art of Alexander Pope*, ed Howard Erskine-Hill and Anne Smith (1979), 169-91.
26. Stack, *op. cit.*, 187.
27. *Characteristics*, II, 282n. Shaftesbury concedes that detachment represses 'the evils of love, ambition, vanity, luxury, and other disturbances' (II, 177), but adds that 'it need not be thought surprising that religion itself should in the account of these [Epicurean] philosophers be reckoned among those vices and disturbances which it concerns us after this manner to extirpate.' *See also* Addison's *Spectator* papers, nos. 237 (1711) and 413 (1712), in which admiration is represented as 'a very pleasing Motion of the Mind', pre-eminently directed towards the contemplation of God.
28. *Anecdotes*, I, 147.
29. Malebranche maintains that admiration is one of the 'weakest and least moving passions' (*Search After Truth*, I, *v, vi*; p.21).
30. Compare Pope to Jervas, August 1714 (*Correspondence*, I, 243), where he defines human vanity as 'a secret insisting upon what they think their dignity and merit, and an inward expectation of such an Overmeasure of deference and regard, as answers to their own extravagant false scale; and which no body can pay, because none but themselves can tell, exactly, to what pitch it amounts?'
31. Pope writes to the Duchess of Marlborough, August 1741 (*Correspondence*, IV, 359): 'Horace, (the first of that name who was no Fool) ... writ a whole Discourse to show, that All folks are mad, (even Poets and Kings not excepted.) he only begs one Favor, *That the Greater Madmen would spare the Lesser.*'
32. Pope's latin text, l.105, and translation ('confounded stuff', l.152) adopts Dacier's reading of the line in pointedly linking 'impunè' with 'legentibus' and not with 'obturem'. Dacier explains, 'cela est plus salé. Il donne un coup de dent à ces Poëtes en les appellant des liseurs outrés qui ont toute honte buë, et dont on ne sauroit se vanger' (IX, 506).
33. *Works*, ed Warburton, VIII, 197, 203.
34. *Essay on Satire*, pp. 29-30:

> What artful Hand the Wretch's Form can hit,
> Begot by *Satan* on a *M---ly*'s Wit:....
> Foe to the Learn'd, the Virtuous, and the Sage,
> A Pimp in Youth, an Atheist in old Age:
> Now plung'd in Bawdry and substantial Lyes,
> Now dab'ling in ungodly Theories;
> But so, as Swallows skim the pleasing flood,
> Grows giddy, but ne'er drinks to do him good:...

Whose softest Whisper fills a Patron's Ear,
Who smiles unpleas'd, and mourns without a tear.

Although the composition of *To Arbuthnot* had a long history, John Butt dates its conception only as far back as 1732 — two years after Harte's *Essay* was published — and the 'Sporus' sketch as a late addition ('Pope's poetical manuscripts', *Proceedings of the British Academy*, 40 (1954), 23-39).

35. *See* James Osborn's note, *Anecdotes*, I, 150.

36. Pope refers to this work in a letter to Cromwell of October 1710 (*Correspondence*, I, 99), and its influence is stressed by Weinbrot, *The Formal Strain: Studies in Augustan Imitation and Satire* (Chicago and London, 1969).

37. Creech in his 'Preface' observes: 'As for ill Nature, Horace requires none, nay disclaims it in a Satyrist ... and how much this method surpasses the rougher handling, every one may imagine who knows that 'tis more grievous to any man to be Ridicul'd than beaten.'

38. Pope commented to Spence on Scaliger's *Poetics* that it was 'an exceedingly useful book in its kind, and extremely well collected' (*Anecdotes*, I, 234).

39. *Quintus Horatius Flaccus accedunt nunc Danielis Heinsii* (Leyden, 1629) — this edition was in Pope's library, and was the chief source for his latin text. (*See* Lillian D. Bloom, 'Pope as textual critic: a bibliographical study of his Horatian text', *JEGP*, 47 (1948), 150-5).

40. Weinbrot (*The Formal Strain*, 68) notes that Johnson's *Dictionary* cites Dryden's 'Discourse' in glossing the secondary meaning of 'declamatory' as 'appealing to the passions'.

41. This letter is also quoted by R. W. Rogers, *Major Satires*, 81-2, and by Aden, *Something Like Horace*, 109.

42. Hunter, in *Essays in Criticism*, 10 (1960), 390-404.

43. Hill to Pope, May 1733; *Correspondence*, III, 370.

44. Compare Dryden's *Discourse* (Watson, 126) where the claims of charity and the Lord's Prayer are fully considered against the issues of revenge, extreme provocation, and the right to defend one's morals and reputation. *See also* P. K. Elkin, *The Augustan Defence of Satire* (Oxford, 1973), 96-8.

45. Brett, *The Third Earl of Shaftesbury: A Study of Eighteenth-Century Literary Theory* (1951), 174-8.

46. 'History, Horace and Augustus Caesar', 409. Weinbrot assumes that Pope was using 'Friend' as an unwitting mouthpiece for his own concerted attack on Horace. Malcolm Kelsall ('Augustus and Pope', *HLQ*, 39 (1976), 117-31) discusses these lines with much discretion in relation to the problem of political compromise.

47. *Anecdotes*, I, 228, 150.

48. *See* Martin Price, *To the Palace of Wisdom*, 164, and the discussion of Pope's relationship to Horace and Juvenal in Raman Selden's *English Verse Satire, 1590-1765* (1978), 128.

CHAPTER SIX

'Kind Self-conceit':
The Dunciad

It has been justly observed that the essential movement of Pope's *Dunciad* is actually one of contraction, rather than expansion, and of contraction as 'a cause, not just an effect'. While in terms of the mock-heroic action Dulness is shown to be extending her influence ever further towards an all-encompassing finale, this becomes possible because we are increasingly made aware of 'the mind as the empire of Dulness'; even in the early three-book ('A') version of 1728, we witness through Theobald's dreaming 'the withdrawal of the individual dunce from the world of art and nature common to all men, into a self-centred, indeed solipsistic world'.[1] Many of Pope's most vivid passages on the anarchy of the mind are already present in this version, but perhaps one of the most cogent signs of the relative seriousness of Book Four, in its apocalyptic closing passages above all, is the weight which Pope gives to the cult of 'Self' as a central element in the cult of Dulness. The goddess roundly instructs her train of followers that they should 'See all in *Self*, and but for self be born' (IV, 480), urging them to instigate a new religious figurehead 'Wrapt up in Self, a God without a Thought' (485), and she culminates her exhortation with the lines:

> All my commands are easy, short, and full:
> My Sons! be proud, be selfish, and be dull.
> (IV, 581-2)

The crowning hour of her triumph indeed has much in common with the Triumph of Vice closing the first dialogue of the *Epilogue to the Satires*:

> Kind Self-conceit to some her glass applies,
> Which no one looks in with another's eyes:

157

But as the Flatt'rer or Dependant paint,
Beholds himself a Patriot, Chief, or Saint.
(*Dunciad*, IV, 533-6)

Like the 'sweet *Nepenthe* of a Court', this is a state of being which presents pure undisturbed self-sufficiency, significantly as a reflection in the imagination, and thus in the lines of verse which follow (537-40), 'Int'rest' is described through the rainbow image which in Pope's writing so commonly denotes the force of imagination.

Self-centredness, then, is seen as the source both of interest, in the narrowest sense, and of whimsy in its most expansive and indeed extravagant manifestations. As a mock-eulogy and mock-'justification' of Dulness, there are certain passages in the 1742 fourth book of the *Dunciad* particularly which can be seen as ironic inversions of the ideal scheme propounded in *An Essay on Man* (though it should be emphasised that only a few passages are as charged with 'high seriousness' as this would imply), and in a number of points the relationship reflects links which subsisted between Book Four and the half-completed 'opus magnum'. In a variety of ways, the 'New Dunciad' is designed to exhibit and dramatise self-love as 'the spring of motion' in a perverted sense, emphasising that force, both paradoxically and seriously, as the root of innumerable vices and barbarities satirised in the poem. In examining this aspect of the work, it would perhaps be best first to give a short account of the 'opus magnum' question as it relates to this theme, and then to consider some of the subjects of Pope's satire as treated in the four books of the completed *Dunciad*.

From the scope of the satire in Book IV it appears that the poem owed much to the plans which Pope laid out in a letter to Swift (March 1736; *Correspondence*, IV, 5) for 'four Epistles, which naturally follow the Essay on Man', as follows:

1. Of the Extent and Limits of Human Reason, and Science,
2. A view of the useful and therefore attainable and of the un-useful and therefore un-attainable, Arts.
3. Of the nature, ends, application, and the use of different Capacities.
4. Of the use of *Learning*, of the *Science* of the *World*, and of *Wit*. It will conclude with a Satire against the misapplication of all these, exemplify'd by pictures, characters, and examples.

Pope's final statement, in particular, invites the application of these plans to the 'New Dunciad'; we also have the evidence of two entries by Spence (dated March 1743 and April 1744) in which Pope asserts that his projected epistle on education ('part of my Essay scheme') was eventually incorporated in the framework of Book IV.[2] In broad terms, these statements encompass a large part of the intellectual scope of the 'New Dunciad', although they do not seem directly to embrace its theological content. Other available evidence concerning the genesis of the poem is also set out by Leranbaum in her study of the 'opus magnum' (pp.131-54); of particular interest is an annotated volume of the three-book *Dunciad* (1736 edition) from the Berg Collection of the New York Public Library, which contains details (and two early sketches) for much of the scheme of Book IV — the virtuosi, Bentley and the universities, and the French governor with his pupils — in Jonathan Richardson's hand. These details are cryptically headed by Richardson 'Canto 2^d' and described as 'altered from the Second MS'; they are discussed by R. W. Rogers, who observes that 'the impossibility of dating the sketch' represents the chief difficulty in the way of ascertaining its context.[3] It may possibly represent an outline for one of the 'Epistles' mentioned by Pope to Swift, but Leranbaum provides detailed evidence to suggest that it is much more likely to be either a proposed revision to Book II of the 1728 *Dunciad*, or an earlier plan for Book II predating the first edition of the poem and revived by Pope after 1740 at the instigation of Warburton.[4] Her conclusion on this point, that 'the annotation is probably a copy of a working draft of *The Dunciad* prior to its first publication in 1728' (146), has important implications for the scope of ideas underlying the three-book *Dunciad*, which would thus anticipate Book IV more fully than might first be supposed; this hypothesis, however, must remain uncertain in the absence of collaborative evidence. At all events, it is very likely that Pope had planned out his satire on abuses in education in some detail before 1736, and that a large part of the outline of Book IV was charted before the advent of Warburton, whom Pope first met in 1740. It is above all the scope of 'Scriblerian satire' which forms the natural link between the three-book *Dunciad* and the 1742 fourth book, a link which is strengthened by the long history of the *Memoirs of Martinus Scriblerus* (finally published in 1741, but in preparation some twenty-five years before that date). At the same time, the Scriblerian concerns — in Kerby-Miller's words, 'their scorn for cant, hypocrisy, and enthusiasm, their fear of disorder and unbridled innovation, their distrust of projectors and schematists, and their contempt for metaphysical systems',[5] — have much in common with the concerns of the *Essay on Man*, and it is not surprising to find that for many years, perhaps from the very beginning, the plans for an extended *Dunciad* and for the 'opus magnum' were closely associated in Pope's mind. The satire of the Scriblerian *Memoirs* is focused on abuses of learning, and within this scope it also constitutes an attack on misplaced intellectual pride, the absurdity of disregarding the claims of the body (the inescapable reminder of our mortal condition), solipsism, and the 'Diseases of the Mind' which Martin ironically chooses as the problem on which to exercise his genius (*Memoirs*, ch. X). Whereas one of the greatest problems of the four-book *Dunciad* lies in the baffling diversity of follies and disorders satirised under the nomination of 'Dulness', the whole poem likewise contains a vital humanistic emphasis on the arrogance of cultivating reason (in its narrowest sense) to the neglect of man's other faculties, leaving the passions to take their own wayward paths without control; or, more dangerously, of subverting reason to serve the passions. As already noted, Pope's attack on excessive self-love and pride as passions which undermine social responsibilities is central to Book IV in particular, and the corruption of culture which is his major concern is shown to subsist through a fundamental disjunction of the head and heart. Dulness as 'Mother of Arrogance, and Source of Pride' fosters all intellectual blindness and prejudice, exalting selfishness as the unremitting attachment to one's mental conception of things, and the combative refusal to allow others to poach on the same territory.

The satire of the 'A' *Dunciad* in particular, concentrating on the ridicule of hack writers, predatory publishers and obtuse critics, repeatedly holds up their pride and self-interest as objects of contempt; a mock-note of 'Scriblerus' considers the would-be writers as presented by the author in the following moralistic terms: 'First, taking things from their original, he considereth the Causes creative of such authors, namely *Dulness* and *Poverty*; the one born with them, the other contracted, by neglect of their proper talent thro' self conceit of greater abilities.' Both in the poem itself and in the battery of prose commentary which (through a variety of tactics) supports it, Pope sets up the vanity and presumption of the dunces as a major target of satire; his mock-apology for the author's satire on their poverty (A.I,41n.) contrives to suggest that their moral degeneracy is wilful and born of their self-interest, yet also that financial necessity is the mother of untold vices including 'Malice' and 'Servility'. Their 'virtues' are, in the passage on the Cave of Poverty and Poetry, ironically inverted to cardinal vices:[6] impudence in the stead of Fortitude, self-imposed deprivation for Temperance, fear for Prudence and slavish time-serving for Justice (A.I,44-52).

This catalogue of ignoble passions springing from self-love is effectively evoked by frequent ironic allusions to classical texts, particularly to the epics of Virgil and Homer; throughout the poem, the heroic virtues of fortitude, magnanimity and social loyalty are inverted and debased through parody. Dulness is inspired to approach Theobald on the occasion of Lord Mayor's Day, an epitome of the state of passive self-conceit to which the hacks, like the public men of Britain, aspire:

> Pomps without guilt, of bloodless swords and maces,
> Glad chains, warm furs, broad banners, and broad faces.
> (I.85-6)

The complacent ritual of power and conquest is shown to have taken over from the active, conscientious exercise of power; Settle as 'City Poet' exists (as Dulness later reassures Theobald) in an equally withdrawn, slavish state of eternal lethargy, 'cloy'd with custard and with praise ... / Safe, where no critics damn, no duns molest' (I.247-9). This is the ideal condition of satiety and solipsism to which Dulness ultimately wafts her followers, not unlike the crowning stupor of the Court ('where no passion, pride or shame transport') described in the *Epilogue to the Satires*, and encountered again among the 'wonders of the Deep' by Smedley (ll.306ff.). Yet this state of stupor is represented as the corollary to the unbridled 'enthusiasm' of the hack ('*Lethe* and the *Land of Dreams* allegorically represent the *Stupefaction* and *visionary Madness* of Poets equally dull and extravagant', II.314n.). In the 'B' text version of this passage, the allegory is amplified to make more explicit the seeming contradiction, how 'the mingled wave /

Intoxicates the pert, and lulls the grave' (II.343-4); and thus visionary madness overtakes Theobald as he lies in the very lap of Dulness, 'a position of marvellous virtue':

> Then raptures high the seat of sense o'erflow,
> Which only heads, refin'd from reason, know.
> Hence, from the straw where Bedlam's Prophet nods,
> He hears loud Oracles, and talks with Gods.
> Hence the Fool's paradise, the Statesman's scheme,
> The air-built Castle, and the golden Dream,
> The Maid's romantic wish, the Chymist's flame,
> And Poet's vision of eternal fame.
>
> (III.5-12)

Sandy Cunningham has noted the close parallel between this passage and the description of the universal human 'Fool's paradise' in the *Essay on Man*, II.263-70,[7] and indeed Pope was engaged in revisions of successive editions of the *Dunciad* while composing that work. The lines from the *Essay*, like those on the ruling passion as the 'peccant part' of the soul, acknowledge that delusions and obsessions very close to those of madness are responsible for keeping mankind in a state of contentment and activity, an acknowledgement which is in its immediate context ironic. Hobbes defines 'Dulnesse' as the condition of having abnormally weak passions, madness as abnormally vehement passions; 'And if the Excesses be madnesse, there is no doubt but the Passions themselves, when they tend to Evill, are degrees of the same' (*Leviathan*, p.140). He also makes a distinction between the active form of madness ('Rage') and the passive ('Melancholy'), a classification which is reflected in the 'B' text by the statues, 'Cibber's brazen, brainless brothers', above Bedlam gates.[8] This motif of madness is a particularly potent one in the *Dunciad*, embracing the apparent oppositions of lethargy and frenetic activity perpetrated through Dulness; in this semi-conscious world, the dunces past and present exhibit their scowls and grimaces, (III.146-8; II.227-32), the Muses themselves are reduced to tortured screams, and the lunatic Ralph to howls which 'make Night hideous' (III. 154, 159). Warburton, in a note to the opening lines of the 'B' *Dunciad* (I.16n.), attempts to account for the conjunction of madness and Dulness according to the Hobbesian understanding of the terms:

The native Anarchy of the mind is that state which precedes the time of reason's assuming the rule of the Passions. But in that state, the uncontrolled violence of the Passions would soon bring things to confusion, were it not for the intervention of Dulness in this absence of Reason; who, though she cannot regulate them like Reason, yet blunts and deadens their Vigour, and, indeed, produces some of the good effects of it: Hence it is that Dulness has often the appearance of Reason.

While his explanation is altogether too schematic, it might justly be observed that in the *Dunciad* as a whole, the operation of Dulness tends to shift from the promotion of meaningless activity to the final overwhelming inertia which is her ultimate objective; thus the games of Book II are arbitrarily suspended in the sleep which is close cousin to death, and so at the end of the poem the poet himself succumbs unprepared to the mighty yawn. Pope's early 'lines on Dulness' (written in 1707) describe it as 'the safe Opiate of the Mind', the soporific of complacency; the phrase 'Opiate of the Soul' is applied to death in the *Epistle to a Lady*, l.91, and indeed the yawn of Dulness is pre-eminently a universal death.

Driving obliquely towards this fulfilment, the passions which persist in the dunces are pre-eminently of the destructive and the reductive kind. Pope's reference to the 'madness' of Dennis (I.104) is backed up with copious notes (TE,V, 72-4), stressing the extravagance of his notorious ill-temper, castigating his alleged spitefulness, and parodying his critical ideal of '*fury* and *pride of soul*' as facets of genius (II. 256n.). A degree of bitterness is in fact often brought out in the notes, modifying the fundamental gaiety and inventiveness of much of the 'A' *Dunciad*. Theobald's despairing sacrifice of his works in Book I (189ff.) is elaborated as though it represented a sudden access of patriotic fervour, ironically and pointedly set against the true nature of Theobald's resolution, which is to sell himself to the cause of faction in the shape of Mist's *Journal*; self-interest, and an attendant indifference to the fate of his literary offspring, are the targets of Pope's abuse. As Dulness eyes Theobald in his floundering (I. 109ff.) Pope makes a play of allusion identifying his state of despair with that of Milton's Satan,[9] and continues the mock-heroic bathos with the opening to Book II, where the exaltation of Theobald is already shaping his visage:

> The proud Parnassian sneer,
> The conscious simper, and the jealous leer,
> Mix on his look ...
>
> (5-7)

Again, Settle later laments his own and Cibber's 'transformation' into serpents at the Smithfield shows (III, 287-90), himself 'Reduc'd at last to hiss in my own dragon', in a seeming parody of the final punishment of Satan and his entourage undergoing their metamorphosis to snakes (*Paradise Lost*, X, 509-32).

Grotesque transformations and miscreations are vivid motifs of Pope's satire on the hacks, reflecting (like the serpents and the aberrations springing from Theobald's 'monster-breeding breast') their own state of being. The whole world of the *Dunciad* is of course in the shaping hands of Dulness, who like her protégées 'with self-applause her wild creation views' (I, 80), and Pope animates and parodies both the creative urge and the responses to such misbegotten pieces. The poets themselves produce the offspring of perverse conjugations:

> All that on Folly Frenzy could beget,
> Fruits of dull Heat, and Sooterkins of Wit.
> (B.I, 125-6)

and the progeny proves as bizarre as the manner of 'witty Fornication'. In the universe of the theatre, above all, the power of making all in one's mental image is supreme, and John Rich literally plays God with his lightning and thunder, riding the whirlwind and directing the storm (A. III, 251-60). 'At pleasure' (255) is the operative phrase in these verses, signifying both complete self-indulgence on the part of Rich and the unlimited power exercised by him over a world of cheap bombast and sensationalism, immediately gratifying to his audiences. In his jibing at the meagre exchange of popular fare between the dunces of the theatre and their gaping audiences, Pope draws attention particularly to the assault made on the passions through the debased travesties of drama:

> To move, to raise, to ravish ev'ry heart,
> With Shakespear's nature, or with Johnson's art,
> Let others aim: 'Tis yours to shake the soul

> With thunder rumbling from the mustard-bowl,
> With horns and trumpets now to madness swell,
> Now sink in sorrows with a tolling Bell.
>
> (II. 215-20)

The same specious appeal dominates Settle's visual extrava-
ganzas, which are eulogised by their creator in similar terms:

> "See now, what Dulness and her sons admire;
> See! what the charms, that smite the simple heart
> Not touch'd by Nature, and not reach'd by Art."
>
> (III. 226-8)

The force of the word 'admire' here clearly denotes the passion in
all its pejorative aspects, the mere overwhelming of the rational
faculties in favour of immediate and unreflective stupefaction.
Yet the motions of the 'simple heart' are represented as equally
delightful indulgence, often indeed as excited ecstasy or 'enthusiasm'; the dunces' creative productions and half-formed
monsters delight as expressions of their own natures, and in their
infantile histrionics they seem to comport themselves very much
as actors within their own discordant theatre, until Dulness finally
'lets the curtain fall' at the close of the poem.

It is in the Games which occupy Book II (Pope's most sustained
mock-heroic episode) that the combative framework is provided
for the dunces to enact their mutual jealousies, acquisitiveness
and arrogance ('Glory, and gain, th'industrious tribe provoke').
Within this scene the pride of the hack poet is transformed
miraculously to abject servility as he emulates his fellows in efforts
to gain patronage; the metaphor of 'tickling' the patron is made
suggestively sexual (see particularly ll. 203-4, 209-10), and the
idea of prostitution is reinforced in the note of 'Scriblerus' on the
prayer to Venus of the unknown youth:

> The satire of this Episode being levelled at the base flatteries of
> authors to worthless wealth or greatness, concludeth here with an
> excellent lesson to such men; That altho' their pens and praises
> were as exquisite as they conceit of themselves, yet (even in their
> own mercenary views) a creature unlettered, who serveth the pas-
> sions, or pimpeth to the pleasures of such vain, braggart, puft
> Nobility, shall with those patrons be ... much higher rewarded.

This is set beside the 'ardour' of the booksellers when placed in sight of the phantom poet as potential fodder (ll.47-8), crowned in the tyrannous arrogance of Lintot's speech ('with me began this poet, and shall end'), a pointed echo of the speech of Antilochus in the games of the *Iliad* (XXIII, 633). Antilochus, as Pope's note to his declaration points out, 'speaks with the Generosity of a gallant Soldier, and prefers his Honour to his Interest ... he is not concern'd for the value of [his prize], but as it was the Reward of Victory' (l.633n.). The inversion of values is emulated in the still greater presumption of Curll, whose 'heroic' qualities are also ironically elaborated in the prose commentary (II, 54n.) and whose predatory zeal and shamelessness distinguish him even above the other duncer: 'Still happy Impudence obtains the prize' (178). Emrys Jones's excellent essay on 'Pope and Dulness'[10] emphasises how compulsively the games express qualities of childishness in the dunces — the contestants' passionate rivalries, dismay at lost prizes, simple-minded satisfaction in conquests — an infantile regression which curiously renders the satire genial, conveying 'a primitive sense of liberation ... completely without self-consciousness', and which is accentuated by the role of Dulness herself as an indulgent mother figure. Their squabbles, however, also represent an extended parody of Book XXIII of the *Iliad*, in which (as Pope notes) even Homer's most dignified heroes succumb to intense rage and grief at the progress and outcome of the contests, 'transported with Trifles', 'betray'd into ... Indecency' (465n.) and illustrate in general how 'passionate Men betray themselves into Follies' (564n.).[11] The spirit of indulgence towards the dunces' antics is qualified by a vivid sense of the low and ludicrous, indeed of the contemptible, underlined by the scatological elements which are here exploited with unusual directness as a means of moral chastisement (A.II, 71-2).

When, in the four-book *Dunciad*, Pope made the decision to exalt Cibber to Theobald's throne, he found the perfect opportunity to develop his satire on impudence and vanity further. Cibber as comic actor is termed 'the Master of the sev'nfold Face' (B.I, 244), and in fact the face as the seat of expression (along with the prominent 'Cibberian forehead', emblem of impudence) becomes a particular focus of Pope's ridicule. Cibber is endowed with the 'bold visage' of natural shamelessness, and the phrase 'never-blushing Head' is used twice, in application both to himself and Norton (III, 231 and II, 417). In his self-sufficiency, Cibber becomes something of an entity, a metaphysical quintessence of self-ness, as the comic adjectival use of his proper name conveys:

> What then remains? Ourself. Still, still remain
> Cibberian forehead, and Cibberian brain.
> (I. 217)

The idea is brought forward again with the 'Cibberian forehead, and Cimmerian gloom' of IV, 532. The 'quintessential' aspect is again enforced by Dulness, who applies to Cibber the cyclical metaphor of eternal recurrence, once more subtly intimating pomposity, solipsism and pride as his attributes:

> All nonsense thus, of old or modern date,
> Shall in thee centre, from thee circulate.
> (III. 59-60)

The metaphor, so dominant throughout the *Dunciad*, is most strikingly opposed to that of the chain or progressive system of connected parts which dominates the *Essay on Man*. Cibber's qualities of plenitude, his sufficiency unto himself, comform perfectly with Dulness' ulterior aims, and are expounded in Pope's prose 'Advertisement' ('one, who from every Folly (not to say Vice) of which another would be ashamed, has constantly derived a *Vanity*'),[12] as well as by Warburton ('Ricardus Aristarchus of the Hero of the Poem'), who observes that vanity is a just substitute for wisdom as each seeks its 'chief support and confidence within itself':

> It being agreed that the constituent qualities of the greater Epic Hero, are *Wisdom, Bravery*, and *Love*, from whence springeth *Heroic Virtue*; it followeth that those of the lesser Epic Hero, should be *Vanity, Impudence*, and *Debauchery*, from which happy assemblage resulteth *heroic Dulness*... (TE,V, 256).

There is a similar inverted relationship between the attributes of Dulness (particularly as she appears in the 'New Dunciad') and the virtues which Pope had outlined for his own epic hero Brutus; the sketch of the Egerton Manuscript reads: 'Benelovence ye First

Principle and Predominant in Brutus. Thence a strong Desire to Redeem ye Remains of his countrymen ... & To establish their freedom and felicity in a Just Form of Governmt ... The Love of his Country induces his Voyage', and superstition, anarchy and tyranny are set up as evils to be combated by these virtues. These are the concerns which deepen the satire of Book IV of the *Dunciad*, with its more desperate emphasis on political and ecclesiastic corruptions. Miriam Leranbaum comments on the 'Brutus' plan,

> this legend must have seemed to Pope eminently appropriate as a framework for developing the themes of Epistle III of *An Essay on Man*. It provided excellent material by which Epistle III's concerns with freedom, benevolence, the nature of good governments and bad, the contrasts between primitive and civilised peoples, and the virtues of self-love transformed into social love could be given concrete development. (p.165)

The outline, together with the subject set out in Pope's letter to Swift (p.158 above), suggests the enormous range of ideas which informed Pope's expansion of the *Dunciad* to its final form. The satire is still conveyed by the frequent interspersal of 'pictures, characters, and examples' — in fact these tableaux are much more distinct and extended than in the 'A' *Dunciad* — but they are contained within an intellectual framework which is richer and more explicit in significance.

One of the central themes is of course that of the first Epistle mentioned by Pope to Swift, 'Of the Extent and Limits of Human Reason, and Science', and in this context there are particularly interesting links with the scope of Walter Harte's *Essay Upon Reason* (1735), with which Pope was so pleased that he was eager to have it taken at first for one of his own works.[13] It is indeed likely that, as Joseph Warton and Alexander Chalmers stated, he had some hand in its composition.[14] The scheme of Harte's poem shares the optimism of the *Essay on Man*, but while it asserts that reason is a faculty fully accessible to man despite the Fall ('Enough remains for ev'ry social end, / For practice, theory, self, neighbour, friend'), there is also a sceptical emphasis on the difficulty of attaining a truly rational balance:

REASON, like Virtue in a Medium lies;
A Hairs-breadth more might make us *mad* not *wise*,...
For *Reason* like a King who thirsts for Pow'r,
Leaves Realms unpeopled, while it conquers more.[15]

(p.7)

The proper exercise of reason should thus consist in recognising
the true limits of that faculty; it represents a 'Point, round which
th'eternal error lies / Of *fools* too credulous, and *wits* too wise'.
Harte draws a truly desperate picture of the all-too-common state
of confusion in which the soul hopelessly labours:

Where *Prepossession* warps the ductile mind,
Where blindfold *Education* leads the blind:
Where *Int'rest* biasses, *ill Customs* guide,
And *strong Desires* pour on us like a tide;...
Where *Zeal* her unknown vow of fury keeps,
And *Superstition* like an Idiot weeps;...
Where *Pride* still list'ning to herself appears,
New forms earth's orbit, and new rolls the spheres.

(p.26)

This view of intellectual and moral chaos is altogether very close
to the world of the 'New Dunciad', and it is also notable that
Harte's terms throughout the *Essay* show a strong interest in the
social and political implications of his exposition (particularly in
his use of metaphor, replete with images of tyranny, kingship, and
anarchy within the microcosm of man, and his references to
superstition as the weakness of reason in attempting to rise to the
conception of God). One is reminded in these references of the
triumphs planned for Brutus in his 'purpose of extending
Benevolence' over tyranny, anarchy and superstition; for both
Harte and Pope, these states are built on the triumph of irrationality, and thus Book III of the *Essay on Man* presents the 'Origin of
Superstition and Tyranny, from the same principle, of Fear'. One
of Harte's most interesting passages concerns the emergence of
the 'Thinking Faculty' from its state of infancy, when it is almost
entirely overborne by the violence of the passions:

... till the Finishing of thrice sev'n years,
Ye Master-Figure *Reason* scarce appears;
Sighs to survey a Realm by right its own,

While *Passion* (fierce co-heir) usurps the throne;...
Sad farce of pow'r, sad anarchy of things,
Where brutes are subjects, and where tyrants kings.
(p.12)

Education is the primary process by which the proper balance of will with impulse may be established, and as such it clearly held much interest for Pope. There can be no doubt that the savage survey of contemporary abuses in education is of paramount importance in the fourth book of the *Dunciad*; it marks the formative stages of all that Pope understands by duncery. C.R. Kropf, in his study of the ideal of wisdom informing the poem,[16] goes so far as to assert that 'the entire final book of *The Dunciad*, not only the two hundred lines usually cited (ll.149-336), is a satire on abuses in contemporary education'. This seems to be true only in a broad sense, but the many threads which connect Pope's exposition of the subject with the themes of the *New Dunciad* are worth exploring. It is apparent that for Pope the educational process concerns not only an ideal of wisdom but an ideal of human nature.

This theme is central to Montaigne's essay, 'Of Pedantry', in which he notes that 'Plato's principal Institution in his Republick is, to fit his Citizens with Employments suitable to their Nature. Nature can do all, and does all';[17] and it is the emphasis on 'nature' in the process of fitting men for society which represents as important an issue in education as the threatened disjunction between 'words' and 'ideas' which Aubrey Williams, like Kropf, makes the focus of his attention.[18] One of the most striking points about Pope's satire on the educational process is that its results are so grossly unnatural; 'Silenus' (Thomas Gordon) presents the youth constricted by every stage of the educational process,

Bounded by Nature, narrow'd still by Art,
A trifling head, and a contracted heart.
(IV. 503-4)

while at the other extreme (but with no better effects) the young fop is presented, shot into premature 'adulthood' by sheer impudence and self-conceit:

> Thou gav'st that Ripeness, which so soon began
> And ceas'd so soon, he ne'er was Boy, nor Man.
> (287-8)

These lines, together with Warburton's explanatory note, are probably indebted to Swift's *Intelligencer* paper no. 9 (1728), an encomium on the 'traditional sloth and luxury' kept up by the educational methods of the upper classes, indulgence and the debauchery of French tutors:

> By these Methods, the young Gentleman is in every Article as fully accomplished at eight Years old, as at eight and twenty; Age adding only to the Growth of his Person and his Vices; so that if you should look at him in his Boyhood through the magnifying End of a Perspective, and in his Manhood through the other, it would be impossible to spy any Difference. (*Prose Writings*, XII, 50).

The pernicious effects of distorting human nature through education were nowhere developed more persuasively than in Locke's treatise *Some Thoughts Concerning Education* (1693),[19] which had an enormous influence on the many surveys of the subject published in the early eighteenth century, and not least upon a number of the *Spectator*, *Tatler* and *Guardian* papers. The tenor of Locke's ideas on discipline and freedom is strongly indebted to other works well known to Pope, including Montaigne's essays and Vida's *Poetica* (1527),[20] and his approach presents a familiar humanistic emphasis on the difference of individuals and their capacities; the *Thoughts* are also a natural successor to the *Essay on Human Understanding*, bearing out the theory of the 'association of ideas' most clearly in responses to reward and punishment. Education is seen as a deliberate moulding of the personality, with ineradicable consequences (Locke, *Thoughts*, § 1, § 45), and Locke is fully committed to the principle of self-discipline which it ideally nurtures:

> He that has not a Mastery over his own Inclinations, he that knows not how to *resist* the Importunity of *present Pleasure or Pain*, for the sake of what Reason tells him is fit to be done, wants the true Principle of Vertue and Industry; and is in Danger never to be good for any thing.

He also stresses the attention that should be paid by every tutor to the desires and attributes of the individual child, the use to which the natural pleasure in knowledge can be put, and the futility and damaging effects of over-severity in physical punishment (§ 46-52). Montaigne's essay 'Of the Education of Children' (Cotton, I, 253; no.XXV) contends that "Tis not a Soul, 'tis not a Body that we are training up, but a man, and we ought not to divide him', and the method he approves is one of 'severe sweetness' rather than the more customary violence, 'than which, I certainly believe nothing more dulls and degenerates a well-descended Nature. If you would have him apprehend shame and chastisement, do not harden him to them.' The idea that education represents the guiding of the passions — the sense of shame and the drive to emulation — to social and rational ends likewise appears in a number of *Spectator* papers, including no. 215 (by Addison), no. 224 (by Pope's friend John Hughes) and no. 408, which has often been attributed (probably incorrectly) to Pope himself.[21] It is also central to George Turnbull's compendium *Observations upon Liberal Education*, published in 1742, which ambitiously aims to present a unified synposis of 'all that hath been said by the ancients or moderns on the subject': 'The great arcanum in education consists in forming self-denial and mastership of the passions, without weakening the vigour and activity of the mind' ('Contents', viii). Viewed in these terms, the educational process becomes a natural corollary to Pope's theory of the passions, and it is in this context that it is put forward in *Spectator* no. 408, which Pope would certainly have read with interest if he was not the author of it:

> The extraordinary Severity used in most of our Schools has this fatal Effect, it breaks the Spring of the Mind, and most certainly destroys more good Geniuses than it can possibly improve. And surely 'tis a mighty Mistake that the Passions should be so intirely subdued.

Locke's contention that 'such a sort of *Slavish Discipline* makes a *Slavish Temper*' (§ 50) is well illustrated in the effects of the spectre Busby, who makes his appearance in Book IV shrouded in Miltonic horror, with due emphasis on 'the Virtue of the dreadful Wand':

His beaver'd brow a birchen garland wears,
Dropping with Infant's blood, and Mother's tears.
O'er ev'ry vein a shudd'ring horror runs;
Eton and Winton shake thro' all their Sons.
All Flesh is humbled, Westminster's bold race
Shrink, and confess the Genius of the place;
The pale Boy-Senator yet tingling stands,
And holds his breeches close with both his hands.[22]

(IV. 141-8)

It is significant that Pope's satire here makes the leap from school to political life in the reference to the 'pale Boy-Senator', which once again implies that adulthood has been permanently set back, and fear made life's dominant passion (148n.).

At the other extreme, Pope's travelling fop (IV. 282-330) represents the alternative pitfall in education, that of over-indulgence; with the combined effects of his mother's dotage, his protection from physical chastisement and his selective instruction, he is presented to Dulness as

Thine from the birth, and sacred from the rod,
A dauntless infant! never scar'd with God.

(283-4)

The folly of indulgence was a favourite topic among educationalists, and Pope links it with the equally popular theme of travel as an extension of education, the merits of which were a point of much debate.[23] In the case of the fop, the tour is undertaken prematurely, immediately after his release from schooling, and in the company of a tutor who merely assists him in cultivating his vices:

Led by my hand, he saunter'd Europe round,
And gather'd ev'ry Vice on Christian ground;

(311-12)

The choice of the verb 'saunter'd' here is probably pointed, since Locke speaks much of the 'Sauntering Humour' (indolence and lack of direction) as one of the worst and most intractable traits that can be encountered in a child (§ 123ff.). Pope's descriptive passage (297-310) powerfully evokes the sense of 'Languor' in the lap of sensuality, and the images are of *public* degeneracy undermining whole cultures, including that of the formerly masculine Romans (299).

In reaching the aim of social utility and social love, the ideal path consists in drawing the child out of its self-centredness through its natural curiosity, the path of pleasure; curiosity is treated by Locke and Turnbull as an 'appetite', ultimately gratified by the perception of 'final causes'.[24] This progression towards the fulfilment of enquiry is expressed in terms of the 'sapiential ladder', the hierarchy of understanding beginning with sensation and culminating in the exercise of reason;[25] it is discussed in somewhat elaborate detail by Harte (*Essay*, p.13), and in simpler terms by the author of the *Guardian* no. 62 (1713), who evokes the ideal delights of schooldays, 'the dawn of reason':

> As our Parts open and display by gentle degrees, we rise from the gratifications of sense, to relish those of the mind. In the scale of pleasure, the lowest are sensual delights, which are succeeded by the more enlarged views and gay portraitures of a lively imagination; and these give way to the sublimer pleasures of reason, which discover the causes and designs, the frame, connexions and symmetry of things, and fills the mind with the contemplation of intellectual beauty, order and truth.[26]

What is significant in this account is that it presents a scheme of intellectual development alongside a natural 'scale of pleasure' which answers the desires of the developing man. When the spectre Busby boasts of the efforts whereby youth are kept from mounting these upper rungs of the sapiential ladder, he is presenting the spiritual counterpart of his delight in thrashing his pupils; the images of constriction and incarceration have a distinctively sadistic turn, and follow relentlessly on from the momentary evocation of delight in lines 155-6:

> To ask, to guess, to know, as they commence,
> As Fancy opens the quick springs of Sense,
> We ply the Memory, we load the brain,
> Bind rebel Wit, and double chain on chain,
> Confine the thought, to exercise the breath;
> And keep them in the pale of Words till death.
> Whate'er the talents, or howe'er design'd,
> We hang one jingling padlock on the mind.
>
> (155-62)

Similarly, Bentley eulogises the work of the universities in 'binding' the brain with cement, presenting the finished product with the challenge,

> Then take him to develop, if you can,
> And hew the Block off, and get out the Man.[27]
> (269-70)

This picture of the fate of the intellectual Tantalus would present the world of the 'New Dunciad' as a kind of training-ground for Hell, as in a sense it is; but Pope's emphasis is, on the contrary, directed to the great compensatory pleasures which confirmed self-absorption, 'a trifling head, and a contracted heart', can offer. Delight is pre-eminently part of the dunces' experience, and part of the feeling for perverse beauty which is so strong in the *Dunciad* as a whole:

> The most recluse, discreetly open'd, find
> Congenial matter in the Cockle-kind;
> The mind, in Metaphysics at a loss,
> May wander in a wilderness of Moss;
> The head which turns at super-lunar things,
> Poiz'd with a tail, may steer on Wilkins' wings.
> (447-51)

It is the theme of the fourth of Montaigne's essays 'That the Soul discharges her Passions upon False Objects, where the true are wanting', and likewise Turnbull, discussing the passion of 'admiration', observes that if it is not properly directed towards 'moral beauty', it will 'worship some false image of it':

> Intelligent love of the polite arts may have too large a share of our affections ... It may warm the mind to a ridiculous extravagant excess, and take it off from more serious and important pursuits. The same may happen with respect to delight in botany, or any other science, and to the love of speculation and study in general. (p.139)[28]

Turnbull's warnings on this head are of course highly derivative, but they provide a succinct commentary which is relevant to the obsessions of the literary hacks, virtuosi and enthusiasts of the *Dunciad*;[29] their compulsions represent both self-indulgence and a presumptuous, unqualified faith in the power of individual reason, 'of which we have most cause to be diffident' (IV. 481n.). Pope's note to the couplet of IV. 500-1 clarifies the meaning of the 'contracted heart' as the final consequence of miseducation:

> A Recapitulation of the whole Course of Modern Education describ'd in this book ... The whole finished in modern Free-thinking; the completion of whatever is vain, wrong, and destructive to the happiness of mankind, as it establishes *Self-love* for the sole Principle of Action.

A potent means of heaping scorn on intellectual pride is to draw particular attention to the body's less dignified but equally insistent claims, as Montaigne does in his essay 'Of the Education of Children' ('how many have I seen in my time totally brutified by an immoderate Thirst after Knowledge? *Carneades* was so besotted with it, that he would not find time so much as to comb his Head, or to pare his Nails'),[30] and as Pope does in his early type-character 'Artimesia', the woman of erudition:

> Yet in some Things methinks she fails,
> 'Twere well if she would pare her Nails,
> And wear a cleaner Smock.
> (TE,VI, 48-9)

Martinus Scriblerus is likewise presented in a sorry physical condition, emphasised by his austere bearing:

> But under this macerated form was conceal'd a Mind replete with Science, burning with a Zeal of benefiting his fellow-creatures, and filled with an honest conscious Pride, mixt with a scorn of doing or suffering the least thing beneath the dignity of a Philosopher. Accordingly he had a soul that would not let him accept of any offers of Charity, at the same time that his body seem'd but too much to require it. (*Memoirs of Martinus Scriblerus*, 'Introduction')

Martin's follies are treated in a more genial spirit than those of the dunces (particularly those of the 'New Dunciad'), but his misplaced 'Zeal' and selfish pride masquerading as dignity are paradigms of duncery. His fervour in the cause of science is also given overtones of indecency by ironic association with sexual passion, a dimension of experience which brings out Martin's highest degree of obtuseness and distortion; he avidly investigates the case of the woman 'marked with a Pomegranate upon the inside of her right Thigh' ('Forthwith was I possessed with an insatiable curiosity to view this wonderful Phaenomenon. I felt the ardour of my passion encrease as the season advanced, till in the month of July I could no longer contain'; p.93). The imbalance of his consitution and extravagance of his self-conceit are depicted as a consequence of his education, marked by the pride and dementia of his father, who starves the child for fear of nurturing 'ungovernable Passions'.[31] Similarly, he suffers the intellectual deprivation of possessing only 'single apprehensions', but 'neither of the other two faculties, the *judicium* or *discursus*', enabling him only to 'form single Ideas with a great deal of vivacity' (*Memoirs*, ch. VIII).

Among the many facets of duncery, Pope thus emphasises that there is a turning of the passions away from their proper paths, into narrow channels springing from self-love which express the imbalance of the whole man. The final initiation into the 'mysteries' of Dulness commences with the libation from 'The *Cup* of *Self-Love*, which causes a total oblivion of the obligations of Friendship, of Honour, and of the Service of God and our Country; all sacrified to Vain-glory, Court-worship, or yet meaner considerations of Lucre and brutal Pleasures' (517n. — 'his Cup &C.'). The jibes at Walpole in this 'allegory' are brilliantly sharpened through Pope's allusion to the nepenthe of Homer (518n.), which is much more than a soporific; the passage cited elaborates its effects in drowning all moral or emotional response:

> Charm'd with that virtuous draught, th' exalted mind
> All sense of woe delivers to the wind.
> Though on the blazing pile his parent lay,
> Or a lov'd brother groan'd his life away,
> Or darling son oppress'd by ruffian-force
> Fell breathless at his feet, a mangled corse,
> From morn to eve, impassive and serene,
> The man entranc'd wou'd view the deathful scene.
> (*Odyssey*, IV.307-14; Pope's translation)

The passions are thus represented either in a state of stupefaction, or in a state of immaturity which resembles a perpetual infancy.

In the first three books of the *Dunciad*, the state of the passions is chiefly conveyed through the 'heroic' actions of the dunces, ironic allusions and the expositions of the footnotes; but when Pope laid out his scheme for the 'four Epistles' to Swift, his final reference to 'pictures, characters and examples' marked out an important dimension of the 'New Dunciad', that is the depth and trenchancy of the many character sketches, drawing Book IV closer to the *Moral Essays* in technique. The longest of these character sketches are executed through self-revealing speeches, and the portraits that emerge show Pope developing a series of familiar types; Bentley's (ll.203-75) is an example of sustained and detailed satire on a recognisable individual, but in its emphasis on his arrogance in every sphere of life it also becomes a pastiche of the scholar–critic as he tends to appear in Restoration and Augustan satires — ignorant, coercive and opinionated. The confrontation of Annius and Mummius displays the archetypal deceitfulness and avarice of the former, the fierce envy of the latter; in all the portraits, the private obsession is allied to a fundamental passion. Although Boyce (*Character-Sketches*, p.108) contends that the 'New Dunciad' shows no sign of Pope's former interest in the idea of the 'ruling passion', it could well be argued that his lines on the subject in the *Essay on Man* are strikingly appropriate to the distortion of the mind exposed in the dunce, particularly in application to the bad effects of education:

> Each vital humour which should feed the whole,
> Soon flows to this, in body and in soul.
> Whatever warms the heart, or fills the head,
> As the mind opens, and its functions spread,
> Imagination plies her dang'rous art,
> And pours it all upon the peccant part.
>   Nature its mother, Habit is its nurse;
> Wit, Spirit, Faculties, but make it worse;
> Reason itself but gives it edge and pow'r;
> As Heav'n's blest beam turns vinegar more sowr.
>   (*Essay on Man*, II. 139-48)

The description in lines 141-2 in particular brings to mind the growth of the intellect through the 'sapiential ladder' discussed above (p.174); there is the same vital link established through the 'gay portraitures of a lively imagination', as also in Harte's account (*Essay Upon Reason*, pp.12-14), tending either to enlarge the perspective, or to foster dangerous delusions, according to how it is developed. With the growth of the ruling passion, as with the narrowing process of a constrictive education, the intensification is potentially destructive; as already argued, Pope concentrates on the notion of the passion as 'the Mind's disease' (l.138), an epithet which very nearly denotes madness.

Pope's concern with the concept of faculties narrowed and at the same time concentrated by their singleness of direction is further expressed in the fact that two of the central figures in the 'New Dunciad', the carnation-grower and butterfly-catcher, are taken directly from the 'Theophrastan' mode as developed by La Bruyère and Edward Young.[32] They are familiar as representations of obsessional types relentlessly pursuing their entrenched, ritual actions, rather than as characters of Cartesian complexity and paradox. None the less, there are hints of complexity in Young's treatment, and doubtless Pope's admiration for *Love of Fame* led him to develop the portrait of 'Florio' from the second Satire (pp.24-5), and the carnation-grower from the idea of Young's following sketch on the tulip crushed by the anti-idolatrous Quaker. Young attempts to moralise the incidents through his guiding motif of 'love of fame', the shallowness of ambition, and particularly the folly of directing this passion to transient objects, but there are further depths in his suggestion that the grower becomes deeply identified with the flower, until the adoration becomes distinctly sexual and the man himself almost joins the tulip species:

> From morn to night has *Florio* gazing stood,
> And wonder'd how the Gods could be so good.
> What shape? what hue? was ever nymph so fair?
> He doats! he dies! he too is *rooted* there.

This last hint of a 'metamorphosis' through mental fixation is lightly echoed in Pope's reclusive seekers of 'congenial' cockles, and more explicitly in the description of the butterfly-catcher in chase of his quarry; the allusion to Milton which is footnoted (427, 28n.) refers to Eve's discovery of her own reflection in the water, and her sense of rapture which (by God's intervention and direction) is to be transformed to love for Adam as a more exalted object of desire. By implication, the butterfly-chaser's passion is an oblique form of solipsism, self-reflecting and almost mechan-istic:

> It fled, I follow'd; now in hope, now pain;
> It stopt, I stopt; it mov'd, I mov'd again.
> (427-8)

The ardour of the pursuit itself perhaps carries echoes of the *Metamorphoses*, with a fine twist whereby the pursuer 'becomes' the pursued. Likewise the sexual passion of the carnation-grower is transferred to his flower, and his anguish at its 'violation' reaches heights of lyricism and depths of despair untouched by Young. The solicitude for the flower, the care in its nurturing, 'christening' and exaltation, is not only sexual but maternal, and the attempt to usurp the role of nature is altogether a source for much more complex irony than it is for Young:

> Did Nature's pencil ever blend such rays,
> Such vary'd light in one promiscuous blaze?
> Now prostrate! dead! behold that Caroline:
> No Maid cries, charming! and no Youth, divine!
> And lo the wretch! whose vile, whose insect lust
> Lay'd this gay daughter of the Spring in dust.
> (411-16)

This grief and rage, however, is overborne by the impudence of the butterfly-collector whose damning 'innocence of mien' reflects total faith in the claims of the standard of success, as well as the mean-minded acquisitiveness which destroys the essence of all that it pursues:

> "Rose or Carnation was below my care;
> I meddle, Goddess! only in my sphere.
> I tell the naked fact without disguise,
> And, to excuse it, need but shew the prize;
> Whose spoils this paper offers to your eye,
> Fair ev'n in death! this peerless *Butterfly*."
> (431-6)

In these speeches, and in the comically fortuitous blundering of one fanatic into the closely-guarded delights of another, there is a fascinating drawing together of the sense of life and the sense of death, which is extended to the spiritual; disproportionate intensity yielding itself all too vulnerably to its own destruction. The negative cycle is perhaps acknowledged and approved by Dulness in her benign dismissal of the contention ('My Sons! (she answer'd) both have done your parts'; 437).[33] Within the wider scheme of Dulness' advent, the temporary 'pertness' of the virtuosi, the compulsive concentration of all their passions and energies on the smallest possible object, suffices to keep them fixed and absorbed in preparation for their final laying to rest. The sinking of self-consciousness is accomplished as effectively through an obsession as through brazen insensibility, and the overweening assurance expressed unapologetically by the butterfly-catcher is experienced vicariously by the relatively innocent carnation-grower in the exaltation of his virgin flower from its 'humble bed' to 'one promiscuous blaze'. Following on from this encounter is the final libation (or inebriation) administered by Dulness, when 'Firm Impudence, or Stupefaction mild' are communicated to all her disciples, in which section (517-41) Pope conveys the drowning of sensibility and the yielding to sensuality through a series of allusions to the *Odyssey*, not only in the stupefying nepenthe but in the charms of Circe reducing men to beasts and in the subversive blandishments of the Sirens. Dulness' final hour is 'all-composing', and here she finally subsumes all with her oppressive, debilitating reign of matronly indulgence and complaisance. Pope begs the Muse to relate how the goddess stifles even the animating force of self-love:

> What Charms could Faction, what Ambition lull,
> The Venal quiet, and intrance the Dull?
>
> (623-4)

but the 'Song' itself succumbs to and is cut short by these same powers. With the dying of passions which are so much castigated in the poem as a whole comes the ultimate death, the Miltonic 'Night' of Dulness, precedent to human existence and human impulses themselves. Significantly, she brings too the death of the imagination:

> Before her, *Fancy's* gilded clouds decay,
> And all its varying Rain-bows die away.
>
> (631-2)

There is a certain paradox in this, in that the very forces which have been taken to exemplify Dulness are finally destroyed by her, 'clos'd one by one to everlasting rest'. Sleep, so often presented in the poem as the medium of dreaming, visionary inspiration, the free reign of discordant passions and madness, becomes finally antithetical to passion.

As B. L. Reid argues, the *Dunciad's* 'new world' has a quality of completeness which draws it nearer to that of the *Rape of the Lock* than might be first supposed; in the latter, 'we see nothing but this world because it is what is left, the trivial absolute created by absolute vanity',[34] while in the *Dunciad* we are presented with an equally unreal, grotesque inflation of vanities and vices, closer to the bizarre, unconscious underworld of the *Rape*. This is perhaps to draw both works together on a restricted level, but the analogies on this level are none the less important. In both cases it is the consistent distortion of perspectives and the totality of the mythic vision composed which has compelling force; in both, the bathos of the mock-heroic is expressed above all in a dominion of the infantile, combining immaturity and a kind of innocence with destructive impulsiveness and the chaos of whimsical indulgence. The concern with destructiveness is much intensified in the *Dunciad's* Book IV, which as already argued has an affinity with the more acerbic, apocalyptic sections of Pope's later satires. With this intensification, the four-book *Dunciad* presents altogether a vividly dramatised exposition of Pope's fundamental assumptions on the subject of moral degeneracy, assumptions which the fourteen-year gap in the publication dates of the two *Dunciads* had done little to alter.

Notes

1. David Sheehan, 'The movement inward in Pope's *Dunciad*', *Modern Language Studies*, 8 (1978), 33-9; 37.
2. *Anecdotes*, I, 151, 134.
3. Rogers, *Major Satires*, Appendix B ('The missing *Dunciad* manuscripts'), pp.120-3. Richardson's outline is set out on a blank page before the title page of the 1736 *Dunciad* volume.
4. Leranbaum, *Pope's 'Opus Magnum'*, 146-7; Richardson seems to have pre-

pared the 1736 text from the MS draft for Pope's use in revising the poem.

5. C. Kerby-Miller (ed.), *Memoirs of the Extraordinary Life, Works, and Discoveries of Martinus Scriblerus* (New Haven and London, 1950), 73.

6. This passage may well reflect the 'two extremes to each of the cardinal virtues' which Pope told Spence had formed an early part of his plans for the 'opus magnum' (*Anecdotes*, I, 134).

7. Cunningham, 'Bedlam and Parnassus; eighteenth century reflections', *Essays and Studies*, (n.s.) 24 (1971), 36-55; 40. Thomas Fitzgerald's poem 'Bedlam', perhaps reflecting the 1728 *Dunciad*, includes a similar catalogue of lunatics (*Poems on Several Occasions*, 1733, 11), concluding, 'In these poor *Bedlamites* thy Self survey, / Thy Self, less innocently mad than They.' The necessity and delights of folly, so memorably eulogised by Erasmus, are very much of a commonplace; cf. James Miller's *An Hospital For Fools: A Dramatic Fable* (1739), in which it is asserted that all men are equally fools, and that 'the Happiness of Mankind is so complicated with their folly, that it is impossible to cure them of the one, without endangering the other too' (26-7).

8. The states of madness represented in the statues are discussed by David B. Morris, 'The kinship of madness in Pope's *Dunciad*', *PQ*, 51 (1972), 813-31.

9. Similarly, the title page to Richard Savage's satire on the hacks, *An Author to be Lett* (1729), bears the motto 'Evil be thou my Good. SATAN'.

10. Jones, 'Pope and Dulness', *Proceedings of the British Academy*, 54 (1968), 231-63.

11. In a synoptic note (n.323), Pope approves the 'more lively Picture of natural Passions' in Homer's games as against Virgil's.

12. Although the 'Advertisement to the Reader' (TE, V, 251) is signed 'W.W.', it was certainly written by Pope as the manuscript is still extant (*see* Leranbaum, 144).

13. *See* Pope's letter to David Mallet of May (June?) 1734 (*Correspondence*, III, 408-9) and to Caryll, February 1735 (III, 450).

14. *See* Leranbaum, 25-6.

15. Compare Pope's *Essay on Criticism*, 50-67, where the same ideas and metaphors are applied to the compass of individual wit:

> Like Kings we lose the Conquests gain'd before,
> By vain Ambition still to make them more.

16. Kropf, 'Education and the Neoplatonic idea of wisdom in Pope's *Dunciad*', *Texas Studies in Literature and Language*, 14 (1973), 593-604.

17. *Essays* (Cotton, I, 206-7); no. 24.

18. Williams, *Pope's 'Dunciad': A Study of its Meaning* (1955), 104-30.

19. See *The Educational Writings of John Locke*, ed J. L. Axtell (Cambridge, 1968).

20. Pope's active role in the eighteenth-century revival of the works of Marcus Hieronymous Vida is documented by D. W. Hopkins and I. D. MacKillop, '"Immortal Vida" and Basil Kennett', *RES*, (n.s.) 27 (1976), 137-47, where it is noted that 'Pope's primary enthusiasm seems to have been for the *Poetica*'. Pope included the *Poetica* in his edition *Selecta Poemata Italorum Qui Latine Scripserunt* (1740); *see also* his letter to Christopher Pitt of July

1726 (*Correspondence*, II, 382-3).

21. *See* Donald F. Bond, 'Pope's contributions to the *Spectator*', *MLQ*, 5 (1944), 69-78.

22. Vida's *Poetica* includes an episode something like Pope's describing the confrontation between the raging tutor and a pupil who drops dead with fear:

> But when his Arms the dire Tormentor shook,
> Storming with Wrath, and rose to give the Stroke
> Of Justice; ah! in an untimely hour,
> A deadly Chill surprize'd the (youthful) Flower:
> Drooping he fell, by Pineing Grief oppress't;
> And joyful Heaven receiv'd an early Guest.

(I quote from Basil Kennett's unpublished translation; see n.20, above.)

23. James Miller's *Of Politeness* (1738), 12-13 (ll.211-50) and Steele's *Spectator* paper no. 364 (1712) both satirise the Grand Tour in similar terms.

24. Locke, *Thoughts*, § 118; Turnbull, *Observations upon Liberal Education*, 126, 132.

25. Kropf (*see* n.16 above) also refers to the importance of this concept.; 602-3.

26. *Guardian* (Tonson's edition, 2 vols, 1747; I, 268-9).

27. Addison observes, in the *Spectator* no. 215 (1711), that '*Aristotle* ... tells us, that a Statue lies hid in a Block of Marble; and that the art of the Statuary only clears away the superfluous Matter; ... What Sculpture is to a Block of Marble, Education is to an Human Soul.' This is almost certainly the source of Pope's mysterious reference in his footnote (270n.).

28. Compare *Spectator* no. 224 (Hughes): 'Active and Masculine Spirits in the Vigour of Youth neither can nor ought to remain at Rest: If they debar themselves from aiming at a noble Object, their Desires will move downwards, and they will feel themselves actuated by some low and abject Passion.'

29. Compare Prior's essay 'Opinion' (*Works*, I, 590): 'The Various Estimate we make as to the value of things cannot be better Illustrated then by the wants we find in the pursuit of our Studies, every Man adding to his heap, and desirous to compleat his Collection; Books, Pictures, Medals, nay Dryed Flowers, Insects, Cockleshels, any thing will do, but then the Cruel Losses which we some times Sustain, ... perhaps a little Boy yesterday at Canterbury tore that Butterfly in Pieces...'

30. Cotton, I, 251.

31. *Memoirs*, 106. Archbishop Tillotson puts forward the objection to wet-nurses seriously (*Six Sermons*, 1694, 105): 'the Child to be sure sucks in the natural infirmities of the Nurse, together with a great deal of her natural inclinations and irregular passions, which many times stick by the Child for a long time after.'

32. Jean de la Bruyère, *Les Caractères, ou les Moeurs de ce Siècle* (Paris, 1688); Pope knew the 1720 Amsterdam edition (in French), and makes appreciative reference to the work in his letter to Judith Cowper of November 1722 (*Correspondence*, II, 142) and in the letter 'The Publisher to the Reader' prefacing the 1728 *Dunciad*. The source of Young's and Pope's sketches is

the section 'De La Mode'.

33. The parting of the two antagonists by Dulness seems to be an echo of the amicable parting and exchange of gifts between Hector and Ajax, after their duel has been suspended by the falling of darkness (*Iliad*, VII, 337-42):

> Forbear, my Sons! your farther Force to prove,
> Both dear to Men, and both belov'd of *Jove*.
> To either Host your matchless Worth is known,
> Each sounds your Praise, and War is all your own.
> But now the Night extends her awful Shade;
> The Goddess parts you: Be the Night obey'd.

34. Reid, 'Ordering chaos: *The Dunciad*', in *Quick Springs of Sense*, ed Larry S. Champion (Athens, Georgia, 1974), 75-96.

Conclusion

Pope's theory of the passions outlined in the *Essay on Man* was by no means a confined exposition within the precepts of philosophical optimism; it represented rather the focal point of ideas which had held his interest from his earliest years as a writer, and which he went on developing through the main body of his works. As a satirist (in particular, a master of the satiric character) and as a moralist, both the subversive and the positive role of the passions held as deep an interest for Pope as for his contemporaries, embracing a range of apparently contradictory notions. All of Pope's works, including the translations of Homer with their commentaries, reflect significantly on his theory of the passions, since all are in some sense of the word philosophical works and all share a concern with the nature of emotional and motivational impulse. In the same way, it is also notable that all of the major writings discussed in this study show a deep concern with the problem of will, which is as central to the poems of selfconscious 'pathos' as to the satires. By contrast, the 'mechanistic', or purely physiological, view of the operation of the passions is as forcefully mocked in the *Dunciad* and other Scriblerian satires connected with Pope as it is in Swift's *Tale of a Tub*.

The meaning of passion represents for Pope not only a subject for detached analysis, but equally for personal moral enquiry; in his arguments on the neccessity of assaulting and arousing the passions through satire there is a commitment to the strength of urgent response which is intimately related to the philosophical reflections expressed in his *Imitations of Horace* and in his own letters. Both as satirist and philosopher, Pope is inclined towards idealism — evoking what he sees as the highest potential for human integrity — but idealism which is often expressed by negation, or deeply qualified by scepticism, the undermining of rationalistic or optimistic defences. The seeming contradictions of attitude are not easily resolved, but something of a reconciliation is propounded in Pope's attraction to a concept of spiritual harmony which may accommodate the variables of controlled feeling; his opposition to the negative ideals which were associated with Stoicism is conventional enough, but none the less forcefully registered. Friendship is above all represented as a paradigm of emotional engagement without turbulence or rupture, ideally (as in his comments on the friendship of Achilles and Patroclus) the attraction of contrasting temperaments towards a responsive dependency. Similarly, the idea of a 'ruling passion' evolved in Pope's mind as an expression both of his scepticism and his optimism, his interest both in complexity and in the possibility of underlying coherence, and above all the sense of conflict within personality which held a particular fascination for him. In applying the concept of *concors discordia rerum* to character, Pope in effect gives as much strength to the discordant elements as to the theoretical pattern of consistency arising from the whole; hence it arises that the ruling passion (often equated with the disruptive force of madness in Pope's descriptions) also occupies the role which the rationalist would assign to 'raison divine' as a directing power.

A general point of especial interest is that in illustrating the ruling passion theory within his social satires, Pope was able to develop his concern with the discrepancies between assumed 'motives' and actual 'aims'(resolving frequently into aimlessness), the redirecting of the passions within a complex society towards diverse secondary gratifications, manifestations of power or the desire of possession. The disparities and conflicts arising from the confusion of the two are viewed as a near approach to madness, in which man appears at best semi-rational, an emphasis which draws Pope closely towards the satiric view of Horace. The frustrations and confinements of sophistication are perhaps his most insistent concern, and it is in his analysis of women that this concern is most imaginatively developed. Comparison of these works with the satires of Young gives a strong sense, not so much of Pope's originality in his perception of the motions of frustration (which were also imaginatively discussed in contemporary analysis of the phenomena of melancholy and 'spleen'), but of the relative depth and clarity in his recognition of the theme, a power to evoke the subtler connections between 'affectations' and psychological traits.

Pope's theory of the passions, like other contemporary expositions of the subject, was fundamentally only a rough and flawed approach to the intricacies of psychology; yet it was within this seemingly limited framework that he was able, like his mentors Burton and Locke, to present insights which are suggestive and often penetrating, and which have a central part in the enduring power of his satire.

Select Bibliography

Unless otherwise stated, all texts listed bear a London imprint; I have consulted the first edition of most works and translations, except in some cases where significant revisions were made, or where Pope is known to have possessed a copy of a later edition (*see* Mack, 'Pope's books', in the third section of the bibliography below). For many of the major literary and philosophical works, I have made use of modern scholarly editions.

Primary Sources

Abbadie, Jacques. *The Art of Knowing One-Self: or, an Enquiry into the Sources of Morality. Written Originally in French* (Oxford, 1695; second edition, 1698); from *L'Art de se connoitre soy-meme* (2 vols, Rotterdam, 1692).

Aristotle. *The Ethics of Aristotle (The Nicomachean Ethics)*, translated by J. A. K. Thomson, revised by H. Tredennick (1953; reprinted revision, 1976).

Bacon, Sir Francis. *Essays and the Advancement of Learning*, edited by A. W. Pollard (1900).

Baxter, Richard. *A Treatise of Self-Denyall* (1660).

Blackmore, Sir Richard. *A Treatise of the Spleen and Vapours: or, Hypocondriacal and Hysterical Affections. With Three Discourses on the Nature and Cure of the Cholick, Melancholy, and Palsies* (1725).

Boileau-Despreaux, Nicolas. *The Works of Monsieur Boileau made English ... by several hands. To which is prefix'd his life ... (made English by Mr. Ozell) and some account of this translation by N. Rowe* (3 vols, 1711-13).

Boyer, Abel. *Characters of the Virtues and Vices of the Age; or Moral Reflections, Maxims and Thoughts upon Men and Manners. Translated from the most refined French Wits ... and extracted*

from the most celebrated English Writers (1695).

Burton, Robert. *The Anatomy of Melancholy, what it is. With all the Kindes, Causes, Symptomes, Prognostickes, and Severall Cures of it ... Philosophically, Medicinally, Historically, opened and cut up* (1621). Edited by Holbrook Jackson (1932).

Chambers, Ephraim. *Cyclopaedia: or, an Universal Dictionary of Arts and Sciences ... compiled from the best authors ... by E. Chambers* (2 vols, 1728); fourth edition, corrected and amended, with some additions (2 vols, 1741).

Charleton, Walter. *Natural History of the Passions* (1674).

Charron, Pierre. *Of Wisdom ... Made English by George Stanhope* (2 vols, 1697); from *De la Sagesse trois livres* (Bordeaux, 1601).

Clarke, Samuel, D. D., Rector of St. James's, Westminster. 'The Government of Passion' (1711), in *Six Sermons on Several Occasions* (1718).

Creech, Thomas. *The Odes, Satyrs and Epistles of Horace. Done into English* (1684).

Dacier, André. *Remarques Critiques sur les Oeuvres d'Horace, Avec une nouvelle Traduction* (10 vols, Paris, 1697).

Dennis, John. *The Critical Works of John Dennis*, edited by E. N. Hooker (2 vols, Baltimore, 1939, 1943).
Remarks on Mr. Pope's Rape of the Lock. In Several Letters to a Friend (1728).

Drayton, Michael. *Englands Heroicall Epistles* (1598-9).

Dryden, John. *'Of Dramatic Poesy' and Other Critical Essays*, edited by George Watson (2 vols, 1962).
The Poems of John Dryden edited by James Kinsley (4 vols, Oxford, 1958).
(and other hands). *Ovid's Epistles, Translated by Several Hands* (1680).

Elwin, W. and Courthope, W. J. *The Works of Alexander Pope* (10 vols, 1871-89).

Erasmus, Desiderius. *Moriae Encomium: or, A Panegyrick upon Folly ... Done into English* by W. Kennett (1709); from *Moriae Encomium* (Paris, 1511).

Esprit, Jacques. *The Falshood of Human Virtue. Done out of French* (1691); from *La fausseté des vertus humaines* (2 vols, Paris, 1677-8).

Fitzgerald, Thomas (Rev.). *Poems Upon Several Occasions* (Oxford, 1733).

Gally, Henry. *The Moral Characters of Theophrastus* (1725).

Garth, Sir Samuel. *The Dispensary* (1699; sixth edition, revised, 1706; this edition is in Pope's collection, with his manuscript annotations).

Select Bibliography

Gay, John. *The Fan* (1714).

Guardian. *The Guardian* (2 vols, 1767).

Harte, Walter. *An Essay on Satire, Particularly on the 'Dunciad'* (1730); among Pope's collection.

An Essay Upon Reason (1735).

Heinsius, Daniel. *Quintus Horatius Flaccus accedunt nunc Danielis Heinsii* (Leyden, 1629). This was the edition in Pope's library.

Hobbes, Thomas. *Leviathan, or the Matter, Forme, and Power of a Common-wealth, ecclesiasticall and civill* (1651); edited by C. B. MacPherson (1968) — Pope owned a copy of the first edition.

Horace. *See* Creech, Thomas; Dacier, André; Heinsius, Daniel; Morris, E.P.

Hughes, John. *Letters of Abelard and Heloise ... Extracted chiefly from Monsieur Bayle* (1718; fourth edition, 1722).

Hutcheson, Francis. *An Essay on the Nature and Conduct of the Passions and Affections. With Illustrations on the Moral Sense* (1728).

Johnson, Samuel. *Lives of the English Poets* (10 vols, 1779-81) edited by George Birkbeck Hill (3 vols, Oxford, 1905).

A Dictionary of the English Language (3 vols, 1755)·

King, William. *An Essay on the Origin of Evil*, translated by Edmund Law (1731); from *De Origine Mali* (1702).

La Bruyère, Jean de. *Les Caractères, ou les Moeurs de ce Siècle* (Paris, 1688); *'Nouvelle édition'* (3 vols, Amsterdam, 1720).

La Chambre, Cureau de. *The Characters of the Passions ... Translated into English* (1650); from *Les Caractères des Passions* (Paris, 1640).

La Rochefoucauld, Francois, Duc de. *Moral Maxims and Reflections ... made English* (1694); from *Réflexions, ou Sentences et maximes morales* (Paris, 1665).

Le Bossu, René. *Monsieur Bossu's Treatise of the Epick Poem*, translated by 'W.J.' (1695); from *Traité du poëme épique* (Paris, 1675).

Le Grand, Antoine. *Man without Passion, or, the Wise Stoick, According to the Sentiments of Seneca. Englished by G.R.* (1675); from *Les Caractères de l'homme sans passions* (Paris, 1663).

Locke, John. *An Essay Concerning Humane Understanding* (1690); edited by P. H. Nidditch (Oxford, 1975).

Some Thoughts Concerning Education (1693); in *The Educational Writings of John Locke*, edited by J. L. Axtell (Cambridge, 1968).

Lowde, James. *A Discourse Concerning the Nature of Man ... With an Examination of some of Mr. Hobb's Opinions relating hereunto* (1694).

Maidwell, Lewis. *An Essay upon the Necessity and Excellency of Educa-*

191

tion (1705), edited by J. Max Patrick (Los Angeles, 1955; Augustan Reprint Society, no.51).

Malebranche, Nicolas. *Father Malebranche's Treatise Concerning the Search After Truth*, translated by T. Taylor (2 vols, Oxford, 1694); from *De La Recherche de la vérité, où l'on traite de la nature de l'esprit* (2 vols, Paris, 1674-5).

Mandeville, Bernard de. *A Treatise of the Hypochondriack and Hysterick Passions* (1711).

The Fable of the Bees; Or, private vices publick benefits (1714).

Miller, James. *Of Politeness* (1738).

An Hospital for Fools: A Dramatic Fable (1739).

Milton, John. *The Poetical Works of John Milton*, edited by Helen Darbishire (2 vols, Oxford, 1952).

Of Education: To Master Samuel Hartlib (1644).

Montaigne, Michel Eyquen de. *Essays of Michael Seigneur de Montaigne ... new rendred into English by C. Cotton* (3 vols, 1685-6; second edition, 1693); from *Essais de messire Michel de Montaigne* (Bordeaux, 1580). Pope possessed two volumes of the first edition, the third of the second edition.

Montfaucon de Villars (Abbé Nicolas-Pierre-Henri). *Le Compte de Gabalis; or, the Extravagant Mysteries of the Cabalists exposed*, translated by Philip Ayres, in Bentley's *Modern Novels* (vol. 2, 1692); from *Le Compte de Gabalis, ou Entretiens sur les sciences secretes* (Paris, 1670).

Morris, E. P. *Horace: Satires and Epistles* (Oklahoma, 1939; reprinted 1968).

Nicole, Pierre. *Moral Essays. Written in French by Messieurs du Port Royal. Faithfully Rendred into English by a Person of Quality* (3 vols, 1677-80); from *Essais de Morale* (Paris, 1671-9).

Nourse, Timothy. *A Discourse Upon the Nature and Faculties of Man* (1697).

Oldmixon, John. *Amores Britannici. Epistles Historical and Gallant, in English Heroic Verse ... In imitation of the Heroidum Epistolae of Ovid* (1703).

Ovid. *See* Dryden, John; Sandys, George; Showerman, Grant.

Plato. *The Republic of Plato*, translated by F. M. Cornford (Oxford, 1941).

Pope, Alexander. *The Twickenham Edition of the Poems of Alexander Pope* — see List of Abbreviations.

The Correspondence of Alexander Pope, edited by George Sherburn (5 vols, Oxford, 1956).

The Prose Works of Alexander Pope, edited by Norman Ault (1936).

(other editions — see Warburton, William; Roscoe, William;

Elwin, W. and Courthope, W. J.
See Mack, Maynard: *Alexander Pope: An Essay on Man. Reproductions of the Manuscripts in the Pierpont Morgan Library and the Houghton Library with the Printed Text of the Original Edition* (Oxford, 1962).

(and other hands). *Peri Bathous: or, Martinus Scriblerus His Treatise of the Art of Sinking in Poetry* (1727), edited by E. Leake Steeves (1952).

(and other hands). *The Memoirs of the Extraordinary Life, Works and Discoveries of Martinus Scriblerus* (1741), edited by C. Kerby-Miller (New Haven and London, 1950).

Prior, Matthew. *Literary Works*, edited by H. B. Wright and M. K. Spears (2 vols, Oxford, 1959).

Quintilian. *The Institutio Oratoria of Quintilian with an English Translation by H. E. Butler* (1920).

Ralph, James. *Sawney. An Heroic Poem. Occasion'd by the Dunciad* (1728; owned by Pope).

Rapin, René. *Monsieur Rapin's Reflections on Aristotle's Treatise of Poesie, containing the Necessary, Rational and Universal Rules for Epick, Dramatick, and other Sorts of Poetry.* Translated by Thomas Rymer (1694); from *Réflexions sur la póetique d'Aristote et sur les ouvrages des poètes anciens et modernes* (Paris, 1674).

Reynolds, Edward. *A Treatise of the Passions and Faculties of the Soule of Man. With the severall Dignities and Corruptions thereunto belonging* (1640).

Robinson, Nicholas. *A New System of the Spleen, Vapours, and Hypochondriack Melancholy: Wherein all the Decays of the Nerves, and Lownesses of the Spirits, are mechanically Accounted for* (1729).

Roscoe, William. *The Works of Alexander Pope ... To which are added a new life of the author ... and occasional remarks by W. Roscoe* (10 vols, 1824).

Sandys, George. *Ovid's Metamorphosis Englished by G. Sandys* (1626; third edition, 1632).

Savage, Richard. *An Author to be Lett* (1729).

Senault, Jean-François. *The Use of the Passions ... put into English by Henry Earl of Monmouth* (1649; second edition, 1671); from *De l'Usage des Passions* (Paris, 1641).

Shaftesbury (Anthony Ashley Cooper, Third Earl of Shaftesbury) *Characteristicks of Men, Manners, Opinions, Times* (3 vols, 1711); edited by J. M. Robertson (2 vols, New York, 1900).

Sheffield, John (Duke of Buckingham). *The Works of John Sheffield Earl of Mulgrave, Marquis of Normanby, and Duke of Buckingham in*

Verse and Prose (2 vols, 1723); edited by Pope.

Showerman, Grant. *Ovid, Heroides and Amores*, translated by G. Showerman (1921; second edition, 1977).

Spectator, The, edited by Donald F. Bond (5 vols, Oxford, 1965).

Spence, Joseph. *Observations, Anecdotes and Characters of Books and Men*, edited by James M. Osborn (2 vols, Oxford, 1956).

Stanley, Thomas. *History of Philosophy* (3 vols, 1656-60).

Swift, Jonathan. *The Prose Writings of Jonathan Swift*, edited by Herbert Davies (12 vols, Oxford, 1939-55).

Tatler. *The Tatler, Edited with Introduction and Notes by G. A. Aitken* (4 vols, 1898-9).

Tillotson, John (Archbishop of Canterbury). *Six Sermons ... of Stedfastness in Religion; Family Religion; Education of Children; the Advantages of Early Piety* (1694).

Turnbull, George. *Observations upon Liberal Education, in all its Branches; containing the Substance of what hath been said upon that important Subject by the best Writers Ancient or Modern* (1742).

Vida, Marcus Hieronymus. *De Arte Poetica* (1527), in Pope's *Selecta Poemata Italorum qui Latine scripserunt* (1740).

Virgil. *Virgil's Aeneis*, translated by John Dryden. *See* Dryden, *Poems*.

Warburton, William. *The Works of Alexander Pope, Esq ... With the commentaries and notes of Mr. Warburton* (9 vols, 1751).

Wollaston, William. *The Religion of Nature Delineated* (1722; second edition, 1724).

Young, Edward. *Love of Fame, the Universal Passion. In Seven Characteristical Satires* (1728).

    A Vindication of Providence: or a true estimate of Human Life. In which the passions are consider'd in a new light (1728).

    Two Epistles to Mr. Pope, Concerning the Authors of the Age (1730; owned by Pope).

Secondary Sources

(1) Books and Dissertations

Aden, John M. *Something Like Horace: Studies in the Art and Allusion of Pope's Horatian Satires* (Kingsport, Tennessee, 1969).

    Pope's Once and Future Kings; Satire and Politics in the Early Career (Knoxville, Tennessee, 1978).

Audra, Émile. *L'Influence française sur l'oeuvre de Pope* (Paris, 1931) (*Bibliothèque de la Revue de la littérature comparée*, vol. 72).

Axtell, J. L. (ed.) *The Educational Writings of John Locke* (Cambridge, 1968).

Boyce, Benjamin. *The Character-Sketches in Pope's Poems* (Durham, N.C., 1962).

Brett, R. L. *The Third Earl of Shaftesbury: A Study in Eighteenth-Century Literary Theory* (1951).

Brower, Reuben A. *Alexander Pope: The Poetry of Allusion* (Oxford, 1959).

Bush, J. N. Douglas. *Mythology and the Romantic Tradition in English Poetry* (Cambridge, Mass., 1937).

Clark, Alexander Frederick Bruce. *Boileau and the French Classical Critics in England, 1660-1830* (Paris, 1925).

DePorte, Michael V. *Nightmares and Hobbyhorses : Swift, Sterne, and Augustan Ideas of Madness* (San Marino, Cal., 1974).

Dixon, Peter. *The World of Pope's Satires: An Introduction to the 'Epistles' and 'Imitations of Horace'* (1968).

Elkin, P. K. *The Augustan Defence of Satire* (Oxford, 1973).

Erskine-Hill, Howard H. (ed.) *Pope: Horatian Satires and Epistles* (1964).

    Pope: The Dunciad (Studies in English Literature, no.49) (1972).

    (ed.) *The Art of Alexander Pope* (1979).

Fairer, David. *Pope's Imagination* (1984).

Hammond, Brean. *Pope and Bolingbroke: A Study of Friendship and Influence* (Columbia, 1984).

Harth, Phillip. *Contexts of Dryden's Thought* (1968).

Hirschman, A.O., *The Passions and the Interests: Political Arguments for Capitalism before its Triumph* (Princeton, 1977).

Hunter, Richard and McAlpine, Ida. (eds.) *Three Hundred Years of Psychiatry 1535-1860* (Oxford and London, 1963).

Jack, Ian. *Augustan Satire: Intention and Idiom in English Poetry, 1660-1750* (Oxford, 1952).

Janetta, Mervyn J. '*The* predominant passion *and its force:* Propensity, Volition and Motive in the Works of Swift and Pope' (PhD thesis, University of York, 1975).

Keener, F. M. *An Essay on Pope* (New York and London, 1974).

Kenny, Anthony. *Action, Emotion and Will* (1963).

Laurie, S. S. *Studies in the History of Educational Opinion from the Renaissance* (Cambridge, 1903).

Leranbaum, Miriam. *Alexander Pope's 'Opus Magnum', 1729-1744* (Oxford, 1977).

Levi, Anthony. *French Moralists: The Theory of the Passions 1585 to 1649* (Oxford, 1964).

Mack, Maynard. *Alexander Pope. An Essay on Man. Reproductions of the Manuscripts in the Pierpont Morgan Library and the*

Houghton Library with the Printed Text of the Original Edition (Oxford, 1962).

(ed.) *Essential Articles for the Study of Alexander Pope* (revised and enlarged edition, 1968).

The Garden and the City: Retirement and Politics in the Later Poetry of Pope, 1731-43 (Toronto, Oxford and London, 1969).

(ed) *Pope: Recent Essays by Several Hands* (Brighton, Sussex, 1980).

Maclean, Kenneth. *John Locke and English Literature of the Eighteenth Century* (New Haven, 1936).

Maresca, Thomas E. *Pope's Horatian Poems* (Ohio, 1966).

Mell, D. C. *A Poetics of the Augustan Elegy* (Amsterdam, 1974).

Monk, Samuel Holt. *The Sublime : A Study of Critical Theory in Eighteenth-Century England* (New York, 1935).

Pagliaro, Harold E. (ed.) *Studies in Eighteenth Century Culture,* vol. II: *Irrationalism in the Eighteenth Century* (Cleveland, 1972).

Price, Martin. *To the Palace of Wisdom: Studies in Order and Energy from Dryden to Blake* (Garden City, 1964).

Rogers, R. W. *The Major Satires of Alexander Pope* (Urbana, 1955; *Illinois Studies in Language and Literature,* vol. 40).

Røstvig, Maren Sophie. *The Happy Man: Studies in the Metamorphoses of a Classical Ideal, 1600-1700 / 1700-1750* (2 vols, Oslo and Oxford, 1954, 1958).

Rothstein, Eric. *Restoration Tragedy: Form and the Process of Change* (1967).

Selden, Raman. *English Verse Satire, 1590-1765* (1978).

Shankman, Steven. *Pope's 'Iliad': Homer in the Age of Passion* (Princeton, 1983).

Sherburn, George. *The Early Career of Alexander Pope* (Oxford, 1934).

Sitter, John E. *The Poetry of Pope's 'Dunciad'* (Minneapolis, 1971).

Spacks, Patricia Meyer. *An Argument of Images: The Poetry of Alexander Pope* (Cambridge, Mass., 1971).

Sullivan, J. P. (ed.) *Critical Essays on Roman Literature: Satire (1963).*

Swedenberg, H. T. *The Theory of the Epic in England, 1650-1800* (Berkeley, 1944; *University of California Publications in English*, vol. 15).

Trickett, Rachel. *The Honest Muse: A Study in Augustan Verse* (Oxford, 1967).

Veith, Ilza. *Hysteria: The History of a Disease* (Chicago, 1965).

Vinge, Louise. *The Narcissus Theme in Western European Literature up to the Early Nineteenth Century* (Lund, 1967).

Warren, Austin. *Richard Crashaw: A Study in Baroque Sensibility* (Louisiana, 1939).

Wasserman, Earl R. *Pope's 'Epistle to Bathurst': A Critical Reading with an Edition of the Manuscripts* (Baltimore, 1960).

Weinbrot, Howard D. *The Formal Strain: Studies in Augustan Imitation and Satire* (Chicago and London, 1969).

    Augustus Caesar in 'Augustan' England: The Decline of a Classical Norm (Princeton, 1978).

    Alexander Pope and the Traditions of Formal Verse Satire (Princeton, 1982).

Wellington, James E. *'Eloisa to Abelard', with the Letters of Heloise to Abelard in the version by John Hughes, 1713* (Miami, 1965).

White, Douglas H. *Pope and the Context of Controversy: The Manipulation of Ideas in 'An Essay on Man'* (Chicago and London, 1970).

Wilkinson, L. P. *Ovid Recalled* (Cambridge, 1955).

Williams, Aubrey. *Pope's 'Dunciad': A Study of its Meaning* (1955).

Williams, Kathleen M. *Jonathan Swift and the Age of Compromise* (Lawrence, Texas, 1955).

Zimmerman, Hans-Joachim. *Alexander Popes Noten zu Homer* (Heidelberg, 1966).

(2) Articles

Ackerman, Stephen J. 'The vocation of Pope's Eloisa', *SEL*, 19 (1979), 445-57.

Aden, John M. 'Bethel's Sermon and Pope's *Exemplum: towards a critique'*, *SEL*, 9 (1969), 463-70.

    'Pope's *To Augustus*, 241-62', *Explicator*, 26 (1968), entry 70.

Alkon, Paul K. 'Johnson's conception of admiration', *PQ*, 48 (1969), 59-81.

Alpers, P. J. 'Pope's *To Bathurst* and the Mandevillian State', *ELH*, 25 (1958), 23-42.

Anderson, W. S. 'The Roman Socrates: Horace and his Satires', in *Critical Essays on Roman Literature: Satire*, edited by J. P. Sullivan (1963).

Atkins, G. D. 'Strategy and purpose in Pope's *Sober Advice from Horace'*, *Papers on Language and Literature*, 15 (1979), 159-74.

Babb, Lawrence. 'The Cave of Spleen', *RES*, 12 (1936), 165-76.

Barbeau, Anne. 'Free will and the passions in Dryden and Pope', *Restoration*, 4 (1980), 2-8.

Beer, Gillian. '"Our unnatural no-voice": the heroic epistle, Pope, and women's gothic', *YES*, 12 (1982), 125-51.

Bloom, Lillian D. 'Pope as textual critic: a bibliographical study of his Horatian text', *JEGP*, 47 (1948), 150-5.

Bond, Donald. 'Pope's contributions to the *Spectator*', *MLQ*, 5 (1944), 69-78.

Brady, Frank. 'The history and structure of Pope's *To A Lady'*, *SEL*, 9 (1969), 439-62.

Butt, John. 'Pope's poetical manuscripts', *Proceedings of the British Academy*, 40 (1954), 23-39.

Cohen, Ralph. 'Transformation in the *Rape of the Lock*', *ECS*, 2 (1969), 205-24.

Crawford, Charlotte E. 'What was Pope's debt to Edward Young?', *ELH*, 13 (1946), 157-67.

Crossley, Robert. 'Pope's *Iliad*: the commentary and the translation', *PQ*, 56 (1977), 339-57.

Cunningham, Sandy. 'Bedlam and Parnassus: eighteenth century reflections', *Essays and Studies*, (n.s.) 24 (1971), 36-55.

Davidow, Lawrence L. 'Pope's verse epistles: friendship and the private sphere of life', *HLQ*, 40 (1977), 151-70.

Dearing, Vinton A. 'The Prince of Wales's set of Pope's Works', *Harvard Library Bulletin*, 4 (1950), 320-38.

Dillon, George L. 'Complexity and change of character in neo-classical criticism', *JHI*, 35 (1974), 51-61.

Douglas, L. 'A severe animadversion on Bossu', *PMLA*, 62 (1947), 690-706.

Douglass, Richard H. 'More on the rhetoric and imagery of Pope's *Arbuthnot*', *SEL*, 13 (1973), 488-502.

Fabian, Bernhard. 'Pope's Konzeption der 'Ruling Passion': Eine Quellenuntersuchung', *Archiv für das Studium der neueren Sprachen*, 195 (1959), 290-301.

Fairer, David. 'Imagination in *The Rape of the Lock*', *Essays in Criticism*, 29 (1979), 53-74.

Fox, Christopher. '"Gone as soon as found": Pope's *Epistle to Cobham* and the death-day as moment of truth', *SEL*, 20 (1980), 431-8.

Frost, William. '*The Rape of the Lock* and Pope's Homer', *MLQ*, 8 (1947), 342-54.

Gillie, C. 'Pope's *Elegy to the Memory of an Unfortunate Lady*', in *Interpretations*, edited by John Wain (1955), 75-85.

Goggin, L. P. 'La Caverne aux Vapeurs', *PQ*, 42 (1963), 404-11.

Goldgar, Bertrand A. 'Pope's theory of the passions: the background of Epistle II of the *Essay on Man*', *PQ*, 41 (1962), 730-43.

Grundy, Isobel. 'Pope, Peterborough and the *Characters of Women*', *RES*, (n.s.) 20 (1969), 461-8.

Gubar, S. 'The female monster in Augustan Satire', *Signs: Journal of Women in Culture and Society*, 3 (1977), 380-94.

Hatzfeld, H. 'The Baroque from the viewpoint of the literary historian', *Journal of Aesthetics and Art Criticism*, 14 (1955), 156-64.

Hopkins, D. W. and MacKillop, I.D. '"Immortal Vida" and Basil Kennett', *RES*, (n.s.) 27 (1976), 137-47.

Hunter, G. K. 'The "Romanticism" of Pope's Horace', *Essays in Criticism*, 10 (1960), 390-404.

Select Bibliography

Jackson, Wallace. 'Affective values in early eighteenth century aesthetics', *Journal of Aesthetics and Art Criticism*, 27 (1968), 87-92.

Jones, Emrys. 'Pope and Dulness', *Proceedings of the British Academy*, 54 (1968), 231-63.

Kalmey, Robert P. 'Pope's *Eloisa to Abelard* and "those celebrated letters"', *PQ*, 47 (1968), 164-78.

'Rhetoric, language and structure in *Eloisa to Abelard*', *ECS*, 5 (1971), 315-18.

Kelsall, Malcolm. 'Augustus and Pope', *HLQ*, 39 (1976), 117-31.

Knight, D. C. 'The development of Pope's *Iliad* Preface: a study of the manuscript', *MLQ*, 16 (1955), 237-46.

Knoepflmacher, U. C. 'The poet as physician: Pope's *Epistle to Arbuthnot*', *MLQ*, 31 (1970), 440-9.

Kreiger, Murray. '*Eloisa to Abelard*: the escape from body or the embrace of body', *ECS*, 3 (1969), 28-47.

Kropf, C. R. 'What really happens in *Eloisa to Abelard*?', *South Atlantic Bulletin*, 41 (1976), 43-9.

'Education and the Neoplatonic idea of wisdom in Pope's *Dunciad*', *Texas Studies in Literature and Language*, 14 (1973), 593-604.

Mack, Maynard. 'Pope's books: a biographical survey with a finding list', in *English Literature in the Age of Disguise*, edited by Maximillian E. Novak (Los Angeles and London, 1977), 209-305.

Mandel, Barrett John. 'Pope's *Eloisa to Abelard*', *Texas Studies in Literature and Language*, 9 (1967), 57-68.

Mell, D. C. 'Pope's Idea of the Imagination and the Design of the *Elegy*', *MLQ*, 29 (1968), 395-406.

Mengel, Elias F. 'Patterns of Imagery in Pope's *Arbuthnot*', *PMLA*, 69 (1954), 189-97.

Morris, David B. '"The visionary maid": tragic passion and redemptive sympathy in Pope's *Eloisa to Abelard*', *MLQ*, 34 (1973), 247-71.

'The kinship of madness in Pope's *Dunciad*', *PQ*, 51 (1972), 813-31.

Moscovit, L. 'Pope's purposes in *Sober Advice*', *PQ*, 44 (1965), 195-9.

O'Hehir, Brendan. 'Virtue and passion; the dialectic of *Eloisa to Abelard*', *Texas Studies in Literature and Language*, 2 (1960), 219-32.

Peake, Charles. 'Swift and the passions', *MLR*, 55 (1960), 169-80.

Pettit, Henry. '*Eloisa to Abelard*: an interpretation', *University of Colorado Studies: Series in Language and Literature*, 4 (1953), 67-74.

Quintana, Ricardo. 'The Rape of the Lock as a comedy of continuity', REL, 7 (1966), 9-19.

Regan, John V. 'The mock-epic structure of the Dunciad', SEL, 19 (1979), 459-73.

Reichard, Hugo M. 'The love affair in Pope's Rape of the Lock', PMLA, 69 (1954), 887-902.

Reid, B. L. 'Ordering chaos: The Dunciad', in Quick Springs of Sense, edited by Larry S. Champion (Athens, Georgia, 1974), 75-96.

Rivers, William E. 'Pope, the Spectre, and Mr Busby', Eighteenth Century Life, 5 (Summer 1979), 43-53.

Rogers, Pat. 'Faery lore and The Rape of the Lock', RES, (n.s.) 25 (1974), 25-38.

Rogerson, Brewster. 'The art of painting the passions', JHI, 14 (1953), 68-94.

Rosslyn, Felicity. 'Awed by reason: Pope on Achilles', Cambridge Quarterly, 9 (no. 3, 1980), 189-202.

Schmitz, Robert M. 'Peterborough's and Pope's nymphs: Pope at work', PQ, 48 (1969), 192-200.

Sena, John F. '"The wide Circumference around": the context of Belinda's petticoat in The Rape of the Lock', Papers on Language and Literature, 16 (1980), 260-7.

'Belinda's hysteria: the medical context of The Rape of the Lock', Eighteenth Century Life, vol. 5, no. 4 (Summer 1979), 29-42.

Sheehan, David. 'The movement inward in Pope's Dunciad', Modern Language Studies, 8 (1978), 33-9.

Simon, Irène. 'An Essay on Man III, 109-146: a footnote', English Studies, 50 (1969), 93-8.

Sitter, John. 'The Argument of Pope's Epistle to Cobham', SEL, 17 (1977), 435-49.

Stack, Frank. 'Pope's Epistle to Bolingbroke and Epistle I i', in The Art of Alexander Pope, edited by Howard Erskine-Hill and Anne Smith (1979), 169-91.

Steadman, John M. 'Achilles and Renaissance epic: moral criticism and literary tradition', in Lebende Antike: Symposium für Rudolf Sühnel, edited by H. Meller and H. J. Zimmermann (Berlin, 1967).

Stumpf, Thomas A. 'Pope's To Cobham, To A Lady, and the traditions of inconstancy', Studies in Philology, 67 (1970), 339-58.

Trowbridge, Hoyt. 'Pope's Eloisa and the Heroides of Ovid', in Studies in Eighteenth Century Culture, edited by Harold Pagliaro (Cleveland and London, 1973), III, 11-34.

Warren, Austin. 'The reputation of Crashaw in the seventeenth and eighteenth centuries', Studies in Philology, 31 (1934), 385-407.

Wasserman, Earl R. 'The limits of allusion in The Rape of the Lock', JEGP, 65 (1966), 425-44.

Select Bibliography

Weinbrot, Howard D. 'Pope's *Elegy to the Memory of an Unfortunate Lady*', *MLQ*, 32 (1971), 255-67.
'History, Horace and Augustus Caesar', *ECS*, 7 (1974), 391-414.
'André Dacier in 'Augustan' England: towards the reclamation of his *Horace*', *Romance Notes*, 7 (1966), 155-60.
Williams, Aubrey L. 'The "Fall" of China and *The Rape of the Lock*', *PQ*, 41 (1962), 412-25.
Winn, James A. 'Pope plays the rake: his letters to ladies and the making of the *Eloisa*', in *The Art of Alexander Pope*, edited by Howard Erskine-Hill and Anne Smith (1979), 89-118.

Index

Abbadie, Jacques, 93
Achilles, 35-9, 47, 59, 64
Ackerman, Stephen J., 30, 31
Addison, Joseph, 8, 34, 59, 62, 143, 151, 155, 172
Aden, John M., 129, 153, 156
Admiration, 136-9, 165
Aggression, 35-8, 41-3, 53, 58, 60-1, 62, 140-51, 162, 163-4, 165, 178
Alpers, P.J., 118
Anderson, W.S., 154
Apathy, 6, 23, 69, 73, 77, 136, 138-9, 144-5, 161, 163, 177, 181-2
Arbuthnot, John, 124, 147, 150
Aristippus, 132, 133
Aristotle, 35, 68, 75, 78
Atkins, G.D., 154
Avarice, 96-9, 101-3, 125, 127, 130

Babb, Lawrence, 57
Bacon, Sir Francis, 71, 119
Barbeau, Anne, 90, 94
Bateson, F.W., 105, 106, 112
Baxter, Richard, 91
Beer, Gillian, 31
Benevolence, 71, 84-5, 102, 107, 128, 150, 152-3, 167-8
Bentley, Richard, 142, 155, 159, 175, 178
Blount, Martha, 1, 116, 145
Body, 6, 12, 19, 21-3, 79, 81, 126, 134-5, 167
Boileau-Despreaux, Nicolas, 119
Bolingbroke, Henry St. John, 1st Viscount, 32, 49, 65, 68, 89, 122, 132-3, 135, 154
Bond, Donald F., 93, 184

Boyce, Benjamin, 109-10, 119, 178
Boyer, Abel, 99
Brady, Frank, 121
Brett, R.L., 151
Bridges, Ralph, 34, 48
Brower, Reuben A., 1, 17, 118
Burton, Robert, 57, 63, 93
Bush, Douglas, 30
Butt, John, 148, 156

Character-Satire, xiii, 104, 108-9, 112, 115, 148, 178-81
Charleton, Walter, 92
Charron, Pierre, 69, 91, 93, 111
Christianity, 3-9, 12, 15, 17, 19-29, 30, 41-2, 72-6, 98-9, 102, 111, 123, 127, 132, 136-7, 151, 176
Cicero, 93, 154
Clarke, Samuel, 70, 92
Cowper, William, 26
Crashaw, Richard, 26, 28
Creech, Thomas, 154, 156
Cromwell, Henry, 10-12, 156
Cunningham, J.S., 162

Dacier, André, 125, 126, 128, 136-7, 138, 140, 147, 153-4, 155
Dacier, Anne, 41
Davidow, Lawrence L., 154
Death, 3-4, 6-7, 19, 27, 58, 60, 79, 84-5, 115, 119, 144-5, 163, 180-1
Dennis, John, 43, 142, 163
Descartes, René, 109-10, 179
Dixon, Peter, 125, 136, 155
Drayton, Michael, 9, 15
Dryden, John, 9-10, 19, 30, 44, 62, 90, 120, 124, 145, 147, 151, 156

Index

Ecstasy, 12, 20, 26-8, 57, 84, 162, 165
Education, 158-9, 169-75
Elkin, P.K., 156
Epicureanism, 16, 70, 87, 92, 124, 129, 136, 154
Esprit, Jacques, 93, 105, 107
Equanimity, 131-40
Eroticism, 7, 11-14, 17, 27, 50-1, 53-5; *see also* Sex

Fabian, Bernhard, 119
Fairer, David, 63
Fitzgerald, Thomas, 183
Fortescue, William, 76
Fox, Christopher, 119
Friendship, 40, 128-9, 150, 152-3, 154
Frost, William, 33

Gally, Henry, 110, 112, 120
Garth, Sir Samuel, 54
Gay, John, 55-6
Goldgar, Bertrand A., 65, 91
Grundy, Isobel, 121
Guardian, The, 171, 174

Hammond, Brean S., 132
Harte, Walter, 124, 141, 144, 156, 168-9, 174
Harth, Phillip, 92
Heinsius, Daniel, 147
Hervey, John (Lord), 143
Hobbes, Thomas, 68-70, 82, 85-6, 91, 106-7, 121, 162
Horace, 112, 122-53, 156; *See* under Pope, *Imitations of Horace*, and also Creech, Thomas; Dacier, André; Heinsius, Daniel; Morris, E.P.
Hughes, John, 17-18, 20-5, 172
Hume, David, 70
Hunter, G.K., 149
Hutcheson, Francis, 71, 92
Hysteria, xii, 57-8, 63

Imagination, 10, 13, 17, 21, 25, 54, 63, 79, 106, 158, 178, 181
Insanity, xii, 83, 92, 103, 114, 162-3, 179, 182

Jack, Ian, 48
Johnson, Samuel, 3, 120, 151, 156
Jones, Emrys, 166
Juvenal, 122, 146-7, 153

Kalmey, Robert P., 30
Keener, Frederick, 118
Kelsall, Malcolm, 156
Kenny, Anthony, 91
Kerby-Miller, C., 160
King, William (Archbishop), 88, 94
Kropf, C.R., 170

La Bruyère, Jean de, 179, 184
La Rochefoucauld, Francois, Duc de, 68, 77, 81, 91, 92, 93, 105-6, 108, 119, 130
Le Bossu, René, 32, 42-5
Le Grand, Antoine, 69, 91, 93
Leranbaum, Miriam, xiii, 65, 95, 113, 118, 120, 159, 168, 182, 183
Levi, Anthony, 91, 111
Locke, John, 132, 171-4
Longinus, Dionysius Cassius, 35, 62
Lowde, James, 70, 92, 94
Luxury, 99, 101, 126-7

Mack, Maynard, 35, 62, 64, 70, 75, 91
Madness, *see* Insanity
Malebranche, Nicolas, 69, 91, 155
Mandeville, Bernard de, 69, 99
Maresca, Thomas E., 122, 132
Mell, D.C., 3
Miller, James, 183, 184
Milton, John, 3, 26, 62, 164, 172, 179, 181
Monk, Samuel Holt, 62
Montaigne, Michel Eyquen de, 92, 96, 104-11, 119, 120, 132, 170, 171, 172, 175-6
Montfaucon de Villars (Abbé Nicolas-Pierre Henri), 50
Morris, David B., 17, 183
Morris, E.P., 125
Motivation, xii, 68-9, 71, 75-6, 83-5, 87, 89, 97-117, 129-30, 137-8, 148, 170-81
Myth, 8-9, 32-3, 62

Nature, 8, 16, 31, 69, 72-3, 75-80, 82, 85, 88, 101, 116, 125, 129, 170-4
Nicole, Pierre, 69, 91, 92

O'Hehir, Brendan, 20, 30
Oldmixon, John, 9, 15
Otway, Thomas, 16
Ovid, *Amores*, 9, 11, 59-60
  Ars Amatoria, 9
  Heroides, 1, 4, 8-17, 19, 24
  Metamorphoses, 8, 10, 56, 63, 180;
  See also Dryden, Sandys

Passions, definitions of, xii-xiii, 62, 67, 73, 74, 78
Pathos, 2-17, 26, 35, 39-41, 48
Persius, 152
Petit, Henry, 17
Plato, 18, 154, 170
Pope, Alexander
  Works: Dunciad, 61, 65, 141, 142, 157-85; *Elegy to the Memory of an Unfortunate Lady*, 1-8, 15, 24-5; *Eloisa to Abelard*, 1, 7, 10-11, 13, 15-29, 39, 53, 61, 64, 76.
  Epistles: To Arbuthnot, 123, 127-8, 132, 140, 142-4, 148, 149, 150, 152, 156; *To Bathurst*, 95, 97-105, 117, 118; *To Burlington*, 28, 84, 96, 97-9, 118; *To Cobham*, 66, 71, 100, 104-13; *To A Lady*, 56, 61, 68, 78, 91, 112-17, 120; *To Miss Blount, With the Works of Voiture*, 113, 116; (see also under '*Imitations of Horace*', below).
  Essay on Criticism, 30, 62, 183; *Essay on Man*, 23, 30, 42, 64-91, 95-7, 102-3, 105-6, 118, 120, 123, 129, 131, 141-2, 158-60, 162, 168-9, 178; *Homer* (translations); *Iliad*, 32-42, 64, 166, 185 *Odyssey*, 32-3, 177; *Imitations of Horace* (see also '*To Arbuthnot*' above); *Satire I ii* ('*Sober Advice from Horace*'), 62, 129-30, 142, 143; *Satire II i* (*To Fortescue*), 122-3, 140, 143, 148,

149-50; *Satire II ii* (*To Bethel*), 125-9, 135, 142; *Epistle I i* (*To Bolingbroke*), 130, 131-5; *Epistle I vi* (*To Murray*), 131, 136-40; *Epistle II i* (*To Augustus*), 143, 146; *Epistle II ii*, 141, 142, 143; *Epilogue to the Satires*, 122, 140, 141, 144, 148, 149, 152-3, 157-8, 161; *Moral Essays* (see also under *Epistles*), 37, 65-6, 76, 78, 90, 113, 117, 123, 125, 129, 178; '*opus magnum*', xi, 65, 95-6, 112, 117, 120, 158, 160, 182; *Pastorals*, 17; *Rape of the Lock*, 33, 42-61, 182; *Sapho to Phaon*, 9, 12-14, 17, 26
Price, Martin, 58, 156
Prior, Matthew, 106, 121, 184
Pride, 52, 57, 71-83, 85, 97-8, 106, 123, 127, 130, 141, 142-4, 150, 160, 176
Pyrrhonism, 71, 92, 96, 104-11

Reason, 69-71, 74-5, 77-8, 80-2, 88, 92, 93, 111, 119, 120, 146, 158, 160, 163, 168-70, 174, 175
Reid, B.L., 182
Religion, *see* Christianity
Reynolds, Edward (Bishop), 70, 92
Rogers, R.W., 124, 153, 156, 159
Rogerson, Brewster, 29
Roscoe, William, 30
Rosslyn, Felicity, 62
Rothstein, Eric, 16
Rousseau, G.S., 153
Ruling Passion, 37, 47, 71, 76, 78-81, 90, 95-117, 119, 120, 129, 178
Rymer, Thomas, 9

Sandys, George, 56, 63
Satire, 134, 140-53 *passim*; *see also* Character-Satire
Savage, Richard, 183
Scaliger, 147, 156
Scepticism, 71, 74, 92, 104-9, 110-12
Schmitz, Robert M., 121
Scrope, Sir Carr, 12-14
Self-love, xii-xiii, 68-9, 75, 77, 83, 84-7, 102, 105, 114-15, 123, 157-8, 160-8, 177-82

Index

Sena, John F., 63
Senault, Jean-François, 76, 92, 93
Sex, 11-14, 17, 50-1, 53, 58-9, 84, 114, 144, 149-50, 165, 176-7, 179-80; *see also* Eroticism
Shaftesbury (Anthony Ashley Cooper, Third Earl of Shaftesbury), 71, 138; *Characteristics:* 77, 87, 91, 136, 138, 145, 151, 152, 155
Shankman, Steven, 62
Sheehan, David, 182
Sheffield, John (Duke of Buckingham), 121
Sherburn, George, 29, 147
Simon, Irène, 93
Spacks, Patricia Meyer, 29
Spectator, The, 8, 34, 59, 171, 172, 184
Spence, Joseph, *Anecdotes:* xi, 8, 72, 93, 96-7, 100, 111, 118, 119, 122, 137, 152, 156, 159, 183
Stack, Frank, 135
Stanley, Thomas, 92, 93, 107
Stoicism, 4-5, 16, 23, 36, 48, 69-78, 87, 93, 99-100, 106, 111, 119, 124-8, 131, 133, 135, 154
St. Paul, 132, 133
Stumpf, Thomas A., 104, 111, 118, 120
Stupefaction, 138-9, 144-5, 161, 163, 177, 181-2
Swift, Jonathan, xi, 66, 73, 89, 119, 120, 128, 140, 158, 171; *Tale of a Tub* 72

Tatler, The, 63, 171
Tillotson, Geoffrey, 21, 29, 30
Tillotson, John (Archbishop of Canterbury), 184
Tonson, Jacob, 9, 30
Trickett, Rachel, 30
Trowbridge, Hoyt, 29
Turnbull, George, 172, 174, 175

Veith, Ilza, 63
Vida, Marcus Hieronymus, 171, 184
Vinge, Louise, 8
Virgil, *Aeneid*, 35, 44, 46, 48, 56, 62, 161, 183
Voltaire, Francois Marie Arouet, 32

Walpole, Sir Robert, 129, 177
Warburton, William, 49, 65, 106, 120, 152, 159, 162, 171
Warren, Austin, 28, 31
Warton, Joseph, 26
Wasserman, Earl R., 99
Watts, Isaac, 28
Wealth, 97-103, 116, 125-6
Weinbrot, Howard D., 3, 118, 122, 152, 153, 154, 156
Wellington, James E., 31
White, Douglas H., xiii, 65, 66, 82, 92
Wilkinson, L.P., 30
Will, 70, 75, 78, 90, 106-7, 115, 124
Williams, Aubrey L., 63, 170
Williams, Kathleen, 92
Wollaston, William, 70, 88, 91, 94
Women, 37, 39-40, 57-9, 112-17, 129-30

Young, Edward, 97, 116, 120, 123, 140, 141, 145, 146-7, 179-80

Zimmerman, Hans-Joachim, 62